JEFFERSON'S ENGLISH CRISIS
Commerce, Embargo, and the Republican Revolution

JEFFERSON'S ENGLISH CRISIS

Commerce, Embargo, and the Republican Revolution

Burton Spivak

University Press of Virginia
Charlottesville

THE UNIVERSITY PRESS OF VIRGINIA
Copyright © 1979 by the Rector and Visitors
of the University of Virginia

First published 1979

Library of Congress Cataloging in Publication Data

Spivak, Burton.
  Jefferson's English crisis: commerce, embargo, and the
    Republican revolution.
  Bibliography: p. 229
  Includes index.
  1.–United States—Foreign relations—1801-1809.
  2.–United States—Politics and government—1801-1809.
  3.–Jefferson, Thomas, Pres. U.S., 1743-1826. I. Title.
  E331.S68   973.4'6'0924   78-13110
  ISBN 0-8139-0805-1

Printed in the United States of America

This book is for the undergraduate students at the University of Texas at Austin

CONTENTS

PREFACE

The United States was born amid European turmoil and did not escape its influence until 1815. A host of able historians have charted America's relationship with the European world between its two wars with Great Britain. This book does not attempt to duplicate their efforts. My subject is Thomas Jefferson's formulation and handling of America's English problem, especially during his presidency. This problem, as I believe Jefferson understood it, extended beyond the external threats of English maritime power and ambition, and involved as well the unwanted growth, within the American Republic, of English political forms, social ideas, and commercial development. Yet I also believe that the commercial goals of Jefferson's English diplomacy encouraged the very kind of national economic development that he found so incompatible with his republican dreams. These goals, particularly the quest for a profitable share of the wartime carrying trade, both complicated America's foreign relations and compromised important republican assumptions about life and labor in what Jefferson once called "this great agricultural country." And, because of their *Englishness*, and Jefferson's complicity in them, the goals also generated tensions in his thought and strains on his policy that eventually found their dramatic release in his famous embargo.

My focus is Jefferson's English policy between 1803 and 1809 and its implications for our understanding of Jefferson's thought and temperament and for our understanding of republicanism, that is, of the ideology of American nationhood. I have tried to clarify the development of policy during these years—including the sharp divisions within the Republican party on wartime commerce and national economic goals and the disagreements within Jefferson's cabinet on the events and issues of 1807: the *Chesapeake* attack in

June, the possibility of war with England during the summer and fall, and the embargo on American foreign shipping in December. Since Henry Adams's classic study of Jefferson's presidency, historians have usually viewed the 1807 embargo as an experiment in peaceable, economic coercion; as an attempt to defend and expand the national interest with economic levers rather than with military weapons. Because the embargo addressed the problems of national defense and economic growth without violence and war, it has become an expression of both Jefferson's pacifism and of his enlightened statecraft. In this interpretative framework, embargo and economic coercion have become one and the same policy.

It is a thesis of this book, however, that embargo and economic coercion, as Republicans in the early national period understood them, were two different policies, not one. An embargo was a *defensive* precautionary policy. It withheld American ships, sailors, and mercantile property from the world's oceans in an attempt to preserve these maritime resources of war. The policy of economic coercion, on the other hand, was an *offensive* tool of commercial diplomacy. Its weapon was usually the American market for imported goods. Economic coercion withheld the American market from foreign nations with whom the United States was at economic odds through the medium of a congressional nonimportation law. Sometimes economic coercion also included a ban on exports to the offending nation through the medium of nonintercourse. Although a coercive policy assumed a competitive, even an antagonistic, world economic order, it also assumed peace and sought to enhance the nation's economic advantage through peaceful retaliation. The differences between the two lines of action found their ultimate expression in different amounts of time. An embargo, because so total, was necessarily short. Economic coercion, because of the more selective nature of its adversary and its less severe impact on the domestic economy, was a potentially longer experiment in competitive commercial diplomacy. In sum, Republicans recognized that economic coercion was largely a peacetime policy of economic reprisal and economic growth, and embargo was largely a prewar policy of isolation and military preparation.

In the aftermath of the English attack on the *Chesapeake* in June 1807 and continuing through the congressional session of October, Jefferson favored war against Great Britain, not the peaceable alternative of economic coercion. A formal embargo was unnecessary during the *Chesapeake* summer because the war scare created by the June outrage served that purpose admirably. When the president did call for an embargo in December, his request grew from the grim realization that French additions to the initial English problems had created a general Atlantic crisis for the American nation. More than anything else, the embargo addressed this dismal development in the Atlantic world, and it offered the United States only "an intervening period" to measure its proper response. The hopes of peaceful coercion did not shape Jefferson's initial request. During most of the embargo's run, it blended into larger strategies of watchful waiting, military preparation, and diplomatic attempts to resolve or at least to make manageable the nation's foreign crisis.

But from its beginning, some Republicans did champion the embargo as a usable weapon of economic coercion. The argument in cabinet for an offensive, coercive embargo elicited from Albert Gallatin pleas that Jefferson not let such a hybrid policy, a "permanent embargo" the Treasury chief called it, a dangerous mingling of two dissimilar traditions, capture and distort the defensive policy. Even Jefferson occasionally wrote in the spring and summer about the importance of giving a fair chance to this "first experiment" in economic coercion. But against these understandable outcroppings of a coercive rationale that reached deeply into Republican soil, we must weigh Jefferson's own appreciation that domestic economic appetites placed the embargo on a short tether, robbed it of time, and therefore spoiled the dream of coercion through isolation. This crucial insight shaped Jefferson's thinking until the autumn of 1808. Only when he lost sight of it did the embargo become the offensive weapon he had never intended it to be. Why he lost sight of it is essentially a story of Jefferson's frustration, and of the political and psychological pressures that can, and usually do, twist policy in unintended directions and challenge the ability of national leaders to control their own devices.

Yet the newfound importance of economic coercion was only part of the embargo's refashioned purpose. During its fifteen months it became bound up, in Jefferson's mind, with concerns that transcended immediate problems and foreign policy and instead centered on the redemption of the American economy and on the protection of the legacy of the Revolution of 1800. In its final meaning, the embargo was both Jefferson's defense and renunciation of American commerce. This paradox helps explain another. When the embargo became implicated in the economic redemption of 1776 and the political survival of 1800, it necessitated the draconian enforcement measures that historians have found so incompatible with Jeffersonian principles. These measures emerged from both Jefferson's anger and his republicanism, and they must be understood as serious attempts to protect those principles from the onslaughts of Federalism, English ways, and the nineteenth century.

I have accumulated many debts and been shown many kindnesses in the course of writing this book, and it is a pleasure, finally, to acknowledge the contributions of others. My father, the late Joseph Spivak, and my mother, Mrs. Eva Spivak, always allowed their sons to choose their own course and careers. For this I am ever thankful. My brother, David, and his wife, Barbara, have spurred this project on since its inception. At the University of Virginia my major professor, Norman A. Graebner, provided me with a perfect model of academic excellence, intellectual rigor, and Jeffersonian civility. Professor Merrill D. Peterson read many drafts of this book when it was a dissertation, helped me clarify both my questions and my answers, and made my pages much better than when he received them. Professor William W. Abbot spent countless hours on a seminar paper many years ago, and in the process taught me most of what I know about using the English language clearly. Martin J. Havran, chairman of the Corcoran Department of History, did me a special favor at very short notice in the summer of 1974. Steven H. Hochman, Professor Dumas Malone's research associate, answered many questions at long distance, and has been a close friend since our Virginia days.

Several of my former colleagues at the University of Texas at Austin read my manuscript and made it better by their efforts. I would like to thank Professors Robert A. Divine, Standish Meacham, Norman D. Brown, and Gwyn Morgan. Professor Richard A. Ryerson was a steady source of encouragement and an able critic. Professor Janet Meisel read none of my book, and knows only as much about my Jefferson as I do about her Welsh barons. But in many ways, she made the completion of this book possible. For her, a special thanks. Professor Thomas K. McCraw of the Harvard Business School improved the style and clarity of two chapters. More importantly, he and his wife, Susan, have been examples of what friendship and the academic world are supposed to be about.

Quotations from the Adams Papers are from the microfilm edition by permission of the Massachusetts Historical Society. For permission to quote from the Joseph Carrington Cabell Papers, I would like to thank the Cabell Memorial Foundation of Charlottesville, Virginia. Miss Olivia A. Taylor kindly gave me permission to quote from letters from the Wilson Cary Nicholas Papers. I would also like to thank Mary McKinney, Mark Kantor, Robin Zorn, and John Youkilis for their help in reading galley and page proofs.

History writing is a cooperative endeavor. Historians cannot prosper without other historians, and none of them can survive without librarians and students. I would like to thank here as well as in my footnotes and bibliography all the Jeffersonian scholars who have helped my work through their own; all the librarians and archivists—especially at the Library of Congress, the National Archives, the University of Texas, the Maryland Historical Society, and the University of Virginia—who have helped me along the way; and all the students who have made me a better historian and a better teacher with the questions they have asked and the answers they have given.

Providence, Rhode Island
June 23, 1978

1

JEFFERSON'S ENGLISH DIPLOMACY
"The God of Peace" or "the Lord of Hosts"

Jeffersonian Economics: Revolutionary Liberalism, American Mercantilism

Between the American Revolution and his presidency, Thomas Jefferson fashioned an ideal theoretical economy that centered on agriculture and the penetration of foreign markets for native American produce. A commercial-agricultural economy would allow the United States to leave its "workshops" in Europe. Industry presumed cities, and these conjured up images of squalor and human unhappiness, of European wretchedness. The social and political implications of industrial development counted as heavily in Jefferson's verdict against a Hamiltonian future as did any economic consideration. The republican scheme bound farmers and merchants in equal and tranquil partnership, tied the fortunes of both to the growth and foreign sale of American produce, and supported Jefferson's passion for peace. But because it assumed an unfettered international market, a republican economy rested on Europe's acceptance of the free trade ideology of Adam Smith.[1]

Part of the utopian dimension of the American Revolution was economic, a body of antimercantilist dogma that comprised America's radical quest for a sane world economy. These "Liberal Sentiments," as John Adams called them, rested on a division between politics and economics, between the state and the individual. The Old World had sacrificed economic freedom to political rivalry

[1] TJ to Elbridge Gerry, May 11, 1785, to P. & V. French & Nephew, July 13, 1785, to John Adams, July 31, Nov. 19, 1785, to G. K. van Hogendorp, Oct. 13, 1785, to William Seward, Nov. 12, 1785, Julian P. Boyd, ed., *The Papers of Thomas Jefferson* (Princeton, N.J., 1950—), 8:142, 292, 332, 633, 9:28, 42 (hereafter cited as Boyd).

and had reared a suffocating system of regulations by which nations warred against their adversaries for influence and status. America's Revolutionary economics deplored this ruinous manifestation of European reaction: the capture and control of the marketplace by the state. After Independence, Jefferson hoped that republican America could liberate the international market on the principle of free trade through the medium of negotiated treaties. These treaties aimed to erase national distinctions in the world market and to embody in international law the fresh concept of "world citizen." If all nations treated "alien" ships and goods as they treated their own, economic activity would follow productive ability, not artifically imposed political power. England was always Jefferson's chief mercantilist villain,[2] but this anti-English stance masked a general revulsion against the whole European practice. But diplomatic efforts to free trade from politics failed, and by 1785 Jefferson began to repose his liberal hopes in the coercive power of a strengthened national congress.[3]

By the mid-1780s, a system of American mercantilism had evolved in Jefferson's thinking and American statecraft because of the failure to create with words and parchment an international order based on the sensible notion of free trade. American policy makers abandoned their innocent yearnings and instead sought remedies equal to national purpose in the coercive power of the American market. John Adams caught the nation's dilemma in 1785: "If we cannot obtain reciprocal Liberality, we must adopt reciprocal Prohibitions, Exclusions, Monopolies, and Imposts. We must not be the Dupes," he warned Jefferson. "All foreign nations are taking an ungenerous Advantage of our Symplicity and philosophical Liberality. We must not, my Friend, be the Bubbles of our own Liberal Sentiments."[4]

[2] TJ to Abigail Adams, June 21, 1785, to William Stephens Smith, June 22, 1785, to Nathaniel Tracy, Aug. 17, 1785, to John Langdon, Sept. 11, 1785, to Edmund Randolph, Sept. 20, 1785, to John Adams, Sept. 24, Nov. 19, 1785, to James Currie, Sept. 27, 1785, to William Carmichael, Nov. 4, 1785, Boyd, 8:239, 249, 399, 512, 538, 545, 9:42, 8:599, 9:15.

[3] TJ to Monroe, May 11, June 17, Dec. 11, 1785, to John Adams, July 7, 1785, to Richard Henry Lee, July 12, 1785, to G. K. van Hogendorp, July 29, Oct. 13, 1785, to John Bannister, Aug. 31, 1785, to Madison, Sept. 1, 1785, to David Hartley, Sept. 5, 1785, to Elbridge Gerry, Oct. 11, 1785, Boyd, 8:149, 229, 9:95, 8:266–67, 287, 325, 632–33, 456, 461, 483–84, 605.

[4] Adams to TJ, Aug. 7, Sept. 4, Nov. 4, 1785, Boyd, 8:354–55, 477, 9:11.

For Jefferson, diplomatic failure was really the failure of reason; his new fascination with congressional power signaled an awareness that force now carried the burden of the nation's economic future. Of Anglo-American relations he wrote in 1786: "Each country is left to do justice to itself and to the other according to its own ideas . . . and to scramble for the future as well as they can; to regulate their commerce by duties and prohibitions, and perhaps by cannons and mortars." Although he mourned the death of America's bright dream of a world economy emptied of political power, the disappointment was short-lived as Jefferson, in characteristic fashion, recovered his optimism by redirecting it. With not too many backward glances, he moved from treaty negotiation to economic retaliation, from free trade to American mercantilism. By 1787 continued negotiations with the French and English not only promised meager rewards but threatened to compromise congressional freedom of action as well. Because the new national congress would "be the less embarrassed in their system in proportion as their hands are less tied up by engagements with other powers," Jefferson was now anxious to lay America's European commercial discussions to rest. And in the interim, before national reform, he viewed separate state retaliations unequal to American needs. The English, he knew, banked on the continued division of commercial power among the thirteen state legislatures to ensure confusion, staggered steps, and weakness. "It remains for us to shew whether they are true prophets," he wrote in April. Commercial expansion now required force, and force required national union. "I love energy in government dearly," he confided to Abigail Adams in July. By 1787 foreign commerce and domestic political consolidation had become intimately connected in Jefferson's view of the American future.[5]

When they came to power in 1801, the Jeffersonians brought with them a well-developed tradition of commercial retaliation that, like the European mercantilism it warred against, was market oriented. It stressed the importance of the American import market and its purchasing power to European, especially English, economic stability, and it hoped to turn a perceived European dependence to the ad-

---

[5] TJ to David Ross, May 8, 1786, to William Carmichael, Aug. 22, 1786, to Nicholas Lewis, April 22, 1786, to Abigail Adams, July 7, 1785, Boyd, 9:475, 10:287, 9:400, 8:265. See also TJ to Monroe, June 17, 1785, to David Hartley, Sept. 5, 1785, to John Jay, Oct. 11, 1785, Boyd, 8:230–31, 484, 607–8.

vantage of America's quest for better foreign markets. The tradition grew from the colonial heritage of merchant boycotts and the failure of the 1780s diplomacy. In the mid-eighties, future Republicans and future Federalists similarly championed a market response to European commercial restrictions. Only "retaliatory measures may induce them [the English] to lend a listening ear to equal propositions," Jefferson believed. "Nothing will bring them to reason but physical obstruction, applied to their bodily senses." His methods ranged from discriminatory taxation to complete nonimportation. This market-oriented, import-oriented tradition of economic coercion never embraced a financially destructive and politically divisive ban on American shipping and foreign trade. It would grant or withhold the privilege of the American market in rhythm with foreign treatment of American exports. It would counter prohibition with prohibition until the European nations accepted the mutual benefits of reciprocal liberalism. And if these methods did not liberalize Anglo-American commerce, they at least would snap a dangerous addiction to British luxuries. "We have all the world besides open to supply us with gew-gaws," he affirmed to James Madison.[6]

Jefferson's New England comrade also favored the discouragement or complete exclusion of English ships and goods from American ports. "Such measures as these," Adams noted in 1785, "would discover to the English that we know our strength and their weakness, and would have probably a greater tendency to influence the ministry . . . than any reasoning which can be used." Alexander Hamilton also connected commercial expansion to the politically harnessed power of the American market. "If we continue united," he wrote in 1788, "we may oblige foreign countries to bid against each other, for the privileges of our markets." "Suppose . . . we had a government in America, capable of excluding Great Britain from all our ports," he asked in *The Federalist* No. 11. "What would be the probable operation of this step upon her politics?"[7]

[6] TJ to Madison, Mar. 18, 1785, to Elbridge Gerry, May 11, 1785, to John Page, Aug. 20, 1785, to David Humphreys, May 7, 1786, Boyd, 8:40, 143, 419, 9:469.

[7] John Adams to John Jay, May 8, June 26, July 19, 1785, quoted in Norman Graebner, ed., *Ideas and Diplomacy: Readings in the Intellectual Tradition of American Foreign Policy* (New York, 1964), pp. 36–40; Alexander Hamilton, "Federalist Number Eleven," in Jacob E. Cooke, ed., *The Federalist* (Middletown, Conn., 1961), pp. 65–73; Frederick W. Marks III, *Independence on Trial: Foreign Affairs and the Making of the Constitution* (Baton Rouge, La., 1973), pp. 52–95.

In the 1790s Hamilton based a different system of economic growth on credit, national banking, funded debt, and industrial development. Because his entire fiscal structure floated on the revenues provided by British imports, he soon lost interest in the kinds of market-oriented retaliatory policies that he had boldly outlined during the ratification debates. In fact, the fiscal requirements of capital formation and incipient industrialization ended the unified efforts of northern and southern nationalists because they required a temporary acceptance of English mistreatment and maritime superiority, a surrender that the southern advocates of commercial agriculture were not prepared to make. Party differences in the 1790s grew from antagonistic conceptions of American economic development. When Hamilton and the Federalists embraced credit and a steady stream of British revenues, they forced into formal Republican opposition leaders and groups that saw in the improvement of foreign trade the surest and safest path to prosperity and national growth. These different economic priorities made the opposition party the sole custodian of the weapon of economic retaliation. What had been developing as an American tradition before 1789 emerged from the partisan struggle over Hamilton's financial reports as the basis of a distinctly Republican foreign policy. Secretary of State Jefferson bonded the association between Republicanism and mercantilism in his own report.[8]

Jefferson's "Report on the Privileges and Restrictions on the Commerce of the United States in Foreign Countries," submitted to Congress on December 16, 1793, outlined the Republican party's strategy of economic growth. The paper reiterated Jefferson's appreciation of the connections between access to foreign markets and agricultural prosperity and the ties between the farming interest and national growth and development. It chided the nation for previously granting favor for restriction. "Free commerce and navigation are not to be given in exchange for restrictions and vexations," Jefferson warned, "nor are they likely to produce a relaxation of them." In-

---

[8] Even before the spokesmen of commercial agriculture found in Hamilton's economic reports a threat to their interests, they argued for discriminatory tonnage duties on English ships, a policy they thought in keeping with the purposes for which the national government had been reformed. See Merrill D. Peterson, "Thomas Jefferson and Commercial Policy, 1783–1793," in Peterson, ed., *Thomas Jefferson, a Profile* (New York, 1967), pp. 104–34.

stead, he recommended that Congress fight its way, with peaceful weapons, toward a freer world economy.[9]

The Jay Treaty of 1794 pushed the loose Republican interests that had formed from disagreement with the Hamiltonian system into open opposition, party organization, and two national campaigns for the presidency.[10] It reminded them of the danger of executive power and thereby confirmed a fundamental premise of their political theory. They saw how a Federalist executive had bartered away a national foreign policy weapon for negligible gain, against the wishes of the farmer-dominated House. The Jay Treaty protected the Hamiltonian orientation and jeopardized the future of commercial agriculture. To secure for "the treasury men" (as Jefferson called the holders of the public debt) their needed revenues on British imports, the Jay Treaty enfeebled commercial policy by denying Congress the power to discriminate against English ships and goods. "A bolder party-stroke was never struck," Jefferson brooded. The Federalist Senate and executive had bound "up the hands of the adverse branch from ever restricting the commerce of their patron nation."[11] For a time the market weapon of economic retaliation had been emptied and reloaded with blanks.

By 1801 Jefferson had developed both a system of national economic growth and a strategy for its attainment. His ideas assumed world peace and centered on American produce and ships and foreign markets and industry. Trade and agriculture were both wedded to the productive power of the nation, and therefore were both fully legitimate. Their weapon was the American market. Wars were for the Old World, the president hoped. "Those peaceable coercions which are in the power of every nation," Jefferson wrote at the beginning of his presidency, "are more likely to produce the desired

[9] Paul L. Ford, ed., *The Writings of Thomas Jefferson* (New York, 1882–99), 6:470-84 (hereafter cited as Ford).

[10] Paul A. Varg, *Foreign Policies of the Founding Fathers* (East Lansing, Mich., 1963), pp. 95-168; Joseph Charles, *The Origins of the American Party System* (Williamsburg, Va., 1956), pp. 91–140; Jerald A. Combs, *The Jay Treaty: Political Battleground of the Founding Fathers* (Berkeley, Calif., 1970), pp. 65–188; Charles A. Beard, *Economic Origins of Jeffersonian Democracy* (New York, 1915), pp. 268–98.

[11] TJ to Madison, Sept. 21, 1795, Andrew A. Lipscomb and Albert Ellery Bergh, eds., *The Writings of Thomas Jefferson* (Washington, D.C., 1903), 9:310 (hereafter cited as Lipscomb and Bergh).

effect." [12] Contrary to ideal hope, the frustrations of prying open better markets, especially in the colonial possessions of the Old World nations, were legion. Perhaps that is why Jefferson soon succumbed to the allures of a different trade; a trade less attractive, a trade connected not to the nation's productive capacity but only to its entrepreneurial ability. Jeffersonian theory mourned European war, but Republican leaders understood the profitable opportunities it opened to the United States "provided," James Monroe once wrote, "our merchants have enterprise. . . . They may turn it to theirs and the general advantage." [13] This wartime carrying trade complicated Jefferson's English diplomacy, ruined his presidency, and finally impelled him to renounce foreign trade completely and to fashion in the midst of the embargo crisis a new political economy that transformed his agrarianism and altered the relationship of the major economic groups within the American Republic.

The Carrying Trade

Between 1793 and 1815 the Napoleonic wars had an important maritime dimension. Both France and England attempted to deny commerce to their adversary as part of an overall strategy of victory. Although their means created problems for neutral nations, they also created opportunities. The most lucrative was the wartime carrying trade, especially in the goods of England's European enemies and their colonial possessions in the Caribbean. The French imperial trade was an important component of French prosperity and during European peace was usually reserved to French ships and merchants. But when pressed by war and the Royal Navy, France gladly opened the trade to neutral carriers. So it was that the United States assumed the role of prosperous middleman, transporting French and Spanish Caribbean and metropolitan goods between colonies and mother countries.

The wartime carrying trade both attracted and repelled Jefferson. His anxiety was part of a larger though less troublesome ambivalence toward foreign trade generally. "You ask what I think on the expediency of encouraging our states to be commercial," he replied to a

[12] TJ to Robert R. Livingston, Sept. 9, 1801, ibid., 10:281–82.
[13] Monroe to TJ, April 12, 1785, Boyd, 8:80.

European correspondent. "I should wish them to practice neither commerce nor navigation, but to stand with respect to Europe precisely on the footing of China. We should thus avoid wars, and all our citizens would be husbandmen." This wish took its intensity from Jefferson's belief that the rural life provided a unique physical setting for individual happiness and social harmony, and from his fear that commerce bred conflict and war. But the wish, taken as a national directive, was as empty of reality as it was powerfully expressive of agrarian dreams. "But this is theory only," he understood, "and a theory which the servants of America are not at liberty to follow. Our people have a decided taste for navigation and commerce. They take this from their mother country: and their servants are in duty bound to calculate all their measures on this datum."[14]

Accepting the importance of commerce, Jefferson's public acts between the Revolution and his presidency aimed to make it compatible with agriculture, national unity, peace, and republican ideas on labor. The first was easiest because farmers needed transportation and shippers needed cargoes. Federalist accusations that he was anticommerce and anti–New England amused more than angered him because they made such little sense. Of all the partisan invective that he had weathered in the campaign, the president wrote in 1801, "one imputation in particular has been remarked till it seems as if some believe it: that I am an enemy of commerce. They admit me as a friend to agriculture and suppose me an enemy to the only means of disposing its produce."[15] A friend to trade because agriculture demanded it, Jefferson hoped the nation might confine its commercial aspirations to the penetration of foreign markets for native American goods. This was a trade the nation was entitled to. Its pursuit held the best chance of avoiding rivalries with other nations that might spawn war. It bound American trade and agriculture to the nation's productive power, thereby blending the shoreline and the interior, the North and South, in a steady and connected economic endeavor. Because peace was its initial environment, it seemed not to require massive naval and military support. In the event of European war, it was the type of trade least likely to provoke belligerent reprisals.

[14] G. K. van Hogendorp to TJ, Sept. 8, 1785, TJ to van Hogendorp, Oct. 13, 1785, TJ to John Jay, Aug. 23, 1785, Boyd, 8:503–4, 633, 426–27.

[15] TJ to William Jackson, Feb. 18, 1801, to the General Assembly of Rhode Island and Providence Plantations, Lipscomb and Bergh, 10:206, 263.

While Jefferson was in Europe in the 1780s, he analyzed closely the probable impact of European war on American commerce. The focus of his analysis was the wartime carrying business, a commerce that England's enemies usually denied the United States when they were at peace. "At first blush," he knew, "a war between [England and France] would promise advantage to us." But it was a seduction that promised abuse. Because of the disparity between English and French naval power, the carrying trade would become no more than a French commerce covered by the American flag. Unneutral in impact on the European struggle, its pursuit would ensure a deterioration in Anglo-American relations, and perhaps war. Disturbing in its foreign consequences, the trade challenged important Jeffersonian assumptions on labor and wealth in republican America. He believed that "a steady application to agriculture with just trade enough to take off it's superfluities is our wisest course." The carrying trade, on the other hand, encouraged "speculation," "a spirit of gambling," and the desire to prosper without labor. Because it fed on war, it was unseemly. Because it broke the intimate connection between the nation's agriculture and its foreign trade, it threatened the harmony of domestic economic interest that Jefferson had hoped would ensure American political tranquillity and regional sympathy. But it was prosperous. Jefferson knew that when European war broke out, many of his countrymen would demand governmental protection for such trade. European war, Jefferson fretted to George Washington, "would convert us into sea rovers under French and Dutch colours and divert us from Agriculture which is our wisest pursuit, because it will in the end contribute most to real wealth . . . and happiness." "Tho we shall be neuters," he wrote in 1787, "and as such shall derive considerable pecuniary advantages, yet I think we shall lose in happiness and morals by being launched again into the ocean of speculation, led to overtrade ourselves, tempted to become sea-robbers under French colours, and to quit the pursuit of Agriculture the surest road to affluence and the best preservative of morals."[16] Jefferson hoped that Europe would compose its differences, but in vain. By the years of his presidency, the carrying trade had become a major ingredient of American commercial prosperity, and its protection the major economic goal of Jefferson's English diplomacy. James

[16] TJ to Wilson Miles Cary, Aug. 12, 1787, to Washington, Aug. 14, 1787, to John Blair, Aug. 13, 1787, Boyd, 12:24, 38, 28.

Monroe in 1804-5 and Monroe and William Pinkney of Maryland in joint mission in 1806 shouldered its preservation as their major diplomatic responsibility.

Quite plainly, Monroe's chore amounted to extracting from Great Britain permission to trade at its military and economic expense. From the outset, Monroe sensed the enormity of the task before him. He also knew that the trade's character was his greatest burden. Great Britain could accurately claim that the United States was posing as a New World innocent, its raw economic urges dressed up in the stylish rhetoric of neutral rights and international law, while it stood poised to profit from English distress. If the United States fed this image, Monroe warned, diplomacy could achieve little.[17]

Other Americans noted the grasping nature of American neutrality. John Randolph of Virginia castigated the administration for marrying American prosperity and peace to the wartime trade. In fact, an English publisher printed one of his congressional attacks on both the carrying trade and the administration's defense of it as an introduction to James Stephen's *War in Disguise* (1805), a piece that accused the United States of mounting an unfair commercial challenge to England's maritime position while Great Britain was mired in continental trouble. Some, like Thomas Cooper of Pennsylvania, thought the United States cheapened its character by fattening on European war. "Nor can I help thinking there is something ungenerous," he scolded Jefferson, "in taking advantage of a period when Great Britain is struggling for her very existence." Others, including a majority of Republican congressmen, opposed strong congressional retaliatory measures in 1806 because the carrying trade—a narrow economic interest, a "fungus" John Randolph called it, a source of profit divorced from the needs of commercial agriculture, an interest that would evaporate when war in Europe ended—was not worth the tangle it was making of American foreign relations, not worth, certainly, the risk of war. The 1806 debates in Congress on the nation's English policy, therefore, were more importantly a discussion of the proper direction for American economic development; of whether, as John Taylor put it, "the God of peace" or "the lord of hosts" should inspire American political economy.

[17] Monroe to Madison, April 15, 1804, Dispatches, Great Britain, Monroe, vol. 11, National Archives (NA).

"Take care of the Commonwealth," he warned James Madison. "It has deeper interest than the carrying trade."[18]

Jefferson never fashioned a personally satisfying defense of the carrying trade that overcame the objections he had raised about it in the 1780s. While president, he fretted that Great Britain would interpret American demands as the desires of a greedy nation, buoyed by the prospects before it, less needy of English trade and friendship, ready and willing to put English distress to American economic purpose. By and large, however, his own anxiety fell before popular desires to amass wealth, national hopes that being merchant to a world at war was an easy road to riches, and a rather smug Republican belief that neutral rights protected American avarice from the onslaughts of the belligerent powers. Wilson Cary Nicholas, Republican congressman from Virginia, thought the carrying trade worth a war, and although most Americans held back from that notion, many shared Nicholas's belief that "the right to buy and sell colonial produce is too dear and too important to be given up." "This is not a trade of little importance," Nicholas wrote Jefferson in 1806, "it is of incalculable value." Nicholas reasoned for the future as well as for the present. Because Europe spent "half [its] time fighting," it was imperative that the United States defend immediately its neutral right to the carrying trade.[19] Jefferson's administration needed little reminding. The May 1806 instructions to Monroe and Pinkney that renewed the negotiations with Great Britain under a joint commission demanded only two things in an acceptable treaty: satisfaction on impressments and protection of the carrying trade.

The Jeffersonians calculated European war too heavily in their accounting of American prosperity. Republican economics pegged national growth and prosperity to the legitimate expansion of peacetime markets for native productions. But Republican leaders made the tragic blunder of twice renewing their English negotiations with eyes riveted on the European war. The administration committed its diplomatic resources to the protection of merchant and shipping profit in the nonnative carrying trade and to the protection

[18] Joseph Buttersworth to Randolph, May 17, 1806, John Randolph Papers, University of Virginia (UVa); Cooper to TJ, Mar. 16, 1806, Jefferson Papers, Library of Congress (LC); Randolph, *Annals of Congress*, 9th Cong., lst sess., p. 557; Taylor to Madison, Jan. 15, 1808, James Madison Papers, UVa.

[19] Nicholas to TJ, April 2, 1806, Jefferson Papers, LC.

of agricultural profit in the temporary and dangerous direct trade with Great Britain's enemies. It harnessed doctrines of international law on behalf of national avarice. "Neutrals have at all times been avaricious and encroachers," Benjamin Stoddert would write Jefferson in 1809. The United States was not the exception to the general rule. "Had we been ever so certain that the belligerent nations would have submitted to [our] encroachments . . . , we should still have decided from regard to our own interest that none should have been made—and we should have still confined our enterprise to a commerce purely American." Stoddert's was not a brief against commerce, but a reasoned statement against a commerce divorced from native American production. To the extent that Jeffersonian policy makers departed from their republican vision of an economic order grounded in the skill of the American producing classes, to the extent that they embraced foreign war as profitable enterprise, they created the dilemmas that confronted them in the last four years of Jefferson's presidency.[20]

Monroe's English Diplomacy

On January 5, 1804, the State Department sent Monroe formal instructions covering his prospective negotiations with Great Britain. Each economic item on the official agenda concerned the European war and the possibilities it opened to American commerce. The instructions were silent on America's peacetime trade, an omission that Madison calculated would make the way "plainer and shorter" to the resolution of the differences that threatened conflict. The State Department wanted four issues settled: impressment, blockade, contraband, and the American trade with the colonial possessions of England's enemies. Success on these four points would improve Anglo-American relations and avoid hostilities. It would also ensure a safe environment for wartime profit taking. The instructions also spelled out certain concessions to England's belligerent needs. If concessions alone did not produce a diplomatic settlement, the instructions ordered Monroe to threaten retaliation: the loss of the American

[20] Stoddert to TJ, Jan. 25, 1809, ibid.

market "to certain important and popular classes of British manufactures."[21]

Madison also sent Monroe a draft of an acceptable treaty. The first three articles concerned impressment. One categorically rejected any British right to take persons off American ships on the high seas. Two additional articles rounded out the American demand. One prohibited the practice involving American citizens within the domains of Great Britain, calling for the immediate release of all victims and "adequate recompense" to allow them "to return to their own country." The other limited the right of English press gangs to approach and board American ships.

Monroe was empowered to make concessions to facilitate England's acceptance of the American position. He could offer congressional legislation to prohibit American citizens from giving "refuge or protection" to any actual deserter from the British navy, army, or merchant marine. He could also commit American local authorities to active cooperation in the capture, confinement, and return of bona fide British deserters. The State Department had anticipated that England might demand American action against its ship captains who enticed British sailors into the American service. This was a thorny question, and the Jeffersonians hoped to avoid it completely. Once the United States admitted that enticement existed, then Great Britain could pile on American shoulders much of the responsibility for British desertion. There was also the practical difficulty of policing American captains in faraway ports. Madison cautioned his diplomat not to discuss enticement and its prevention "but in the event of it being made an indispensible condition" to British agreement on the impressment articles.[22]

While the administration recognized Great Britain's interest in keeping its naval service manned at adequate levels and accepted England's legitimate concern with desertion, there was little a republican government could do to coerce popular respect for England's needs and to police the activities of American captains in foreign ports. Although Madison pledged American help both in the capture of deserters and in the reduction of the number of British

[21] Madison to Monroe, Sept. 12, 17, 1804, Mar. 6, 1805, Diplomatic Instructions, All Countries, vol. 6, NA.
[22] Madison to Monroe, Jan. 5, 1804, ibid.

seamen jumping to American ships, he also instructed Monroe to emphasize the serious obstacles to effective American cooperation in these matters. Consequently, the State Department's position hung on the hope that promises and good intentions would soften English resistance to American goals.

Impressments aside, Monroe's diplomacy had an overriding economic purpose: to neutralize the threat of British maritime power to the sources of profit created by the European war. Blockade, contraband, and the carrying trade were the essential issues. Central to the administration's understanding of a safe environment for wartime trade in 1804 was the definition of legal blockade. This emphasis rested on a commonsense realization that as powerful as the Royal Navy was, it was not omnipotent. Great Britain could not physically blockade all the ports of its enemies. What England could do, and what it had done in the past, was to blockade them on paper. Blockade by pronouncement exaggerated England's control of the world's trade well beyond its physical resources and, when combined with a reserved right to capture neutral vessels after they had violated paper blockades, unfairly extended the reach of the English navy. It was the promulgation of paper blockades that had resulted in so many confiscations and condemnations of American vessels in the previous Anglo-French war. Then Great Britain, in Madison's words, had carried the policy to "extravagance." "The whole scene," he later observed, "was a perfect mockery in which fact was sacrificed to form, right to power and plunder." England's bloated claims posed a serious threat to the rich American trade with the colonial possessions of France and Spain. As early as 1804, the reemergence of a "paper system" was discernible. When war with France resumed, England declared Martinique and Santo Domingo in a state of blockade even though "the whole naval force applied to the purpose was inconsiderable." Paper blockades were shifting, mercurial, and arbitrary. Their power to disrupt American trade, coupled with their capriciousness, made them the most important item on the Jeffersonian English agenda.[23]

On the permissible scope of blockade hung England's ability to restrict American trade. Contraband and the carrying trade, therefore, did not absolutely require treaty stipulation. Although the State

[23] Ibid.

Department sent Monroe draft articles that defined contraband in narrow military terms and sought protection for the carrying trade, formal success on these points was not necessary because the abolition of paper blockades would restrict England's ability to enforce its definition of contraband and because existing admirality law—most notably in the case of the ship *Polly*—already secured the carrying trade to the workable doctrine of the broken voyage.

The *Polly* decision (1800) had given the United States most of the benefits of the unattainable "free ships free goods" doctrine. Long a Jeffersonian dream, this doctrine rested on the happy assumption that during war peaceful nations should suffer as little economic interruption as possible consistent with honest belligerent needs. It recognized a belligerent right to stop neutral trade in military contraband and to enfeeble its opponents through blockades to the limits of its actual naval power. Neutral nations could trade in all goods not contraband of war and between all places, including the colonial possessions of the belligerent nations, not under physical blockade. Different British notions buttressed by the Royal Navy and admiralty courts ruined the dream. But it was a compelling ingredient in Jefferson's enlightened universe, and even as his diplomacy struggled to achieve much less, it pained him to let it go. As late as 1806, while keeping a running record of cabinet discussions on the scope of American demands, he first wrote of "giving up" the free ships principle in exchange for a British return to the recently overturned *Polly* decision, only to scratch out the telling phrase and insert "not insisting on."[24] At any rate, "free ships free goods" was not essential to the carrying trade in the spring of 1804 because the *Polly* decision was still in force.

In *Polly*, the court held that neutral nations could pursue a European and colonial trade denied them in peacetime provided the voyage was interrupted or "broken" by an importation into the neutral country. Accordingly, an American vessel could not carry a colonial cargo of England's enemy directly to a foreign port, but it could pick up the colonial cargo, stop in an American port, unload, pay duties, reload, and set out again. Ideally, *Polly* aimed to confine American trade with the colonial possessions of England's enemies to the needs of American domestic consumption. Practically, it tried to erode

[24] TJ, "Notes on Cabinet Discussions," Mar. 5, 1806, Jefferson Papers, LC.

America's advantage over British merchants with cumbersome and costly double voyages. American ingenuity shrank the cost and the annoyance and turned the broken voyage to the purposes of both the free ships ideology and sizable commercial profit. When war in Europe resumed in 1803, breaking the voyage became largely a charade. Congressional statute allowed the American merchant to "draw back" the duties paid on importation if the cargo was reexported within a certain period of time. Often merchants did not even pay duties, but simply posted security. Cargoes went unloaded, and ships unchanged. When England complained that breaking voyages with an honest importation was done more on paper than in fact, the State Department answered that American commercial regulations were not England's concern.[25]

On the British judicial meaning of importation rested the ability of American merchants to live comfortably and profitably within the requirements of the broken voyage. The *Polly* ruling had happily supported the needs of American trade. "It is not my business," the judge held in that case, "to say what is universally the test of a bona fide importation. I am strongly disposed to hold that it would be sufficient that goods should be landed and duties paid. If these criteria are not resorted to, I should be at a loss to know what should be the test." Why the American satisfaction with this British emphasis on importation? Because other components of England's maritime system, most notably the Rule of 1756 and the doctrine of "accustomed commerce," denied to neutral nations a trade with England's enemies that those nations did not grant the neutral country in peacetime. Ironically, *Polly* technically destroyed the American carrying trade but actually protected it by calling it by another name. Its requirement of importation transformed the colonial produce into native American stock. The future destination of the now American goods, so long as they were not contraband, was limited only by blockade.[26]

The Jeffersonians in Washington had lofty hopes for Monroe's mission.[27] He may have fostered unreasonable expectations by displaying too much optimism in his initial dispatches back to the State

[25] The words of the British judge in the *Polly* case were quoted in a letter from Madison to Monroe, April 12, 1805, Diplomatic Instructions, All Countries, vol. 6, NA.

[26] Ibid.

[27] Madison to Monroe, April 15, 1804, ibid.

Department.[28] In fact, harsh realities hounded Monroe throughout his stay in London. He began his discussions with a government, the Addington ministry, that he knew would not survive beyond the early stages of diplomacy. Nonetheless, Monroe prepared a treaty draft covering the fundamental issues outlined in his January instructions which he presented to Addington's foreign secretary, Robert Jenkinson, Lord Hawkesbury, on April 7, 1804, and in it Monroe showed a pragmatic eye for the status quo when leaving matters as they stood was the best available option and did not work a hardship on American interests. His draft included stipulations on blockade and impressment but omitted contraband and American trade with the colonial possessions of England's enemies. He was sure that Great Britain would not accept the American definition of contraband, and he believed that the *Polly* decision temporarily protected the American carrying trade, albeit through the annoying medium of the broken voyage. Ignoring the whole question of the carrying trade, therefore, sacrificed no American interest and avoided a more complicated diplomacy. Jefferson and Madison, less confident that the mercurial admiralty courts afforded dependable security, wanted *Polly* written into treaty law. But because the *Polly* cushion still existed, they would have accepted a treaty silent on the carrying trade if it satisfied American demands on impressment and blockade.[29]

After he presented his ideas to Hawkesbury, Monroe waited for the collapse of the Addington ministry and the end of diplomatic instability. "A few days will reduce this mess to a certainty," he wrote Madison in early May, promising to begin earnest discussions with Hawkesbury's successor when the new government came to power. Ironically, the Addington coalition lasted long enough to outline certain assumptions that defined the English position throughout the negotiations. On April 12 Hawkesbury told Monroe that England would not consider neutral questions apart from the larger issue of Anglo-American trade. He also insisted that the Jay Treaty form the foundation of any new commercial accord. Monroe quickly rejected

[28]Monroe to Madison, Mar. 18, 1804, Dispatches, Great Britain, Monroe, vol. 11, NA.

[29]Project of a Convention presented to Lord Hawkesbury, April 7, 1804, *American State Papers: Foreign Relations* 3:92; Monroe to Madison, Sept. 8, 1804, Dispatches, Great Britain, Monroe, vol. 11, NA; Madison to Monroe, Mar. 6, 1805, Diplomatic Instructions, All Countries, vol. 6, NA.

its relevance to the present negotiations. These antagonistic positions revealed the fundamental differences that separated Great Britain and the United States and eventually produced a war.[30]

No accomplishment of the Federalist administrations had more angered the Republicans than John Jay's in 1794. In it, agriculture, democracy, and national independence had suffered at the hands of the Hamiltonian credit interest, aristocracy, and Great Britain. For the Jeffersonians, it was a nagging reminder of American economic bondage to Great Britain and a symbol of American inferiority. It constrained the United States beneath its aspirations and abilities and unfairly rewarded the country's transatlantic rival. The memory of the Jay Treaty shadowed the negotiations because beneath the raw economic urges to profit from the Napoleonic wars, Republican goals centered on establishing a new and better status for the United States in its relations with Great Britain and, by extension, the Old World. Colonial remembrances jarred uncomfortably with national assertions in the Republican imagination, and their antagonism gave Jefferson's English diplomacy its dramatic meaning.

Hawkesbury's quiet insistence that the Jay Treaty shape the deliberations warned Monroe of a British design to preserve its status at the expense of American desire. Although nagged by doubts of the propriety of American demands, Monroe gradually embraced the assumption that diplomacy could accomplish little because Great Britain already saw itself at war against American maritime ambition. Whenever hopeful predictions crept into his dispatches and private letters home, they owed more to a bad habit of seeing British concession in personal civility and to a worry that his esteem at home depended on his success abroad. Not until he committed his reputation and his political future to the treaty that he and Pinkney initialed in late 1806 did he depart from the grim conclusion he reached during the agonizing months of 1805: "No event is deemed more unfavorable to Great Britain than the growing importance of the United States, and it is the primary object of her government to check it, if not crush it."[31] But before the negotiations turned ominous they became merely boring, as Monroe waited patiently for Addington's successor.

[30] Monroe to Madison, April 15, May 3, 1804, Dispatches, Great Britain, Monroe, vol. 11, NA.

[31] Monroe to Madison, Oct. 18, 1805, ibid., vol. 12.

Although English political instability created immediate problems for American diplomacy, there was always the hope that the new ministry, when formed, would be more receptive to American positions. Hawkesbury's hard line made any changes in personnel welcome. In the spring of 1804 Monroe reported to Washington that political change in England was imminent. Pitt, Grenville, and Fox were all in opposition. Rumors in May had the entire opposition on the verge of coalition. Political talk had Pitt forming the new government, Grenville heading the home office, and Fox taking charge of foreign affairs. But Monroe was very cautious about the diplomatic implications of English political change. Expect only "a change of men," he warned Madison, not "a change of measures." Even if Charles James Fox, the American hero, entered the cabinet, "he will have to be a party man."[32]

As it turned out, the king would not yield to William Pitt's demands, and Charles Fox stayed out of the new government. It was not altogether new; it simply added Pitt and his supporters to the core of the old one. The new men, especially Pitt and his foreign secretary designate, Dudley Ryder, second Baron Harrowby, were devoted supporters of the English maritime system and unsympathetic to spending too much for American accord while war raged in Europe. From Madison's point of view, the new government offered little improvement on the old.[33]

At his first meeting with the new foreign secretary, Monroe managed to squeeze between pleasantries a word of his anxiety to get on with official business. Harrowby parried with predictable excuses: he would need time to study Anglo-American affairs, and the European war was more important to England at the moment than an American treaty. He was so busy, Harrowby claimed, that he had not yet read the draft that Monroe had presented to Hawkesbury. Drawing from Harrowby a promise to read it, Monroe took his leave. When two weeks passed and Monroe had still not heard from the Foreign Office, he requested another audience. The second meeting, held

[32] Monroe to Madison, Mar. 18, May 3, June 3, 1804, ibid. The best treatment of English politics during this period, indeed on the English dimension of the Anglo-American controversy before the War of 1812, is Bradford Perkins, *Prologue to War: England and the United States, 1805–1812* (Berkeley, Calif., 1961).

[33] Monroe to Madison, June 3, 1804, Dispatches, Great Britain, Monroe, vol. 11, NA.

on May 30, duplicated the first. Harrowby had not read the draft, offered no assurance that he would soon get to it, and cautioned Monroe that American affairs were distinctly inferior to England's immediate concerns. By midyear, Monroe had lost his earlier optimism. "I now consider these concerns as postponed indefinitely," he wrote Madison on June 3. The English were stalling, and he would not ask for another interview. The resumption of negotiations now depended on British initiative.[34]

More seriously, Monroe informed the State Department that when the negotiations resumed, they would fail. So much pointed to that conclusion. Harrowby's conduct during the May 30 interview had been chilling, "calculated to wound and irritate. Not a friendly sentiment toward the United States or their government escaped him." Communication between the British Foreign Office and the ambassadors of the European neutrals was increasing. If Russia and Sweden joined England's coalition, thereby leaving the United States the only maritime neutral, England's mishandling of American commerce would assume menacing proportions.[35]

As significant was Monroe's midyear assessment of the Pitt ministry. The new government would attempt to distinguish itself from its predecessor by "more enterprising measures" against the United States. In the last European war it was Pitt who had pushed British policy to "an extraordinary harassment of neutral commerce." Soon to come was "a change of policy toward us." It would grow from Great Britain's fear of American potential. Because Monroe located England's refusal to negotiate neutral issues in its unfair desire to restrict American economic growth, his "most earnest advice" was to expect the worst. Consequently, he asked his superiors to buttress his diplomatic position with displays of strength, especially the threat of a congressionally imposed loss of the American market to British industry.[36] Monroe's counsel took the shape of the historic Republican remedy for European abuse. So too did his understanding of the sources of British policy mirror a compelling set of Jeffersonian beliefs. Unable to accept that the girth of their neutral demands both mortgaged negotiations to the unattainable and embarrassed Republican assumptions on the course and ethics of American economic de-

[34] Ibid.
[35] Ibid.
[36] Ibid.

velopment, the Jeffersonians instead found ample reason for impending failure in the plain fact of British jealousy. By marrying their economic demands to the sacred quest for American independence, the Republicans masked economic desires with the innocent face of a good and simple people struggling to be free.

Before he departed for Spain to discuss the Florida boundary, Monroe's remaining months in London convinced him that the United States might be better off without a formal treaty. Changes in personnel had not altered official policy, and Harrowby was as insistent as Hawkesbury had been on the importance of the Jay Treaty to all subsequent achievements. In proper Republican fashion, Monroe rejected the relevance of a document that institutionalized American inferiority, deprived Congress of its right to single out Great Britain for economic punishment, and mocked American potential. "We must begin de novo," he told Harrowby. "Our interests are better understood at this time than they then were."[37]

Not only did Monroe reject the utility of the past treaty; he tried, in keeping with his instructions, to avoid any discussion of Anglo-American trade. Perhaps the Jeffersonians feared a diplomatic contest over the whole range of commercial issues. At any rate, the European war spared them the chore. The war opened the English Caribbean islands as well as a treaty could, and the *Polly* decision anchored the American carrying trade with England's enemies to the broken voyage. Agreement on impressments and blockade would protect the nation's seamen and honor and round out a very attractive environment in which to mount profit and make inroads into British maritime superiority. So Monroe asked Harrowby to forget both the Jay Treaty and a new Anglo-American commercial accord. The United States refused to take unfair advantage while Great Britain was preoccupied with European war. Instead, it wished "to postpone the regulation of their general commercial system till the period should arrive when each enjoying the blessings of peace, might find itself at liberty to pay the subject the attention it merited." But Harrowby would not touch either blockade or colonial trade without reference to the larger question of America's commercial relationship with Great Britain.[38]

[37] Monroe to Madison, Aug. 7, 1804, ibid.
[38] Madison to Monroe, Jan. 5, 1804, Diplomatic Instructions, All Countries, vol. 6, NA.

Unable to make progress on any question of neutral trade, Monroe turned to impressment. He repeated the demands he had outlined to Hawkesbury, but now added what he had omitted from the draft that he had presented to the English government in April: an American pledge of cooperation in the capture and return of bona fide British deserters. Monroe's omission owed mostly to Madison's desire not to have the issue of American cooperation raised until absolutely essential to an agreement. But as a tardy and verbal addition to the written proposals of April, the pledge lost much of its credibility. Harrowby was lukewarm. He doubted if the American government could stop ship captains from enticing or accepting British seamen into the American service. Nor did he believe that republican government was strong enough to oblige state and local authorities to capture, detain, and eventually return English deserters. "The bias and the spirit of the people would be against it," he told Monroe, regardless of the good intentions of American leaders.[39]

Little was accomplished in the summer of 1804, and in August, Monroe told Madison that he had "little hope of bringing [the negotiation] to a successful conclusion." The American diplomat tried to put the best gloss on his work, and in the process contradicted his own pessimistic observations on English motivation.[40] Although his reassessment was understandably motivated by a desire to place his efforts in the best possible light, it also revealed a more subtle and pragmatic attitude toward the sources of international rivalry. Monroe began to stress the protections afforded by the *Polly* decision. He now spoke of concluding his business "by a postponement of it." He asked his superiors to appreciate the constraints that European war placed on official England. "Much allowance must be given to Britain's military struggles on the Continent," he reminded Madison. The broader contexts of European war and English survival seemed to make Great Britain's stubbornness less ominous and allowed Monroe to deny that Anglo-American relations had reached a crisis point or that the outstanding issues required a formal treaty.[41]

[39] Monroe to Madison, Aug. 7, 1804, Dispatches, Great Britain, Monroe, vol. 11, NA.

[40] Monroe to Madison, Sept. 17, Oct. 3, 1804, Monroe to Hawkesbury, Sept. 29, 1804, John Henry Purviance to Madison, Oct. 18, 1804, Harrowby to Purviance, Jan. 11, 1805, ibid.

[41] Monroe to Madison, Aug. 24, Oct. 3, 1804, ibid. See also Madison to Monroe, Nov. 19, 1804, James Madison Papers, LC, microfilm, reel 7.

By the beginning of September, he was set to depart for Spain. He would spend several months on the Continent. By the time he returned, the status quo had altered considerably, and he faced the difficult task of winning back the protections for the carrying trade that British admiralty decisions had taken away.

By the beginning of March 1805, the administration had analyzed Monroe's dispatches up to the moment he interrupted his English diplomacy to journey to the Continent in search of East Florida. Madison now instructed Monroe to emphasize how much the United States would cooperate in the interests of settlement, and he gave him the arguments. A Virginia law punishing ship captains who accepted British deserters into the Virginia merchant marine proved how empty was the English fear that local authorities would refuse to respect England's maritime needs. Congressional laws that obliged American merchants to post security against violating physical blockades further revealed an American commitment to fair compromise. Such laws, state and national, were proof enough "of our good faith." But if they failed to coax reciprocity from England, Madison empowered his diplomat to threaten economic reprisals.[42]

Retaliation took the shape of Jeffersonian statecraft dating from the Revolution: the loss of the American market to British ships and industry. Its implementation, however, created problems. Although the president bristled at the English notion that the United States was wedded to "Quaker principles,"[43] he loathed the thought of war. Consequently his encounter with weapons of force, whether economic or military, was hesitant. In brandishing their weapon, the Republicans aimed to create the impression of peaceful anger, of a beleaguered nation driven to extreme measures that it would gladly forsake if diplomacy offered the smallest indication of an English commitment to candid discussion and the quiet composition of differences. The Jeffersonian threat was almost apologetic. Both moods reflected their temper. Whether anger informed with civility could perform its anticipated good works was another matter.

In the spring of 1805 the American threat spoke to British impressments. Barring new onslaughts on American commerce, the United States would tolerate existing levels of maritime hostility

[42] Madison to Monroe, Mar. 6, 1805, Diplomatic Instructions, All Countries, vol. 6, NA.

[43] TJ to Thomas Cooper, Feb. 18, 1806, Jefferson Papers, LC.

without responding in kind, but not the continuation of impressments. This Monroe was to make clear. But in 1805 the admiralty courts overturned the *Polly* decision, thereby endangering the most profitable form of wartime commerce. In two cases, one involving the *Aurora* in March and the other the *Essex* in May, English judges held that the goods' ultimate destination determined their national character, and if the ultimate destination was a French or Spanish port, the Rule of 1756 and the doctrine of "accustomed commerce" still applied. The *Polly* rule that the payment of import duties proved an honest importation and therefore transformed the national identity of the cargo was no longer sufficient because the Americans had abused it. In the case of the *Essex*, the ship had landed in Charleston. After the payment of duties, it proceeded to Havana. The judge held that the owner's "intention was from the beginning to send the cargo to a Spanish colony." He also tied the misadventure of the *Essex* to a raft of similar American frauds aimed at illegitimate profit.[44]

These decisions struck at a major ingredient of American prosperity. The average annual amount of American reexportations up until 1803 was $32 million. Three years later the average swelled to over $60 million.[45] The *Aurora* departure from the *Polly* rule released new fears in Washington that Great Britain reckoned its treatment of American commerce not on considerations relating to the European war but, in Madison's words, "on the value of it to the United States." It galled Jefferson that England denied a trade to the United States that it carried on with its enemies. If such was the basis of British policy, then America "must calculate by the same standard."[46] The defense of the carrying trade was fast becoming the chief economic reason behind the administration's consideration of congressionally imposed nonimportation of British goods. Alarmed by the overturn of the *Polly* decision and armed with Madison's advice, administration threats, and sundry memorials from merchants to Jefferson and the Congress, Monroe asked for an immediate interview with England's new foreign secretary, Henry Phipps, third

[44] The opinions of both the Nassau Admiralty Court and the Whitehall Appeals Court can be found in Dispatches, Great Britain, Monroe, vol. 12, NA.

[45] Madison to Monroe, April 12, 1805, Diplomatic Instructions, All Countries, vol. 6, NA; Perkins, *Prologue*, p. 23.

[46] Madison to Monroe, April 12, 1805, Diplomatic Instructions, All Countries, vol. 6, NA.

Baron Mulgrave, a Britisher especially hostile to the challenge of American trade.[47]

Monroe and Mulgrave met several times in August and exchanged in almost ritual fashion pleasant formalities and antagonistic principles. The clutter of "accustomed commerce" and "free ships free goods" was choking the diplomatic process, so Monroe placed his lofty principles aside and got down to cases. "On what footing," he asked Mulgrave, was the British government "willing to place the carrying trade"? Monroe wanted a simple return to the *Polly* days, but Mulgrave defended the recent admiralty and appeals rulings. When Monroe warned that the United States would not sit idly by while the British courts "cut up by the roots the commerce of the United States," Mulgrave remained silent.[48]

In August, Monroe not only reported stalemate back to Washington but also stated his belief that the court rulings were actually disguised ministerial policy. The credibility of his conspiracy charge turned on the presence of several cabinet members on the appeals court. By letting judges speak for it, the government both changed policy and escaped responsibility for the change. Thus it deviously accomplished its true aim: "the promotion of the navigation of this country at the expense of the United States." Because the courts and not the ministry had engineered the destruction of the broken voyage, Monroe saw England anticipating little more from the United States than diplomatic whining. In time, as he understood the British tactic, the new restrictive policies would spread quietly over the ocean and achieve cabinet legitimacy. That the British were afraid to adopt the new policies openly and would therefore repudiate the court decisions if pressed by the American government was a crucial assumption of Monroe's analysis. To avoid the American challenge, Mulgrave was avoiding Monroe. With hope in hand, the Republican diplomat decided to press the matter to conclusion.[49]

[47] Monroe to Madison, Aug. 16, 1805, Dispatches, Great Britain, Monroe, vol. 12, NA.

[48] Monroe to Mulgrave, July 31, Aug. 8, 12, Oct. 10, 1805, Mulgrave to Monroe, Aug. 5, 9, 1805, Monroe to Madison, Aug. 16, 20, 26, 1805, minutes of a conversation between Erving and Hammond, Aug. 30, 1805, Monroe to Gen. John Armstrong, Sept. 2, 1805, ibid.

[49] Monroe to Madison, Aug. 16, 20, 25, 1805, ibid.; Monroe to Madison, Oct. 26, 1805, Madison Papers, LC, ser. 2, reel 25.

From October to the end of 1805 Monroe laid stress on the idea of British malevolence. England's treatment of the United States comprised a "studious" attempt to thwart the challenge of American potential to England's inflated maritime status. Although the means changed with circumstance, it moved against American commercial growth whenever opportunity allowed. It had refrained from overturning the *Polly* decision until Russia and Sweden were locked safely in the third coalition. Monroe's England found the United States both frightening and contemptible. One English eye focused on American commerce, the other on the American government. Each perception opposed the other, and both together comprehended the English schizophrenia. Awesome as England found American commercial potential, the challenge that it posed was puny because the government behind the entrepreneurial American was "popular" and therefore "incapable of any great, vigorous, or persevering action." England's America, frailly republican, beset with domestic political tensions, confused by the subtlety of English policy, and fearful of political conflict at home if it acted forcefully abroad, was a docile tiger. Ultimately it would submit tamely to hostile court rulings, an inferior treaty, or no treaty at all. For these reasons, Monroe suggested strong measures—military buildup and nonimportation legislation—to his superiors. If the United States did no more than complain, England would expand its restrictive policies to the complete "prostration and pillage of our commerce throughout the entire war."[50]

Monroe's beliefs about British intentions governed his advice to his country. Demands and treaty proposals based on morality and international law were sorely ineffectual because Great Britain would concede nothing to a rising commercial enemy. Although Monroe did not coin the phrase, by the end of 1805 he was accusing Great Britain of waging disguised war against the United States. Its struggle against Napoleon camouflaged its crusade against American commerce. It was tempting but false to assume that English harassment grew from and would end with the European war. Unless crucial issues were settled immediately, even at the risk of war, an England freed from Napoleonic threat would become an unchallenge-

[50] Monroe to Madison, Oct. 18, Dec. 11, 25, 1805, Dispatches, Great Britain, Monroe, vol. 12, NA; Monroe to Madison, Nov. 16, 22, 1805, Jan. 10, 1806, Madison Papers, LC, ser. 2, reel 25.

able Goliath. As he wrote Madison: "It seems to be a question, simply, whether we will resist their unjust pressures at this time or defer it to some further opportunity." Monroe favored a present stand. "With her force concentrated in this quarter," England could neither annoy the United States nor "protect her commerce and possessions elsewhere which would be exposed to our attacks."[51]

Monroe did not advocate war in the fall of 1805; he merely argued that if his worst apprehensions about England's attitude were correct, war was better now than later. His dispatches and private letters vacillated between continued talks, economic retaliation, war, or even a protective embargo until European forces produced a more serene ocean. His advice was fuzzy because distinctions between various policies were blurred. All were really interconnected. Clearly, further discussion without a show of force was futile. Unless the United States challenged English notions of American timidity, diplomacy was wasted effort. From argument, civility, and mastery of the texts of international law, Monroe wrote Madison, "we can expect nothing." A negotiated settlement rested on transforming the English opinion of the United States, and that, in turn, required "prov[ing] that we can and will do them more harm than they can expect advantage from adhering to their present course." In short, victory at the conference table presumed prior congressional economic reprisal. Yet such actions might anger the British and spoil any chance for a diplomatic settlement. Two considerations prompted Monroe to advise immediate and highly visible military preparation: a prudent belief that American nonimportation might trigger massive scenes of commercial abuse or even an English declaration of war and a diplomat's instinct that both negotiations and economic retaliation required public displays of military activity were they to be effective. His counsel moved in the direction of simultaneous economic reprisal and military buildup; the first to buttress his position and to show England the economic alternative to diplomatic failure, the second "to protect ourselves against unexpected and unfavorable results which are always to be guarded against."[52]

Gloomy as was Monroe's analysis, other less dismal perceptions of

[51] Monroe to Madison, Oct. 18, Dec. 11, 25, 1805, Dispatches, Great Britain, Monroe, vol. 12, NA.

[52] Monroe to TJ, Sept. 26, 1805, Jefferson Papers, LC; Monroe to Madison, Jan. 10, 1806, Madison Papers, LC, ser. 2, reel 25.

British policy and motivation were also compatible with the facts. And this he knew. Although the bulk of his observations supported and fed a Jeffersonian view that always transformed England's policies into morbid anti-American obsessions, sometimes Monroe rejected apocalyptic thinking and suggested, instead, cautious optimism. America need not think the worst. Its deepest fears sprang from a perception of malevolent British design. But robbed of their conspiratorial pattern, recent English actions did not spell American disaster. Almost buried beneath the mountains of anti-British writing that Monroe sent back from London were questions and observations that both minimized the English threat and mocked his abundant arguments for strong economic and military action.

At year's end in 1805 Monroe asked his superiors, what was the precise nature of the English assault? What American economic interests were actually, not potentially, threatened? All that now lay exposed to English power was the carrying trade. By his own admission, Monroe's spirited objections to the *Essex* decisions were politically motivated, necessary to allay the suspicions in New England about a southern president long considered in northern quarters as unsympathetic to the needs of the maritime states. But should the United States go beyond formal complaint and embrace the disturbing policies of economic sanctions and military action? For the sake of the carrying trade, should the United States antagonize the British Lion? Strong congressional action might lead to a raft of unpleasantries: a more comprehensive attack on American commerce that contained ruinous implications for American agriculture as the *Essex* decisions had not; southern political opposition to administration policies that made agricultural prosperity hostage to New England's carrying trade; dislocation of the steady Jeffersonian effort to retire the public debt; confusion in America's foreign relations with France and Spain; war with England. Could the administration assume solid congressional and popular support if it risked all this on behalf of a narrow economic interest? Such were Monroe's chilling reminders of the dangers implicit in a rugged defense of the carrying trade.[53]

Unable to resolve his own ambiguity, Monroe's thinking bounced between national assertion and national restraint, between his south-

[53] Monroe to Madison, Nov. 22, 1805, Feb. 2, 1806, Madison Papers, LC, ser. 2, reel 25.

ern roots and his national position. His indecision mirrored congressional and presidential uncertainty. Celebrate as Jefferson did Madison's legalistic defense of the carrying trade ("I send you a pamphlet," he wrote a friend in February 1806, "in which the British doctrine that a commerce not open to neutrals in peace shall not be pursued by them in war is logically and unanswerably refuted"), the old doubts still gnawed.[54] Was the carrying trade a worthy American economic aspiration? That question had haunted Jefferson since the beginnings of the disintegration of European peace in the 1780s. To friends who questioned the wisdom of binding American peace to wartime carrying profit, Jefferson countered with anti-British venom, preachy justifications, and angry declaimers of wrongdoing that all betrayed anxiety over the rectitude of American demands.[55] In 1805 the carrying trade had Jefferson's support, but only if pamphlets and persuasion could secure it. His doubts on the propriety of the whole business left him lukewarm to strong economic action then being championed by congressional advocates of the wartime commerce. Jefferson's ambivalence and the South's refusal to risk trade and war in a bareknuckled defense of the North's economic interest ensured that Congress's 1806 response to the *Essex* decisions would be less than forceful. The carrying trade confounded Monroe's analysis, eroded Jefferson's commitment to vigorous action, and divided the Republican majority in Congress. Its defense required not only jeremiads against English villainy but a full discussion of American policy as well. Republicans could unite against their British enemy, out of habit if nothing else, but because they could not agree on the proper shape of the nation's economy, coherent policy eluded them. A commercial or military defense of the carrying trade required the public marriage of American prosperity to European war. At this, Monroe, Jefferson, the South, and much of the Congress balked. Divided on both the ends and the means of America's English policy, many Republicans, Jefferson included, favored the least damaging policy of forgoing strong action, continuing quiet diplomacy, and, perhaps, limping along without a formal treaty. The *Essex* decisions galled, but their economic cost was bearable, and combating them strenuously posed more problems than it solved.

[54] TJ to Pierre Samuel Dupont de Nemours, Feb. 12, 1806, Jefferson Papers, LC.

[55] TJ to Thomas Cooper, Feb. 18, 1806, ibid.

The end of 1805 found Monroe preparing to return home. He conveyed his departure time to both Madison and Mulgrave and hoped his abundant analyses would help his superiors see their way to a consistent line of policy. While the American was placing his affairs in order, Pitt's health failed. At the turn of the new year, William Pitt died. That event rekindled Monroe's optimism and convinced him that he could now obtain an advantageous treaty, not only for the carrying trade but for native American commerce and the safety of American sailors as well. "The death of Mr. Pitt," he wrote Madison in January 1806, "is a very important event the tendency of which you will readily perceive." When Charles James Fox became England's new foreign secretary, Monroe's enthusiasm was boundless. For months, he clung to the hope that Fox would fulfill American expectations. In his desire for success, Monroe forgot his realistic reminder to Madison of two years before that if Fox entered the government, he would enter as "a party man."[56] While Monroe pondered diplomatic possibilities in London, the American Congress turned its attention to the proper response to the English crisis.

[56] Monroe to Madison, Jan. 22, 28, Feb. 12, 1806, Dispatches, Great Britain, Monroe, vol. 12, NA.

2

PLANTERS AND MERCHANTS
The Republican Party and the English Threat

The Congress

English problems headed Congress's agenda when it convened in December 1805. Jefferson's annual message outlined the major foreign policy concern—the *Essex* decisions and their probable impact on America's carrying trade—and reminded Congress of its obligation to provide "an effectual and determined opposition to a doctrine so injurious to the rights of peaceable nations."[1] On the proper national response, congressional Republicans would debate and divide for months. Geography and occupation shaped the battle lines. New England and middle state Republicans insisted on tough economic retaliation because of their regions' sizable investment in the wartime carrying business. Southern Republicans opposed bold action because their region gained little from the carrying trade and stood to lose much if Anglo-American commerce was disrupted. An early argument over which congressional committee should hammer out American policy anticipated the sectional divisions that followed. At first, the president's message was routinely assigned to the Ways and Means Committee, chaired by John Randolph of Virginia. For weeks no report or recommendations emerged. Finally, the northern Republicans, led by Jacob Crowninshield and Barnabas Bidwell of Massachusetts, succeeded in transferring the president's message to the entire House, sitting in Committee of the Whole. Never again in the Ninth Congress would the northern commercial interest achieve so clear a victory in matters relating to England's treatment of America's wartime carrying trade.[2]

[1] TJ, Fifth Annual Message, *Annals of Congress*, 9th Cong., 1st sess., p. 13.
[2] Ibid., pp. 258–62, 342–43, 410–12.

On Wednesday, March 5, the congressional consideration of America's English policy began. With proposals of varying severity on the floor and without the anchor of administration direction or preference, the discussion of policy, at times repetitive, was comprehensive. All possible ramifications were considered: impact on domestic revenues and debt retirement, on American trade, on the agricultural South, on the English nation, and on war and peace. The debates ranged across a wide spectrum that encompassed a practical concern for trade and profit and an emotional obsession with republicanism and national honor. Although paeans on American independence and laments on British villainy abounded, especially from the lips of the carrying trade's supporters, these dramatic expressions neither shaped the argument nor established its focus. The disagreements within the congressional Republicans followed sectional economic lines. The *Essex* decisions threatened no significant southern economic interest. To win southern support for the carrying trade, it fell to the North to prove that the implications and tendencies of England's recent maritime rulings imperiled the South's commodity trade. National action hung on the outcome of this attempt. As it turned out, southern Republicans dismissed this northern fascination with potential consequences and insisted on forming congressional policy on the facts as they now stood. These facts posed no antagonism between southern crops and English courts.

Northern Republicans wanted Congress to combat the *Essex* decisions with a complete boycott on the importation of English goods. Sponsored by Andrew Gregg of Pennsylvania, this policy reflected traditional Republican assumptions on commercial statecraft because its heart was the redeeming power of the American market. Gregg defended his proposal precisely in these terms. He called the *Essex* rulings judicial cover for illegal plunder. Since all English policy, ministerial and maritime, emerged from greed, only the threat of economic loss greater than the ill-gotten *Essex* gains could force England to align its treatment of American trade within the reasonable framework of international law. It was England's very greed that promised happy results from an energetic experiment in nonimportation. The other side of greed was fear, Gregg reasoned, and England was "too well acquainted with her own interest, to persevere in this lawless system at the hazard of losing customers." Rather than lose the profitable American market, England would retreat from the *Essex* rulings.[3]

Many problems immediately confronted the congressional defenders of the carrying trade. One of these, ironically, was the trade's legality. Was the carrying business a proper goal of an honest neutrality? Or did the weight of historical precedent and a reasonable construction of fairness support England's *Essex* claims? Both questions touched on the dignity of American demands. At times Gregg let escape his own doubts on the trade's propriety, as when he told his colleagues that he had "no intention of entering into a discussion of abstract questions." He warned against legalistic debates that might snarl American commerce in "the perplexing difficulties" of the British system and mortgage American economic activity on the oceans to endless discussions, prosecutions, court battles, and bewildering and shifting judicial rulings. Often Gregg skirted the legal quagmire completely and camped on the firmer ground of English conspiracy, antirepublicanism, and anti-Americanism. Was there any doubt, he rhetorically asked Congress, "that all [England's] commercial maxims, and the whole system of her conduct, discover a manifest intention, a fixed determination, to consummate the ruin of the commerce of this country"? For all of this, however, the questions of propriety and dignity called for answers. To that end, to square American economic activity with the ethical assumptions of republicanism, the trade's defenders distinguished between a legitimate carrying trade and the excessive, nefarious activities of a certain class of merchants (usually foreigners sailing under American colors, Gregg believed) that complicated the nation's external relations. This illicit activity was traffic in contraband and the violation of legal blockades. "But," Gregg pleaded, "in withholding protection from these lawless adventurers, let us not withdraw it from the real American merchants."[4]

Gregg's distinction between legal and illegal carrying trades was empty. Blockades and contraband had nothing to do with the carrying business, and their mention only clouded the issue. But the distinction was not without purpose or significance. By creating and

[3] Gregg, ibid., pp. 538–55.
[4] Gregg, ibid., pp. 541–43.

chastising an unseemly carrying entrepreneur, the North discovered a wholesome carrying enterprise within the bounds of respectable and worthy labor. In the North's hands, the carrying and direct trade became synonymous and equally important to the American farmer. This was the necessary fiction in the North's attempt to harmonize all American economic activity and to establish intimate and reciprocal connections between New England and the South and between the nation's seaboard and its interior. But only a common enemy could energize this potential coalition. That common enemy, of course, was England.

An accelerating English assault on the nation's economic freedom, the existence of which was pointed to endlessly by the carrying trade's defenders, became of the utmost importance to their goal of blending together the competing domestic interests whose divisions threatened unified and forceful policy. This argument was a recasting of the Revolutionary pattern of perception that in the 1760s and 1770s had loaded on the separate actions of several British ministries the crime of conspiracy against all American liberty. So it was in the early nineteenth century in the realm of economic freedom. For the present, only the carrying trade lay exposed to English power. If its destruction went unchallenged, attacks on the nation's direct trade would certainly follow. No longer a limited economic interest, the carrying trade had become the forward line of defense for the freedom of American commerce itself. Speaking of the *Essex* rulings, Crowninshield of Massachusetts observed: "Can we put up with such decisions? Can we agree to them? I desire to know whether the whole carrying trade of the United States will not eventually be sacrificed? By the carrying trade, I mean the direct trade to and from the colonies as well as to Europe. If we acquiesce in their capturing a part, Great Britain will extend her captures still further, and make a sweep of our whole trade."[5] Most northern Republicans who supported the Gregg resolutions did not adopt the argument that the wartime carrying business and the direct trade in American goods on American ships were really synonymous. But their attempts to find southern support for an essentially northern interest led them to argue that the *Essex* decisions endangered all American commerce, and American agriculture as well. Nathan Williams, a New York

[5] Jacob Crowninshield, ibid., p. 554.

Republican, noted that "the question is not so much . . . the carrying trade . . . as whether we shall be allowed to retain any free commerce upon the ocean at all." English desires for maritime dominion were known commodities. American potential posed a significant threat to England's bloated commercial position. England's jealousy of America's future was the real issue. The carrying trade was only the immediate object, judicial rulings the immediate tactic, the Napoleonic wars the immediate pretext. All were small disguises for outsized British ambition. The suppression of "the rapid and lofty soaring of the American eagle" ultimately defined British policy.[6]

Once the supporters of the Gregg resolution had established a plausible connection between the carrying trade and the safety of all American commerce, they dwelt little on that particular interest, focused instead on American trade in American goods, and framed their arguments on the obvious and important relationship between commerce and agriculture. Although American society was primarily rural, Gregg reminded his audience, rural vocations were meaningless without commerce. The merchant "is a necessary link in the chain of our society. While he is searching a market for the productions of the farmers, he is discovering something that may contribute to their convenience and comfort. There is mutual dependence betwixt him and the farmer." By enveloping the carrying trade in the legitimating folds of American native commerce, the Greggites robbed it of its peculiar characteristics: transport, not productivity; war, not peace. The circle was now complete. The carrying trade had become shorthand for American commerce, and American commerce the transformer of agricultural work into economic profit and social status.[7]

In Gregg's hands, complete nonimportation had much to commend it and contained little risk to America's peace, comfort, trade, or fiscal system. Great Britain depended on the American market to consume upwards of $30 million of exports annually. "By attacking them in their warehouses and workshops we can reach their vitals," Gregg promised. Commercial and industrial hardships in England "would raise a set of advocates in our favor" and ultimately transform policy at the highest official levels. Nor would complete nonimporta-

[6] Williams, ibid., pp. 578–79.
[7] Gregg, ibid., p. 543.

tion cripple America's economy, or imperil the revenue and the retirement of the national debt. American merchants were enterprising. If denied British trade, "they will resort to other countries, and
no doubt they will find goods to answer our purposes quite as well as
many of the gewgaws we get from England." As to the future of
American agricultural exports, Gregg was on shakier ground. On
the price of exports, he confessed, there would be "momentary inconvenience." But the world market hungered for American productions. Soon they would find sufficient outlet at adequate price.
Once the import-export market righted itself along non-British lines,
revenues would again increase and the retirement of the national debt
not suffer. And if the export price schedule stabilized slightly below
American expectations, Gregg asked, "are we to put a few cents difference in the price of a pound of cotton, or tobacco, or a barrel of
flour, or a quintal of fish in competition with the honor and general
interest of our country?" Most likely, however, the United States
would not suffer even the inconvenience of diminished prices. The
beauty of nonimportation was that its ruinous implications for the
British economy would change England's policy before commercial
war between the two nations set in. Rather than suffer industrial and
commercial slumps and their resulting political traumas, Great Britain would capitulate to the power of the American market.[8]

Celebration of the American merchant, his skills and ingenuity,
glorification of the rural life, bold assertions on the power of the
American market, and untested assumptions on the domestic impact
of nonimportation comprised the arguments of the pro-Gregg congressmen. Their rosy logic required them to wink both at the disparity of military power between the United States and Great Britain
and at the obvious realities of the world market that had plagued
American economic development since the Revolution. What of England's primacy in the Atlantic trading area? Since Jefferson's and
Adams's futile efforts in the 1780s to find economic partners capable
of supplying and consuming as much as England did, the United
States had labored under a mortifying dependency on Great Britain.
Subservience owed mostly to English commercial and industrial
power; credit obligations and a common culture compounded it.
Trumpet as the Jeffersonians might the strength of the American

[8] Gregg, ibid., pp. 545–47.

market and England's dependence on American purchasing power, the sword cut two ways. Of this the South was sure. If England could not send finished goods to the United States, English imports of American grain, cotton, and tobacco would decline. Other nations had neither the money nor the commodities of exchange to fill the void. Commercial war against Great Britain entailed formidable risks that could not be argued away by denigrating the English economy, touting the creativity of the American entrepreneur, or exaggerating the economic power of England's European rivals.

The pro-Gregg forces in Congress differed among themselves on the domestic implications of the policy, on its probable impact on Great Britain, and even on the wisdom of an American commercial future. The scattering of southern supporters voiced more realistic impressions on the probable costs of the policy than did their northern brethren and revealed a more sensible regard for England's commercial and military power. Ironically, most of the southern support for Gregg's motion, with the exception of Congressman John Jackson of Virginia, a relative of James Madison whose congressional defense of the carrying trade almost recapitulated Madison's 1806 pamphlet, was anticommercial and echoed the thinking of Pennsylvania's John Smilie. Foreign commerce was a national curse, Smilie believed, not a national blessing. Its pursuit had complicated American foreign policy, threatened war, and lured the seaboard people into expectations of easy riches without appropriate labor. "I have been led to think," he confessed to his colleagues, "that the situation of the people of the United States, separated from the rest of the world by an ocean of three thousand miles, possessing an immense region of land, having full employment for all her people in the cultivation of the earth—having from the variety of her climate and the differences of her soil, the means of supplying herself, not only with all the necessaries of life in abundance, but with many of its comforts, and even some of its luxuries—from these considerations I have been led to think . . . we should have been a happier people without commerce."[9]

But the nation was commercial. The 1787 compact that created it was binding and perpetual and had established the federal government as the protector of all consenting interests and regions. Ob-

[9] Smilie, ibid., p. 583.

ligation, honor, and Union impelled several southerners and a few northerners to defend an economic interest that they held in small regard. Their position was strangely ambivalent. Nonimportation was for them both a defense of commerce and a way to escape its clutches and purify the American people. They revealed their deepest wishes when they voiced the hope that from the peaceful experiment in commercial warfare might emerge a self-sufficient national economy and a more spartan American: less sophisticated, less urbane, less English; the child of the simple American of their Revolutionary memory. "We might want the fine clothes we wear" if nonimportation became law, Smilie noted, "and our wives might be deprived of their silk gowns." "But would this diminish our happiness," this northern agrarian asked? Certainly not. The valuable and necessary commodities that Americans could not acquire elsewhere, they could make for themselves, as their fathers had. Nonimportation would encourage self-reliance and improve the national character. By breaking a foolish and dangerous addiction to English luxury, the United States would strengthen its economy and independence, and fortify its people. The revival of "that spirit of industry which our large importations have almost annihilated" would encourage "family manufactures," the bedrock, along with agriculture, of a self-reliant, independent, and republican economy. Defended in this fashion, nonimportation was not a foreign policy maneuver, but a bracing opportunity to enhance the morals and the safety of the world's only republican nation. Even if it had no visible impact on English policy, these good works would stand as its valid accomplishments.[10]

The Gregg resolution ran into immediate difficulty. For much of Congress, its defense amounted to nothing more than unfounded celebrations of American courage and foolish slaps at English might. Southerners had particular grievances that made their opposition distinctive. They questioned both the propriety of a republican nation pursuing a wartime commerce unrelated to the productive energies of its people and the economic implications for the agrarian South of the methods the North had chosen to defend its carrying business. Other criticisms also found widespread support in Congress, ones that centered on peace and on national finances. These objections made the defeat of the nonimportation advocates as much a national as a southern enterprise.

[10] Ibid., p. 588.

Since the national founding in 1787, foreign and fiscal policy had intersected in a variety of crucial ways. The need for sufficient revenue to float the national debt, to retire annually part of its principal, and to pay the operating costs of government severely cramped the freedom of America's commercial policy.[11] Republican principles, popular expectations, memories of imperial taxation policies, and constitutional provisions had all but eliminated land, direct, excise, and export taxes from the pool of available government revenue. All that remained were taxes on land sales and import duties. As the nation's largest supplier of finished goods, England was, therefore, intimately connected to the smooth running of the government's finances. In part, Jefferson's long-standing effort to multiply the sources of foreign industrial supply revealed a fear of fiscal slavery to England. These attempts had failed, largely because of negligible alternative trading partners, the chains and allures of English credit, and American preference for English goods. Jefferson himself once refused to buy a French harness, although his comrade Lafayette had made the purchase a point of republican honor, because the English variety was superior.[12] Ridicule as they would English "gewgaws," Americans who could afford them bought them.

When Jefferson became president, England's power over the nation's fiscal health was both significant and recognized. When the cabinet first discussed potential economic responses to the *Essex* decisions in the autumn of 1805, Albert Gallatin had warned that "every measure of retaliation which we may adopt, however well calculated for that object, will diminish the revenue."[13] In late 1805 Republican Senator Samuel Smith from Maryland, who would support a moderate nonimportation policy on a limited range of English goods in 1806, spelled out the compelling relationship between foreign policy and fiscal necessity: "It is indeed a mortifying thing that we cannot in an effectual manner resist the insults and injuries of G[reat] B[ritain]. . . . We have no revenue but that arises from importation. We have eight million dollars annually to pay for the ex-

[11] Paul Varg ably explores this tension in his *Foreign Policies of the Founding Fathers*, especially in chap. 5, "Credit versus Markets: The Origin of Party Conflict over Foreign Policy."

[12] Jefferson replied: "It is not from a love of the English but a love of myself that I sometimes find myself obliged to buy their manufactures" (TJ to Lafayette, Nov. 3, 1786, Boyd, 10:505).

[13] Gallatin to TJ, Nov. 21, 1805, Jefferson Papers, LC.

tinguishment of the public debt and the interest thereon besides all
the expenditures of internal government, the army and the navy. If
we by non-importation cut off that great source of revenue, how are
we to meet the payment?"[14] Joseph Clay, a Republican from
Pennsylvania, reminded his colleagues that revenues from English
imports supplied almost half of the government's $12 million in
yearly assets. By existing appropriation, the government was
pledged to the retirement of $8 million of debt during the next fiscal
year. Where was the money to come from? His answer lay in the
prohibition of only those English imports which the nation could
secure elsewhere. "Let us carry such a system into effect," Clay insisted; "one which, as it will do us little [fiscal] injury, is likely to be
permanent, and will therefore have a permanent influence on Great
Britain."[15] What Clay did not say, however, was that a "permanent"
influence and a significant influence are not the same thing. What
was good for the nation's finances was not at all bad for Great Britain.
When push came to shove, the nation's Republicans valued fiscal stability far more than the carrying trade. John Randolph reminded his
colleagues that the prompt payment of the Revolutionary War debt
was a cardinal purpose of Jeffersonian politics. The Republicans, he
noted, had aimed "to convince an unbelieving world that a debt, once
funded, might be paid off, without the intervention of a sponge."
Nonimportation menaced so bright a Jeffersonian promise.[16]

The Gregg resolution rested on the simple assumption that the
nation's major geographic regions and economic interests stood
similarly threatened by England's recent maritime rulings. The advocates of total boycott had shouldered the herculean chore of dem-
onstrating that carrying and direct trade, commerce and agriculture,
and the North and South were uniformly interested in prompt and
vigorous congressional action. Under close scrutiny, the unities that
the boycott supporters had hastily pasted together dissolved. The
South opposed the Gregg resolution because the English market was
vital to southern agriculture, because England's inability to export to
the United States would cripple the English market for southern

[14] Smith to [?], Dec. 19, 1805, Samuel Smith Letterbooks, Samuel Smith Papers,
LC.

[15] Clay, *Annals*, 9th Cong., lst sess., pp. 549–52.

[16] Randolph, ibid., p. 595.

produce, and because the *Essex* decisions did not affect the English market for American agricultural commodities.

The southern Republicans proved their case with abundant data on both the southern percentage of total American agricultural exports to England and the English percentage of the total market for southern exports. Both sets of data underscored the contemporary market realities that the Greggites had tried to ignore. In 1802, for example, the southern commodities of tobacco, rice, tar, pitch, and rosin contributed $8,450,000 to the total of domestic produce exported to Great Britain, which the Treasury Department valued at $18,727,000. For 1803, the corresponding figures were $11,000,000 and $22,700,00. For 1804, the figures read $9,400,000 and $19,000,000. The figures on England's share of southern agricultural exports were as revealing. Average annual exportations of tobacco for 1802, 1803, and 1804 amounted to $6,140,000. Of this amount, England took more than half, $3,290,000. For the same years, annual cotton exportations averaged $6,970,000. England's annual share was $5,630,000, in excess of 80 percent.[17] Was the carrying trade worth the disruptions to the southern economy that these figures almost guaranteed? Republican Peter Early of Georgia thought not. "Do not gentlemen ask too much when they require us to jeopardize the whole agricultural interest of the nation for the sake of that which in our opinion produces no benefit to that interest? Is it not expecting too much of us to suppose that we will consent to surrender the certainty of good markets and high prices for our produce, and brave the danger of total stagnation, for the purpose of embarking on a hazardous contest with Great Britain for the carrying trade?" If agriculture would suffer generally, southern agriculture would suffer the most. Its productions were particularly wedded to the British trade. Middle state wheat and flour were more continental in destination. Only in times of famine and scarcity did England consume a significant share of Pennsylvania exports.[18]

In steady litany, Early's southern colleagues echoed his disbelief. What was the "pivot" on which everything turned, David R. Williams asked from the floor of Congress. "The carrying trade."

[17] Ibid., pp. 624–25.
[18] Early, ibid., p. 623.

"This is the grand pivot on which the whole machinery of national honor, and dignity, and wrongs, and insults, are made to turn." The interest was insufficiently national to justify a response that promised such gloomy consequences for the agricultural South. Christopher Clark from Virginia asked "whether it is correct or proper that the great interests of the country should be given up to a trade only continued in time of war, and in which but a few men are interested?" He thought not. "Let it not be here understood that I am an enemy of commerce," he continued. "I am its friend. Without it agriculture would be nothing." But the *Essex* decisions against the carrying trade threatened neither the nation's direct commerce nor its agriculture. Clark's fellow Virginian, John Wayles Eppes, put the matter squarely in dollars and cents. "The carrying trade which this measure is intended to protect," he noted, "yields a revenue of eight hundred and fifty thousand dollars; so that for the protection of eight hundred and fifty thousand dollars, we put at hazard a net revenue of five million four hundred and thirty-two thousand dollars. . . . A nation, deliberately forming a commercial regulation, by which it risks millions to protect thousands, manifests more zeal than wisdom." Until the trade that promoted these millions was attacked, a response on the order of magnitude of Gregg's was completely inappropriate.[19]

Clark, Early, Williams, Eppes, and many other southerners attacked the Gregg proposal because of their fidelity to the agricultural pursuits of their region.[20] Their vocabulary was primarily economic, but their concern also touched on the propriety of American demands and probed the limits of their definition of worthy republican labor. Should a republican nation pitch its tent on the ground of wartime profit taking? Should the United States desire a trade not founded on American productivity, and therefore unrelated to the vocational pursuit established by Jeffersonian principle as most conducive to national peace and social happiness? Did neutral rights legitimate a

[19] Williams, ibid., pp. 643–50; Clark, ibid., pp. 659–66; Eppes, ibid., pp. 666–86.

[20] The tug of southern economic interests was so compelling that George Washington Campbell of Tennessee, a rare southern defender of the North's carrying trade, still opposed the Gregg motion because of its negative implications for American revenue and southern crops (ibid., pp. 706–24).

trade that was born in war and would die when peace returned to Europe? Should the United States embrace a morally questionable trade and for it risk its revenue, its native commerce, and its peace? These questions all hung on the trade's rectitude, and they disturbed the majority of southern congressmen. Their opposition to the economic and fiscal consequences of nonimportation was forceful and direct. But on the morality of the trade they hung back because, although questioning the trade's ethics, they dared not formally challenge them. To do so equaled an attack on New England, on Madison's conception of neutral rights, on Monroe's diplomatic attempts to overturn the *Essex* decisions, on the administration itself. Only those southerners who were rabidly anticommercial, anti–New England, and anti-Madison (perhaps antiadministration as well) extended their arguments from economics and diplomatic prudence to morality and republican outrage. Chief of these was John Randolph of Virginia.

By 1806 Randolph was fast breaking with Jefferson's administration. Although chairman of the Ways and Means Committee and still a powerful figure in the party, Randolph's extreme opposition to administration policies was destroying his political significance as it elevated his stature among his band of loyalists.[21] His penetrating criticisms were always uncompromising, sarcastic, directed against what he perceived to be assignable villainy behind objectionable policy, and usually public. Regardless of the issue—nonimportation, Jefferson's attempt to secure French help in wrestling the Floridas from Spain, the Yazoo land case, the impeachment of Federalist judges—he used it to track his larger quarry: Republican backsliding, the impending triumph of Federalism, and the complicity of leading Jeffersonians, especially James Madison, in both.[22] The asperity of his language and the completeness of his indictment embarrassed and angered many, including Thomas Jefferson, who shared

[21] John Nicholas to Wilson Cary Nicholas, April 2, 1806, Wilson Cary Nicholas Papers, LC.

[22] Randolph's hatred of Madison was complete: "If the man, who has given the bias to our affairs, from their true bearing and direction, to federalism, be elected to the Presidency (for which he is straining every nerve, supported by all the apostates of our party—the feds and a *few* good, but misguided men) we are gone, forever!" (Randolph to Caesar Rodney, Feb. 28, 1806, Rodney Family Papers, LC).

his anxieties. Randolph did not care. For him, the Republican party was already "ruined past redemption."[23]

Randolph's sense of accomplished tragedy freed him from political responsibility and allowed him to voice in exaggerated form concerns that lay at the heart of southern Republicanism. Madison's defense of the carrying trade and the president's official adoption of it foretold to these men the final triumph of New England, commerce, and Federalism over the South, the agrarian life, and Republicanism. Already the New England way was corrupting the South, making Richmond and Norfolk indistinguishable from Boston and Salem and forcing Randolph, in his attempt to make sense of it all, to shift occasionally from the traditional North-South focus that comprehended much of the southern complaint to the more subtle and revealing seaboard-interior antagonism. "If this great agricultural nation is to be governed by Salem and Boston, New York and Philadelphia, and Baltimore and Norfolk and Charleston, let the gentlemen come out and say so."[24] The sectional varieties of Randolph's divided America comprised a struggle between productive and parasitical labor, and the carrying trade, unless renounced, would feed on the South as it fed on war. His New England was "goaded by a spirit of mercantile avarice," blinded by its "infatuation" with easy riches, and peddling the nation a bill of goods.[25] The least that Randolph demanded was common sense. America was not England's match, either economically or militarily. Nonimportation ensured agricultural havoc if not war. "The proper arguments" for those who said differently, he believed, were "a straight waistcoat, a dark room, water gruel, and depletion." War would stretch executive power and warp the Constitution. And "for what?" Randolph demanded. "What is the question in dispute? The carrying trade. What part of it? The fair, the honest, and the useful trade that is engaged in carrying our own productions to foreign markets, and bringing back their productions in exchange?" This was all the nation was entitled to, and all an agricultural republic should desire. Such trade naturally bound together commerce and agriculture and promised debt

[23] Randolph to George Hay, Jan. 3, 1806, John Randolph Papers, 1801–1834, ser. 2, LC.

[24] John Randolph, *Annals*, 9th Cong., 1st sess., p. 557.

[25] Ibid., p. 556; John Randolph to Joseph Hopper Nicholson, Nov. 8, 1805, Joseph Hopper Nicholson Papers, LC.

retirement, sound prosperity, and peace. Neither the *Essex* decisions nor the Royal Navy threatened it. Not for the nation's honest commerce, Randolph brooded, "but for this mushroom, this fungus," would New England's "spirit of avaricious traffic plunge us into war."[26]

Both the nature of the carrying trade and the consequences of forceful policy in its defense doomed the Gregg resolution in the Ninth Congress. The majority refused to accept the fanciful notion that the United States could better England in either a commercial or military encounter. "Ever since my memory," noted Josiah Masters, "the approaching ruin of Great Britain has been frequently foretold; after all the vain attempts, they yet regulate the commerce of the world." An American challenge to England's commercial power, he cautioned his colleagues, would surely end in "disgrace" and economic ruin.[27] Nor did the majority accept the argument that the *Essex* decisions foreshadowed impending English forays against all American trade, and therefore intimately involved the South in New England's concern. Strong action like the Gregg proposal, John Dawson of Virginia argued, was inappropriate "until it shall be seen that Great Britain perseveres in a system of measures calculated to check and destroy our rising greatness, and eventually the independence of our country."[28] Until then, continuing negotiations coupled with modest economic reprisal was the nation's wiser policy.

From the wreckage of the Gregg motion there was clearly emerging by mid-March a congressional consensus. Its foundation, as David R. Williams noted, was Congress's obligation to support and not cripple the diplomatic process. The majority agreed that Gregg's version of economic reprisal, apart from its disastrous fiscal and economic results, would undercut further negotiations with Great Britain. But the majority also sensed that further diplomacy without

---

[26] John Randolph, *Annals*, 9th Cong., 1st sess., pp. 555–74, 591–605. Other southern Republicans shared Randolph's misgivings and saw in the discussion of the carrying trade a significant argument about America's traditions and its future. The key question for them was whether the republic would extend its economic and social values into the future or betray them in pursuit of unrepublican and "English" goals: "Look at the people of England," Nathaniel Macon of North Carolina observed, "legally free, but half their time fighting for the honor and dignity of the Crown and the carrying trade" (Macon, ibid., pp. 686–92).

[27] Masters, ibid., pp. 580–83.

[28] Dawson, ibid., p. 748.

some show of strength would probably accomplish little. Needed was a prudent policy that threatened neither Monroe's diplomacy or national prosperity. Congress's final determination admirably fitted these requirements. The act that was passed in April, sponsored by Joseph Hopper Nicholson of Maryland, banned the importation of certain British goods in an attempt to inflict the most harm on England at a cost bearable by the United States. Most of the goods on the proscribed list could be gotten elsewhere, thereby assuring little domestic suffering and political opposition. Its enforcement was postponed seven months to ensure a smooth transition to other foreign markets and to portray the measure for what it was: a reminder that unless diplomacy produced positive results, England would lose part of its important American market. Southern Republicans almost unanimously supported modified nonimportation. They recognized a national duty to act on behalf of an economic interest their region did not share. They simply placed limits on that obligation by refusing to endorse policies they thought risked too much. The passage of partial nonimportation allowed the South both to honor the national compact and to preserve the bases of its own prosperity.[29]

The President

President Jefferson had long advocated economic retaliation against English commercial harassment. During the first session of the Ninth Congress, his private correspondence generally applauded economic countermeasures against England's recent maritime rulings. Yet his own policy instincts were more clouded than his easy praise of the power of the American market suggests. An intellectual fascination with economic weapons was part of Jefferson's understanding of American foreign policy, embedded deeply in the history of Republican statecraft. But in early 1806, he balked at their use. He perceived "great" and "irreconcilible" differences among congressional Republicans on "our affairs with England," and their confu-

[29] Ibid., pp. 700–878.

sion mirrored his own.[30] He favored some positive action to buttress diplomacy, but when weighed against the particular nature of the existing English threat, the probable domestic costs of total nonimportation, and the wide assortment of diplomatic problems and goals confronting the administration, especially the acquisition of the Floridas, complete nonimportation appeared too strong a remedy.

Jefferson's administration had long coveted the Spanish Floridas.[31] All its attempts to acquire them peacefully had failed, and for this the president blamed not only Spain but France as well. Consequently, the summer of 1805 found him flirting with an English alliance both to prop up his Spanish diplomacy and to ensure a successful outcome to the ever-growing possibility of a Spanish-American war. What most concerned Jefferson in the summer of 1805 was the imminence, according to intelligence reports, of European peace. Without war in Europe, the United States had little diplomatic leverage and faced the unpleasant thought, if it chose to fight for the Floridas, of war with Spain and France without their simultaneous military involvement on the Continent. Against this, he wrote Madison on August 4, "we ought to provide before the conclusion of a peace." Spain and Napoleon were procrastinating, Jefferson believed, "because peace in Europe shall leave us without an ally," "off our guard," and "friendless." He therefore proposed to Madison an "immediate" and "effectual treaty of alliance" with England "to come into force whenever a war shall take place with Spain and France." This type of alliance ideally suited Jefferson's Spanish diplomacy but ill suited Madison's concern with the *Essex* decisions and England's challenge to America's carrying trade. "It being generally known to France and Spain that we had entered into a treaty with England," he assured Madison, "would probably insure us a peaceable and immediate settlement." And if war broke out, England's participation on the Con-

[30] TJ to William Branch Giles, Feb. 26, 1806, Jefferson Papers, LC; Samuel Smith to [?], Feb. 28, 1806, Samuel Smith Papers, UVa; John Smith to Wilson Cary Nicholas, Jan. 25, 1806, William Pennock to Wilson Cary Nicholas, Feb. 8, Mar. 19, 1806, John Taylor to Wilson Cary Nicholas, Mar. 19, 1806, Wilson Cary Nicholas Papers, UVa.

[31] See Thomas Perkins Abernethy, *The South in the New Nation* (Baton Rouge, La., 1961); Isaac J. Cox, *The West Florida Controversy, 1789–1813* (Baltimore, 1918); and Arthur B. Darling, *Our Rising Empire, 1763–1803* (New Haven, 1940).

tinent and in the West Indies would ensure its success. The president was committed to this new direction in English policy, regardless of its implications for the nation's carrying trade. "We should lose no time," he reiterated on August 29, "in securing something more than a neutral friendship from England."[32]

Jefferson's plan rested on optimistic assumptions about the cost of English cooperation. It also seemed to presume that after European peace, England would again go to war on behalf of America's desire for Florida. Madison made this point, and Jefferson readily agreed that alliance was feasible only during the present European war.[33] This raised serious problems. If the closeness of European peace created the pressing need for an English alliance, it also seemed to point toward an American war with Spain in the very near future. Madison also found it incredible that Jefferson believed England would accept alliance on the terms he had outlined. The president's version of a fair Anglo-American connection bound England to fight Spain and France if the United States could not use the shadow of English power to coax from them a peaceful settlement of the Florida question. But if England's promised support helped acquire the Floridas, the United States was not bound to fight on behalf of England's European goals. Madison did not see "much chance that she will positively bind herself not to make peace whilst we refuse to bind ourselves positively to make war." Second, if the United States did enter the European war, it reserved the freedom to withdraw after it attained the Floridas, regardless of the state of England's wartime goals. Such an arrangement England would never buy, unless the sale included chunks of America's commercial future. And what would England demand? Nothing occurred to Madison, he wrote Jefferson, that "would be admissible to us and satisfactory to her." Finally, the secretary of state doubted the wisdom of the entire maneuver because of the recent *Essex* decisions. Alliance with England would anger the merchants, discredit Madison's recent writings on American neutrality, and commit the nation's carrying trade to the whim of the Royal Navy. Rather than broach the subject to England

[32] TJ to Madison, Aug. 4, 29, 1805, Madison Papers, LC, reel 8; TJ to Madison, Aug. 7, 17, 27, 1805, ibid., ser. 2, reel 25; TJ to Madison, Oct. 11, 1805, Jefferson Papers, LC.

[33] Madison to TJ, Aug. 20, 1805, TJ to Madison, Aug. 27, 1805, Madison Papers, LC, ser. 2, reel 25.

at all, Madison thought it far wiser to instruct American diplomats in Paris to plant in French ears "the apprehension of an eventual connection between the U.S. and G.B." Such rumors might enhance American ambition in Florida. They would not prohibit the United States from dealing energetically with England if it persisted in the policies outlined in the *Essex* rulings.[34]

By the fall of 1805 Madison's tactful objections and Gallatin's complete opposition had appreciably diminished Jefferson's enthusiasm for English alliance.[35] Intelligence that forecast a lengthy European war diminished its importance. Continued Spanish involvement on the Continent would give the United States ample time to make another effort at peaceful settlement, but not through the Spanish Court. The president now wanted to work in Paris through the American minister in France, John Armstrong, and with money. His plan was to "bait" France with cash.[36] And if America could not buy French influence, it would then go to war against Spain and claim the Floridas as a spoil. With Europe still at war, France would pose little problem, and England's help, either for diplomacy or for war, would not be necessary. "Should we now be forced into war," he wrote Madison at the end of October, "it [has] become much more questionable than it was whether we should not pursue it unembarrassed by any alliance and free to retire from it whenever we can obtain our separate terms."[37] Here Spanish matters stood at the beginning of the 1806 congressional session. American options blended money, French cooperation, military threats, and war. Although England was not as important to the nation's Spanish concerns as Jefferson perceived in the summer, still the Spanish business placed limits on America's English policy. Total nonimportation entailed much domestic unpleasantness and might lead to war. Either would sidetrack the acquisition of the Floridas. Nor was England completely irrelevant to the future of Spanish policy. If France did not cooperate, in spite of a healthy American bribe, the need for

[34] Madison to TJ, Sept. 30, Oct. 5, 1805, Jefferson Papers, LC.

[35] Gallatin to Madison, Aug. 5, 1805, Madison Papers, LC, reel 8.

[36] Madison to TJ, Oct. 16, 1805, TJ to Gallatin, Oct. 23, 1805, TJ to Madison, Oct. 23, 1805, TJ to Wilson Cary Nicholas, Oct. 25, 1805, TJ to Samuel Smith, Nov. 1, 1805, Jefferson Papers, LC; see also Lawrence S. Kaplan, *Jefferson and France* (New Haven, 1967), pp. 113–19.

[37] TJ to Madison, Oct. 23, 1805, Jefferson Papers, LC.

English friendship might again surface. Wanting space to maneuver above all things, Jefferson opposed nonimportation because it would effectively destroy English friendship as a potential weapon in his French and Spanish diplomacy.

Although the president had no direct connection with either the Gregg or the Nicholson approach, he eagerly embraced the Marylander's proposal when the opportunity arose.[38] Its moderation was its greatest asset. In February 1806 Jefferson instructed Armstrong to cite the probable exclusion of some English goods from the American market to predispose France in America's favor. By protecting his English options, partial nonimportation had become a usable weapon in the president's French diplomacy.[39]

Two other considerations prompted Jefferson to reject comprehensive nonimportation in favor of a more judicious policy: the character of the American trade and the changed composition of the English government. At the moment, the *Essex* decisions threatened only the carrying trade, an important component of the nation's prosperity, yet a business that troubled Jefferson the agrarian even as Jefferson the president struggled to justify and to protect it. Like his southern congressional brethren, he would not risk the nation's peace and the South's prosperity for its sake. Although Madison's writings and State Department instructions had stamped the carrying trade with administration approval,[40] Jefferson hoped its defense could be diplomatic, quiet, and painless. Although the future of Republicanism in New England and the party's claim to national leadership required its defense, his southern heart was not in it. In 1806 the president drifted, and let Congress bicker over policy. When a workable majority preference emerged, he endorsed it. Modified nonimportation preserved foreign policy options, guarded the Republican party's northern flank, reminded England of America's concern and economic power, and posed no insurmountable barrier to the new English government's willingness to deal fairly. On this last consideration, Jefferson now counted most.

[38] TJ to Monroe, Mar. 16, 18, 1806, ibid.

[39] TJ to Gen. John Armstrong, Feb. 14, 1806, ibid.

[40] Madison was deeply committed to the pamphlet he wrote in defense of the carrying trade. For him, it was a labor of love as well as an affair of state (Madison to TJ, Oct. 5, 1805, ibid.). The complete pamphlet, *An Examination into the British Doctrine concerning Neutral Trade*, can be found in Gaillard Hunt, ed., *The Writings of James Madison* (New York, 1908), 8:204–374.

After Pitt's death, the president's optimism on the outcome of the British negotiations had increased. When Charles James Fox took over the British end of the discussions, it soared. Jefferson's image of Fox's "honesty," "good sense," and political influence made any congressional action seem inappropriate. By the end of March, even modified nonimportation had become an embarrassment. "We had committed ourselves to a line of proceedings to meet Mr. Pitt's policy and hostility," Jefferson advised Monroe. "It ought not to be viewed by the [new] ministry as looking towards them at all." So Monroe was to assure the British government.[41]

The Diplomats

Fox's presence in the British cabinet generated as much fragile optimism in Monroe as it did in Jefferson. Ultimate disappointments would prove as large as the initial hopes. Both shaped the contradictory nature of Monroe's advice. On February 12, 1806, he predicted success for his mission. Two weeks later, he suggested the postponement of congressional retaliatory action. In the second week of March he again pleaded that Congress not spoil his opportunity with hasty action. Before Pitt's death, Monroe had pegged British intransigence to fundamental issues of economic growth and international status that divided the two nations and required an American demonstration of power and spirit. But when Fox entered the Foreign Office, Monroe ignored the still harsh realities and instead equated British attitude with Fox's good manners. Ignoring Fox's private warning that the rest of the cabinet did not share his opinions, Monroe continued to advise his superiors that additional American conciliation would produce a relaxation in English policy.[42] By the spring, however, the American was again despairing. Fox had been vague and evasive in their March 28 interview. He would not discuss the colonial trade, British seizures, or the admiralty decisions. The

[41] For Jefferson's optimism, see TJ to Thomas Paine, Mar. 25, 1806, to William Jarvis, April 16, 1806, to John Tyler, April 26, 1806, to Jacob Crowninshield, May 13, 1806, to John Brown, June 9, 1806, to Levi Lincoln, June 25, 1806, to John Page, July 3, 1806, to Barnabas Bidwell, July 5, 1806, Jefferson Papers, LC; for his embarrassment over partial nonimportation, see TJ to Monroe, May 4, 1806, ibid.

[42] Monroe to Madison, Feb. 12, 28, Mar. 11, 1806, Dispatches, Monroe, Great Britain, vol. 13, NA.

most hopeful note of the entire interview was Fox's seductive remark that court decisions did not necessarily echo cabinet opinion. Spirits dampened, Monroe retracted his winter optimism and advised Madison to press for the immediate passage of coercive legislation.[43]

Negotiations foundered in April and May. Much of the stalemate owed to the obvious difficulties imposed on the process by American economic aspirations and the English refusal to abide them. Sharing responsibility were Monroe's foolish overestimation of Fox's power, his inability to define and follow a steady diplomatic path, and his confusion on what the Jeffersonians in Washington considered essential to settlement.

Although the State Department's 1804 instructions had not demanded treaty protection for the carrying trade, the *Essex* decisions of 1805 elevated treaty guarantees for that enterprise to sine qua non importance; indeed, it alone among outstanding economic issues carried this important status. However, although the carrying trade was more important in the 1806 instructions, both sets allowed Monroe, at his discretion, to trade "free ships free goods" for the "broken voyage" protection of the recently overturned *Polly* decision. (Madison was still loath to abandon the higher ground. He told Monroe to inform the English that while America would never "yield" its free ships principle, it would "omit" it in the pending negotiations.)[44] But when Fox suggested compromise on the colonial trade and pointed to the broken voyage (the landing of goods in American ports, the payment of duties, and the changing of American ships) as a likely basis of discussion, Monroe rejected the suggestion and insisted on what he had never asked from Hawkesbury, Harrowby, or Mulgrave: a principled and antiquated neutral right to trade in all goods not specifically contraband and between all ports not actually blockaded by British ships. "I perceive that your minimum and maximum are the same," Fox noted, and he closed the interview.[45]

The administration also valued the future of the colonial trade more than financial compensation for past seizures. Although the

[43] Monroe to Madison, Mar. 31, April 3, 1806, ibid.

[44] Madison to Monroe, Jan. 5, 1804, Diplomatic Instructions, All Countries, vol. 6, NA.

[45] Monroe to Madison, April 20, 1806, Dispatches, Monroe, Great Britain, vol. 13, NA; Monroe to Madison, April 28, 1806, *American State Papers: Foreign Relations*, 3:17–18.

January 1804 instructions had authorized Monroe to demand compensation, they had specifically ordered him to trade it for future protection if the opportunity arose. But Monroe linked the two together in his conversations with Fox in late March. He was intractable at the wrong time. Both his faith in Fox and his demands on the foreign secretary were too great. When the American bound the past to the future and the free ships doctrine to the carrying trade, he lost Fox's ear and ensured diplomatic frustration. Monroe chalked up his difficulties to cabinet malice. He decided to let Fox soften official England while he awaited the arrival of William Pinkney and the new State Department instructions covering their joint mission.[46]

Monroe's and Pinkney's combined efforts would differ in goals, significance, and difficulty from the task that had been charged to Monroe alone. His solitary efforts had attempted to protect America's non-English wartime trade while avoiding the larger question of America's commercial relationship with Great Britain. These efforts had snagged on England's refusal to treat neutral issues apart from the general Anglo-American commercial connection. Jefferson did not want a full-dress discussion of Anglo-American commerce. He preferred to deal with neutral issues as the need arose. Loathing the Jay Treaty, he feared entrapment in another similar pact. But in 1806 he had lost control of policy, and in March the Senate had passed a resolution demanding the elevation of Monroe's diplomatic status to minister plenipotentiary, the addition of another negotiator to the newly created joint commission, and the enlargement of its official agenda to include all outstanding commercial issues between the two nations. Jefferson resisted. One of the two senators who waited on the president with the resolution later reported that "he was absolutely determined not to do it." Jefferson finally bowed to political pressure and recommended Monroe and William Pinkney of Maryland for the joint enterprise. Diplomacy's increased agenda in 1806 represented a Jeffersonian defeat and a British victory.[47]

"After having decried the former Administration for a British treaty," a Federalist friend warned Republican Barnabas Bidwell of

[46] Monroe to Charles James Fox, April 26, 1806, Dispatches, Great Britain, Monroe, vol. 13, NA; Monroe to Madison, May 20, 1806, *American State Papers: Foreign Relations*, 3:126; Monroe to TJ, June 20, 1806, Jefferson Papers, LC.

[47] Samuel Smith to Wilson Cary Nicholas, Mar. 21, 1806, Wilson Cary Nicholas Papers, acc. no. 5533, UVa.

Massachusetts, "you cannot surely blame us for a [political] retaliation in case of a Republican British treaty." The "present administration having the benefit of one British treaty and the vices attending it
and of twelve years experience ought now to make a better one than
the former." The cards were on the table. On trial was the Republican claim to national leadership. For three years the administration
had avoided tangling with the English on what Bidwell called "the
complicated subject of commerce." The New Englander warned
Jefferson that "the British nation has more practical experience with
commerce than ours and will probably gain some advantage."[48]
Bidwell's anxieties mirrored a nagging Republican concern. The
president also feared engaging the English on the mysteries of commerce. American simplicity, a virtue, would always lose to British
commercial sophistication, a vice. Commerce itself rested on stratagem and manipulation, and those not practiced in it had better leave
it alone. On why he wanted only limited discussion of neutral issues
with the English, Jefferson wrote Madison: "An American con-
tending by stratagem against those exercised in it from their cradle
would undoubtedly be outwitted by them." After Fox's death in
June 1806, Jefferson's fears again spoke to the complexities of commercial negotiations. To Monroe he observed, "I fear that one of
those appointed to negotiate with you is too much wedded to the
ancient maritime code and navigation principles of England, too
much practiced in the tactics of [commercial] diplomacy to negotiate
a just treaty."[49] It was 1794 all over again. The memory of Jay's
Treaty troubled Madison when he sent Monroe a private letter accompanying the official State Department instructions. These covered both neutral issues and the commercial relationship between the
United States and Great Britain. "The commercial one will be
doubtless felt by you in all its delicacy," Madison cautioned. "I need
not suggest the expediency of guarding against the particular vices of
that of 1794."[50] The Jeffersonians feared engaging the English in
their métier, and were seemingly convinced of ghastly defeat once the

    [48] Bidwell to TJ, June 21, July 28, 1806, Jefferson Papers, LC.
    [49] TJ to Madison, Mar. 19, 1803, Madison Papers, LC, ser. 2, reel 25; TJ to
Thomas Mann Randolph, Oct. 10, 1806, to Monroe, Oct. 26, 1806, Jefferson Papers, LC.
    [50] Madison to Monroe, April 23, 1806, Dispatches, Monroe, Great Britain, vol.
13, NA; Madison to Monroe, "private," May 17, 1806, Madison Papers, LC, reel 9.

New World's virtuous farmers confronted the merchants, sharpsters, and bankers who formed the core of an unwholesome British intelligence. Fox's death compounded the gloom. From the moment William Eden, Baron Auckland, replaced Fox, Pinkney joined Monroe, and a full discussion of Anglo-American trade swallowed up the limited war-related goals that Monroe had pursued, the English affirmed the worst Jeffersonian apprehensions.

Great Britain did not want a rupture with the United States in 1806. On the other hand, as the London *Times* editorialized in June 1806, neither did it think the United States could "expect that we shall surrender to them the smallest particle of that equitable system of maritime policy to which we owe our greatness and our prosperity." Auckland, England's chief negotiator, was a skilled veteran of French commercial dealings and a long-standing member of the Board of Trade.[51] The *Times* accurately captured his sentiments. He would yield nothing that might endanger what he considered the supporting structure of British greatness.

Predictably, Auckland immediately suggested that the new round of discussions build on the Jay Treaty. Although the Americans rejected the idea and thought they had won Auckland's "acquiescence" in their desire to begin "de novo," the spirit if not the actual stipulations of the "federal treaty" overshadowed the negotiations from August until the end of the year. Throughout setbacks threatened America on all fronts: the colonial trade, impressment, access to both East India and the British West Indies. England's diplomats insisted that the negotiated tonnage restrictions of the Jay Treaty limit future American access to the British West Indies. But these had been so excessive and humiliating that President Washington in 1794 had insisted, successfully, on the deletion of the whole West Indies article from the Jay Treaty. The Americans again refused them and Auckland countered with a proposal equally as damaging to America's West Indies trade. The new proposal aimed to thwart American competition in the rich Caribbean-Europe-Asia trade. But instead of restricting the entry of American ships into the islands, it supported England's monopolistic goals by controlling the size and destination of exportations of colonial cargoes on American ships. It required that the United States import into American ports all the colonial

[51]Perkins, *Prologue*, pp. 122–23.

produce it took from the British islands, required American merchants to pay high duties on importation, and forbade the remission of duties (drawbacks) to the importer on English colonial produce subsequently reexported from the United States. To complete the destruction of the colonial trade, Auckland's proposal abolished American drawbacks on enemy produce as well. The combined effect worked to reduce America's entire Caribbean trade to a volume roughly equal to the needs of the American home market; together with tonnage restrictions and paper blockades, it would accomplish the frustration of America's bid for a sizable share of the Caribbean-European-Asian trade. The Americans rejected the scheme at first, but in the end they accepted something quite similar.[52]

The protection of American sailors promised to fare as badly under Auckland's scheme as did the future of the carrying trade. He made clear that Great Britain would never negotiate away its right to board American ships and seize British deserters. Auckland would discuss the protection of bona fide American citizens from royal press gangs. But success here was unlikely because the discussions brought out antagonistic definitions of citizenship, England maintaining that birth determined it, the United States proclaiming the individual's right to choose his own national identity. Auckland's next demand overshadowed this knotty definitional problem. England would not even discuss impressment until the American Congress had suspended the nonimportation act.[53]

The American handling of nonimportation reduced a potential strength and symbol of national assertiveness to an episode bordering on farce. Because the president and Congress insisted on moderate measures that did not jeopardize trade, peace, agriculture, and the national debt, the congressional bill was too weak to frighten England; "a milk and water bill," John Randolph accurately called it, "a dose of chicken broth to be taken nine months hence."[54] Second, as modest as it was, the American negotiators tried to keep it a secret. Monroe's and Jefferson's generous hopes for Charles Fox convinced them that conciliation, not intimidation, was the better part of wis-

[52] Monroe and William Pinkney to Madison, Sept. 11, 1806, *American State Papers: Foreign Relations*, 3:133–34.

[53] Lords Holland and Auckland to Monroe and Pinkney, Sept. 4, 1806, ibid., 3:133.

[54] Quoted in Peterson, *Thomas Jefferson and the New Nation*, p. 829.

dom. In his first meetings with Fox, Monroe almost apologized for its passage, as Jefferson had instructed him to do. When Auckland took over the negotiations, the Americans never mentioned nonimportation even though official England could easily read about it in the newspapers. During an August 28 meeting Auckland finally inquired about the congressional law. Monroe and Pinkney replied timidly. They had not mentioned it, they said, "for fear that it would be considered as waved as a menace." Auckland immediately demanded a copy of the law and on September 4 informed the Americans that England would interpret the failure to suspend it as a sign of hostility. The implication was clear: the continuation of the talks hung on America's backing down. When Pinkney and Monroe countered that they could not recommend suspension without solid progress on impressments and the carrying trade, Auckland replied that his presence at the conference table was proof enough of England's good intentions. Unwilling to see the negotiations end, the diplomats counseled retreat and buttressed their plea with promises of decent commercial provisions. The administration had little choice but to comply. It still longed for an acceptable treaty and peaceful relations with Great Britain. Failure to suspend the congressional law might halt the entire diplomatic process and place responsibility for the collapse of the negotiations on American shoulders. Although Fox's death had wilted much of Jefferson's spring and summer optimism, an additional suspension risked nothing but time, protected the administration from domestic political attacks, kept diplomacy afloat, and would allow the United States to play the hand fully and thereby measure England's ultimate intentions toward American commerce and seamen.[55]

Before the administration learned that its diplomats had signed a treaty with Great Britain, it had analyzed their dispatches and pri-

[55] Monroe and Pinkney to Madison, Sept. 11, Nov. 11, 1806, *American State Papers: Foreign Relations*, 3:133–39; U.S. State Department Report on Progress of British Negotiations, Nov. 27, 1806, Jefferson Papers, LC. The administration decided to suspend the nonimportation act on Nov. 28, and the bill authorizing suspension passed Congress on Dec. 5 (TJ to U.S. Senate and House of Representatives, "Report on the progress of the negotiations pending between the United States and Great Britain, recommending Suspension of the act prohibiting certain importations," Dec. 3, 1806, ibid.; Madison to Monroe and Pinkney, Nov. 28, Dec. 3, Dec. 5, 1806, *American State Papers: Foreign Relations*, 3:141).

vate letters through November 11.[56] Based on this foreign intelligence, Jefferson knew that the final treaty would probably be silent on impressments and yet contain positive commercial provisions. He appreciated the conflict between impressment failure on the one hand and commercial success on the other, but his instincts were to let Congress balance the two and make the final determination. "Under this dilemma," he wrote both Madison and Gallatin, "had we not better take the advice of the Senate?" He also asked them to meet in cabinet the following day to iron out an administration policy regarding the English negotiations.[57] Madison, however, opposed letting the Senate balance the pluses and minuses. He knew that the "negotiation risked a good deal on the question" of impressments. But he also knew of England's nonbinding promise to reduce its impressment activities in exchange for the treaty's formal silence on the issue. There was also the heady possibility, based mostly on Monroe's assurances, of significant commercial gains on, in Madison's words, "the other points of greatest interest, the colonial trade and blockades." Thinking that additional discussions might "surmount" the "difficulties," the secretary of state favored keeping the diplomatic track open.[58] In the end, the administration opted for neither senatorial decision nor additional diplomacy but rather for a pleasant scheme that would preserve America's commercial weapons against future contingencies, avoid a binding treaty sweetened a bit with English promises yet still dangerously silent on the impressment issue, and attain, "informally," the commercial benefits that the treaty might have delivered. To that end, the cabinet agreed to instruct Monroe and Pinkney to arrive at "an understanding" between England and the United States to both "act in practice on the very [commercial] principles proposed by the treaty." To show American good faith and to encourage English acceptance of future relations grounded in amicable informality, the cabinet also unanimously agreed "to continue [indefinitely] the suspension of the non-importation act."[59] Here matters stood at the beginning of February,

[56] TJ, Notes on Cabinet Meeting, Feb. 2, 1807, Jefferson Papers, LC.

[57] TJ to Gallatin, Feb. 1, 1807, Albert Gallatin Papers, New York University (NYU), microfilm, reel 13; TJ to Madison, Feb. 1, 1807, Jefferson Papers, LC.

[58] Madison to [?], Feb. 2, 1807, Madison Papers, LC, reel 9.

[59] TJ, Notes on Cabinet Meeting, Feb. 2, 1807, Jefferson Papers, LC; Madison to Monroe and Pinkney, Feb. 3, 1807, Diplomatic Instructions, All Countries, vol. 6, NA.

two months after Monroe and Pinkney had signed the treaty, thereby invalidating their superiors' desire for a painless yet positive informality.

In November and December the Americans completed their diplomacy and reported its results back to Washington. They had agreed to a British offer to ignore impressments in the final treaty in exchange for a British promise in a nonbinding note to balance more carefully the needs of the Royal Navy against the legitimate grievances of the United States. Although this tactic totally violated their instructions, there was little else they could do. Against the absence of a formal impressment article, they weighed Anglo-American stability, the avoidance of war, and their hope for decent commercial articles.[60]

The Treaty

Impressments, blockade, contraband, the carrying trade, Anglo-American commerce: these were the essential issues separating England and the United States. By the American ministers' final appraisal of their work, the treaty was a failure, worse than they had anticipated when they counseled suspension of the nonimportation act. The East India trade fared worse than in 1794. England insisted on crippling American trade with its Caribbean possessions through either tonnage restrictions on American entry to the islands or control of the destination of colonial produce in American bottoms. Consequently, the treaty, as in 1794, stood silent on the British West Indies. The United States still occupied the ground of England's "most favored nation," but this only rewarded it with the same pile of restrictions that England visited on the rest of the world. The new treaty also incorporated the Jay Treaty explanations of legitimate grounds for the capture of American vessels by British cruisers. The United States gained a little on contraband; food was left off the proscribed list, but naval stores remained on it. The final stipulation on blockades guaranteed misunderstanding and costly litigation because of foggy language. Essentially, the article allowed each nation to follow its own definition of blockade. The threat of paper blockades and

[60] Monroe to Madison, Jan. 11, 1807, James Monroe Papers, LC, microfilm, reel 3.

paper navies, then, was still quite real. And what of ports that fell under blockade after the commencement of American trading voyages? Great Britain agreed that American vessels could not be captured for violating a blockade unless they were first warned of its existence. But the treaty did not define what constituted a warning. Whether it meant at the port in question by British naval presence or by ministerial announcement in faraway London was left unclear. On both the meaning of blockade and adequate warning, linguistic fuzziness promised judicial headaches or physical capture for American merchant vessels. The treaty, of course, was completely silent on impressments. And what the American diplomats considered their greatest success—the protection of the wartime carrying trade with England's enemies—showed serious flaws under close examination.[61]

Monroe wrote personal letters to both Madison and Jefferson defending the treaty he had helped negotiate. More accurately, he wrote excuses and apologies. "No aid has been derived in this business from any neutral powers," he explained. The United States had waged the battle for neutral rights alone. And what of England's continental involvement? Monroe reminded his superiors that the United States had made its demands "at a time when the very existence of the [English] country depended on an adherence to its maritime pretensions." So scant were the concrete gains that Monroe cited the conclusion of any treaty whatever as an accomplishment that enhanced both the Republican party and the United States. "The movement has drawn the attention of Europe," he boasted, "and will make us better known and more respected as a power."[62]

Jefferson's initial reaction to the finished treaty was anger and implied rejection. He received the document a short time before the scheduled congressional adjournment and in the midst of a painful migraine attack. On the last day of the session a Senate delegation asked him if Congress would be kept in special session to consider the treaty. Jefferson had only glanced at it. Missing was an article on impressment; included was England's insulting claim of a right to dissolve the treaty unilaterally if the United States did not combat

[61] The full text of the treaty can be found in *American State Papers: Foreign Relations*, 3:147-51.

[62] Monroe to TJ, Jan. 11, 1807, Jefferson Papers, LC; Monroe to Madison, Jan. 11, 1807, Monroe Papers, LC, reel 3.

future French restrictions on American commerce. The treaty oppressed him, the migraine deepened the gloom, and Jefferson snapped that he would not keep the Senate in session to consider it.[63] The administration's final rejection of the treaty, however, came with much care. In fact, it tried desperately to salvage it, so great was its fear of continued drift, worse treatment in the future, and war. In the end, the omission of impressment did not weigh as heavily as did the glaring economic shortcomings, the sale of the Republican weapon of nonimportation for negligible gain, and the shocking news, ferreted from the customs records by Gallatin, that an equitable compromise with the British on impressment would cripple the American merchant marine.

Upon receiving the treaty, the administration set in motion a comprehensive examination of all its commercial provisions. Jefferson carefully studied and made notes of the entire document, and came down heavily against acceptance in its present form.[64] The administration also consulted leading lights in the American mercantile community. Out went confidential requests to Jacob Crowninshield, Republican merchant from Salem, Massachusetts; Samuel Smith, merchant prince from Baltimore; William Jones, future president of the Second National Bank from New York; and Tench Coxe, philosopher of American economic growth from Philadelphia.[65]

These men of commerce uniformly recommended rejection. Crowninshield thought the treaty "would operate in a thousand ways to the injury of this country." The document was riddled with obvious defects; apparent victories disappeared under close analysis.[66] On the carrying trade, for example, Monroe's last dispatches had prepared the administration for the worst: not only the requirement of the broken voyage but also storage of the cargo for one month and its reshipment in a different vessel.[67] Storage and transfer stacked the deck against American merchants in the highly

[63] Peterson, *Thomas Jefferson and the New Nation*, p. 861.

[64] TJ, Notes on the Monroe-Pinkney Treaty, Mar. 21, 1807, Jefferson Papers, LC.

[65] Madison to Coxe, Mar. 27, 1807, to Jones, Mar. 7, 1807, to Crowninshield, Mar. 28, 1807, Madison Papers, LC, reel 9; Madison to Smith, Mar. 3, 14, 1807, Samuel Smith Papers, LC; Madison to Smith, April 12, 1807, Samuel Smith Papers, Maryland Historical Society (Md. Hist. Soc.).

[66] Jacob Crowninshield to Madison, Aug. 18, 1807, Madison Papers, LC, reel 9.

[67] Robert Smith to Samuel Smith, Feb. 9, 1807, Samuel Smith Papers, LC.

competitive colonial trade. The final provisions of the treaty appeared less oppressive; gone were the storage and transfer requirements. In their place England only asked forfeiture of a part of the import duties usually drawn back by the American merchant upon the reexportation of the colonial produce. This England argued would fairly equalize the operating costs between American merchants and their English counterparts, whose set costs were higher because of England's involvement in war. At first glance, the carrying trade stipulation appeared sound. John Randolph thought the article in complete accord with American needs and pegged administration opposition to both it and the whole treaty on Madison's rivalry with James Monroe for the presidential succession.[68] Even Samuel Smith on first reading thought it adequate, especially because its ratification would stabilize relations with England and reduce insurance costs enough to compensate for the partial loss of import duties.[69] After a closer study, however, Smith revised his earlier estimation of the article because parts of it directly threatened profitable activities and because the fuzzy language of the whole package created dangerous amounts of vagueness that the English courts might use to imperil the entire business.

The Monroe-Pinkney treaty confined the American carrying trade to the Caribbean-American-European connection. Non-English colonial goods could only be sent to Europe, and only European goods reshipped back to the colonies. Thus Great Britain preserved for its own merchants the Asian and North African trade.[70] The wording of the treaty also supported an argument that American reexportations were limited to the mother country of the colony of origin. On this and other points, Smith was sure, England would make such arguments. "The article is so worded," he wrote Madison, that it "open[s] a wide field for the constructive powers of the British Admiralty judges." Potential disagreements, costly litigations, and probable seizures and condemnations were legion. The treaty, for example, required the importation of colonial goods into the United States and the "payment" of duties. Most American merchants never

[68] Randolph to Joseph Bryan, Mar. 29, 1808, John Randolph Papers, Virginia State Library; Randolph to James Mercer Garnett, Mar. 7, 1807, John Randolph Papers, LC; Randolph to Monroe, Mar. 26, 1808, ibid., ser. 2.

[69] Smith to Madison, Mar. 14, 1807, Samuel Smith Papers, UVa.

[70] Jacob Crowninshield to Madison, Aug. 18, 1807, Madison Papers, LC, reel 9.

actually paid the duties in cash; this aspect of the American revenue system was a tissue of paperwork involving the mere posting of bond and security. What if England, with treaty in hand, insisted on actual payment? Such an interpretation would either bankrupt the merchant class or destroy the insurance industry. But without actual monetary payment, according to a strict reading of the treaty, England could capture and condemn all American vessels plying the carrying trade. As the treaty stood, Smith confessed, he would not send out his own maritime property.[71]

Although the treaty established a permanent Anglo-American trading connection, the clauses regarding the carrying trade and other neutral issues were only temporary; to operate, according to their precise wording, through the duration of "present hostilities." These different time frames also posed serious dangers. First, if Great Britain made peace with its enemies and war broke out again, the United States would find itself locked in a treaty arrangement that gave no protection to its wartime carrying trade but still denied it methods of protest short of war. On the other hand, if European peace became permanent, the United States could not negotiate peacetime carrying trade privileges with England's former enemies, as remote as that possibility was, without violating its treaty with Great Britain. The treaty's worst reading, then, one consistent with its language, granted the United States a limited carrying trade riddled with financial pitfalls during only the duration of the present round of European war. For these reasons, Smith counseled rejection.[72]

Tench Coxe spelled out the longest list of specific grievances and placed them in their most far-reaching and threatening context. In page after page, he dissected the document with each observation linking Great Britain's overriding purpose to the British accomplishment of twelve years before. "The whole scope of the treaty, like Mr. Jay's," he believed, "is to secure depredations on the part of G[reat] Britain from reciprocity and to secure to her the advantage which reciprocal rules may give." The United States had given much for little. Most galling, it had bartered for insufficient gain the right to single out Great Britain for future economic retaliation. Nor could another bout of diplomacy improve the treaty. Coxe advised the

---

[71] Samuel Smith to Madison, April 3, 15, 1807, Samuel Smith Papers, LC.

[72] Samuel Smith to Madison, April 15, 1807, ibid.

prompt termination of all negotiations. "I am of the opinion," he confided to Madison, "that considering the attachments of G[reat] Britain to the navigation act, the jealousy of our commercial capacities and growth, their spirit of monopoly, and the temper of the preponderant part of the ministry, this treaty is not likely to be ameliorated to eligibility in a commercial sense." Madison agreed. "The lights thrown on the treaty by the gentlemen consulted," he wrote Jefferson, illuminated its adverse implications for American commerce, "particularly the colonial trade." Jefferson concurred. "The more it is developed," he noted in April, "the worse it appears." [73]

As bad as the treaty appeared, the administration struggled to find reason to accept it, or at least to continue the negotiations in good faith. When Jefferson had expected decent commercial provisions, he had been willing to accept a treaty that was silent on impressment. Now that he knew the extent of the commercial defeat and that its denseness and subtleness defied correction, he returned to impressment to salvage a treaty. Only after he learned from Gallatin that fair dealings with the English on impressment contained immensely negative implications for the nation's commerce did the president finally give up on Monroe's and Pinkney's efforts.

The United States had always demanded not only England's abandonment of impressment but also the return of American seamen who had already been pressed into the Royal Navy. This demand, in fairness, presumed a corresponding American return of bona fide English sailors who had jumped (or had been lured) into the American service. The administration had tried to avoid this issue because even the discussion of the possibility of numerous British sailors on American vessels supported England's charge of American enticement and, by extension, divided responsibility for impressment between aggressive British captains and grasping American ones. Consequently, the diplomats skirted the issue. Taking care not to admit the presence of British deserters on American ships, they promised Great Britain the full cooperation of local authorities in their return. England had always rejected a treaty obligation to return American sailors in exchange for a nonenforceable pledge from Washington that American municipal authorities would

[73] Coxe to Madison, April [?], 1807, Madison to TJ, May 3, 1807, Madison Papers, LC, reel 9; TJ to Madison, April 25, 1807, Jefferson Papers, LC.

cooperate in the return of English sailors. The hope for an impressment article, slim as it was, rested on the incorporation of full reciprocity into the treaty: England's renouncement of impressment and
return of its victims; America's rejection of enticement and return of
its prey. As a last effort to win an impressment article, the Jeffersonians considered mutual redress. In their attempt, they finally confronted the size of the English presence on the American merchant
marine.

On Madison's suggestion, the secretary of the treasury estimated
the total number of seamen employed on American vessels and its
composition by nationality: American, English, and other foreign.
He used both available tonnage figures and the monies paid by
sailors into the hospital fund to make his approximation, and he
based his analysis on the 1805 numbers, the most recent. Gallatin
computed the entire tonnage at 1,100,000, broken down into:
foreign trade, 740,000; whaling trade and fisheries, 60,000; coasting
trade, 300,000. On average the foreign and coasting trade required
six persons, officers and crew, for every hundred tons and the whaling and fishing industry eight persons for the same tonnage. All this
computed to 64,000 sailors in the American merchant marine. With
the crews on small crafts estimated at 5,000, the total figure became
69,000. The hospital fund figures supported this estimation. The
total fund for 1805 was $60,000. At the rate of $1.60 per sailor,
37,500 seamen paid hospital duties. Adding to this number the
seamen who were exempt—fishermen (4,500), officers and small
boys (20,000), small craft crews (5,000)—the total figure became
67,500. The crucial part of the total was the number of able seamen
employed in the foreign trade, because very few English deserters
were small boys, few of them joined the fishing, whaling, coasting, or
small craft trade, and few of them became officers, ordinaries, or
cooks. The total number of able seamen involved in the foreign trade
was 18,000. Of these 9,000 were English by American definition of
nationality, exactly half.[74]

Gallatin's data rendered equitable compromise on impressment
undesirable from America's point of view. Even if England returned
all American sailors and "abstained from impressing in the future,"
he noted, a fair exchange was defeat. Even if England accepted all the

[74] Madison, Observations in Cabinet Meeting, Feb. 2, 1807, Jefferson Papers,
LC; Gallatin to Madison, April 13, 1807, Madison Papers, LC, ser. 2, reel 25.

commercial changes the United States might demand, he further explained, "there is no advantageous modification in our commercial regulations with them which could indemnify us for the relinquishment of their seamen on our part." "That measure," he grimly concluded, "would more effectively curtail our commerce than any restriction they can lay upon it." Commerce and impressment had finally blended. Jefferson now understood that saving American victims from royal press gangs and ensuring their future safety through treaty stipulation would ravage the nation's foreign commerce. As he wrote to Madison: "Mr. Gallatin's estimate of the number of foreign seamen in our employ renders it prudent I think to suspend all propositions respecting our nonemploiment of them."[75]

The cruel news that the United States could only avoid the impressment of its sailors at prohibitive costs to its foreign commerce dampened administration spirits. The president thought "our best course is to let the negotiation take a friendly nap." Gallatin and Madison wondered if that was possible. Various fears oppressed them. Madison fretted that both the rejection of the treaty and an abrupt termination to the talks risked "a very dangerous posture of things." They might produce new levels of English harassment with ensuing Federalist political gains at home. If nothing else, continuing the discussions ensured a reasonable stability, both at home and abroad.[76]

New State Department instructions incorporated the strategy of procrastination. They detailed all the changes the United States desired: on impressment, the colonial trade, blockades, and the British trade. Missing was any mention of the return of British deserters. Included were reminders of the levers of force at America's disposal: nonimportation, a ban on American shipments of food and naval stores to Great Britain, and war. The State Department's official image of an Anglo-American war was a happy one. In the contest, England would lose a valued customer and a source of supply, as well as Canada, the British West Indies, and the scores of merchant vessels that would surely fall to American privateers. These were empty

---

[75] Gallatin to Madison, April 13, 1807, TJ to Madison, April 21, 1807, Madison Papers, LC, ser. 2, reel 25.

[76] TJ to Madison, April 21, 1807, ibid.; Madison to TJ, May [?], 1807, Madison Papers, LC, reel 9.

boasts. The administration had already rejected both commercial and military war as viable policy alternatives because the issues at stake justified neither and endangered too much. Nor did the administration expect a second round of diplomacy to change significantly the accomplishment of the first. Its new goals were interminable discussion, diplomatic charade, delay, and the maintenance of the status quo. "As long as the negotiations can be honorably protracted," Madison advised Monroe, "it is a recourse to be preferred, under existing circumstances, to the alternatives of improper concessions or inevitable collisions."[77]

Means and Ends in Republican Statecraft

The three and one-half years that Monroe and Pinkney spent in London were barren of results but nonetheless significant for what they said about Republican aspirations and statecraft and for what they did to Republican perceptions of Great Britain. The Jeffersonians entered the negotiations full of pleasant expectations. They would discuss neutral trade, ignore Anglo-American commerce, and achieve a negotiated settlement pegged to the profit and status needs of the growing nation. Republican notions of "useful" and "honest" neutrality both legitimated the wartime goals and promised their peaceful attainment. So Jefferson hoped. "We shall thus become what we sincerely wish to be," he wrote in July 1806, "honestly neutral and truly useful to both belligerents: to the one [England] by keeping open a market for the consumption of her manufactures, while they are excluded from all other countries under the power of her enemy; to the other [France] by securing for her a safe carriage of all her productions, metropolitan or colonial, while their own means are restrained by their enemy."[78] No longer graspingly neutral, Jefferson's America had become a beneficent servant to a war-torn and suffering world. Only if England accepted the logic, propriety, and utility of Jefferson's definition of "honest neutrality" could the United States anticipate either trade or peace at little cost. England did not,

[77] Madison to Monroe and Pinkney, May 20, 1807, *American State Papers: Foreign Relations*, 3:166–73.
[78] TJ to James Bowdoin, July 10, 1806, Jefferson Papers, LC.

and the United States found itself at year's end with no policy except drift.

Innocent and self-serving perception, the enormity of the American demands, and the misuse of economic weapons scuttled the diplomacy. Jefferson placed his faith in reason and a noble image of American purpose because his own doubts on the rectitude of American neutral goals precluded much stronger a defense. Both the nature of the trade and the probable economic and fiscal consequences of commercial retaliation frightened Jefferson from its use. The results were almost complete congressional freedom, a weak brand of retaliation that accurately represented southern Republican leanings, and the administration's unsure and almost apologetic application of the weapon in the English negotiations. Compromised at creation and in usage as it was, however, America's pre-*Chesapeake* diplomacy clarifies what the Jeffersonians meant by economic coercion and casts new light on the embargo of 1807. Coercion faithfully mirrored its historical antecedents as colonial policy in the 1760s and 1770s, national policy in the 1780s, and Republican policy in the 1790s. It aimed to replace war and it encompassed the congressional denial of the American market to British ships and manufactured goods. This market-oriented, import-oriented tradition never embraced a financially destructive and politically divisive ban on American shipping and foreign trade.

But there was another tradition: the tradition of embargo, a policy that anticipated war, that sought to preserve its military resources and buy time for its preparation, and yet also sought to spare war by communicating clearly a resolve to fight. Republican William Findlay's 1806 recollections of the 1793 congressional debates distinguished between both traditions. After the United States had received word of the British orders-in-council of June 1793, Congressman Madison introduced a series of economically punitive countermeasures. While they were being debated and before any final determination had been made, Congress received notification of England's November 1793 order "which authorized a higher degree of aggression than had been heretofore committed." Consequently the American Congress immediately passed a thirty-day, then a sixty-day embargo. The embargo, Findlay recalled, "was not intended as a permanent measure, nor expected to have any permanent effect." Its purpose was to avoid untimely war and "to secure what was yet in our harbors until Congress might have time to deliberate" on policy.[79] As it turned out, the House of Representatives passed a nonimportation bill, but the full Congress authorized a diplomatic mission to England that both stalled the implementation of economic coercion and finally produced the Jay Treaty. But the point remains: in 1793 when Republicans spoke of economic coercion and embargo, they understood the distinctions and honored the differences. Republicans recognized that the policies of economic coercion and embargo rested on different amounts of time, addressed foreign threats of unequal gravity, and signified different lines of national action; they recognized that one was largely a peacetime policy of economic reprisal and economic growth, and the other a prewar policy of isolation and military preparation.

These distinctions also shaped Republican thinking in 1806. During the congressional debates on the proper American response to the *Essex* decisions, Elbridge Gerry of Massachusetts traced in careful detail the differences between economic coercion (nonimportation) and embargo. Writing to Madison, he analyzed the available American responses to impressments and England's recent maritime rulings. He saw little utility in economic coercion, which he specifically described as the nonimportation of English goods, and saw little likelihood that diplomacy would yield positive results. Instead, he suggested continuing the talks, regardless of their promise, combined with "a general embargo on our commerce until the issue of negotiations shall be known." Such a policy would avoid unnecessary confiscations, prevent precipitate and untimely war, and allow the United States "to employ the interim in effectual preparations for war by land or sea." Three weeks later Gerry again wrote Madison and distinguished between the two types of policy: economic coercion, which embraced nonimportation and conformed to the Republican tradition of economic war, and embargo, which lay outside that tradition and aimed toward either miraculous settlement or successful war by both broadcasting a resolve to fight and purchasing time for effective preparation. "Should Congress . . . adopt commercial restriction or an embargo," Gerry concluded, "I have not the least doubt that the measure would . . . meet with vigorous support."[80]

[79] Findlay, *Annals*, 9th Cong., 1st sess., pp. 615–16.
[80] Gerry to Madison, Feb. 7, 26, Mar. 12, 1806, Madison Papers, LC, reel 9.

Finally, Jefferson opposed the Monroe-Pinkney treaty, in part, to protect the weapon of economic coercion. The treaty's most-favored-nation clause would "yield the principle of our nonimportation act," he brooded, "the only peaceable instrument for coercing all our rights."[81]

Since the 1780s, Jefferson's rationality, his humanism, and his peaceful spirit had shaped a personal quest for the discovery of non-violent forms of national defense. The means he had settled on was the economic power of the American market and its utility as a foreign policy weapon. This intellectual commitment to the soundness of economic weapons was always there, intruding and demanding a hearing whenever the need for policy arose. But during his presidency, theory and policy never converged. In 1806 neither the English threat nor policy ramifications justified the experiment. Later on in 1807, he would find the English threat so malevolent and outsized that he favored war, not the peaceful substitute of economic coercion.

Finally, the failure of diplomacy, so quickly followed by the *Chesapeake* attack in June 1807, gave form to a loose collection of impressions about Great Britain that were staple components of Republicanism itself. The resultant image was of British hatred, of persevering British attempts to thwart American growth and to deny the nation a standing in the international community which its ideology, its energy, and its institutions deserved. The image not only made sense of British actions and of America's diplomatic failure; it also elevated the importance of the Republic itself. The image of British treachery carried with it a corresponding idea of American rivalry and potential greatness. Jefferson thought the futile bout of diplomacy proved that Great Britain was still wedded to "ancient principles," and still "anti-american." Madison thought that the British demands were "not sought in a belligerent right or even in a policy merely belligerent, but in one which had no origin or plan but those of commercial jealousy and monopoly."[82] That Great Britain was fighting imperial France and yet giving worried looks to the

---

[81] TJ, Notes on Cabinet Meeting, Feb. 2, 1807, Jefferson Papers, LC.

[82] TJ to Madison, May 1, 1807, ibid.; Madison to Monroe and Pinkney, Feb. 3, 1807, Diplomatic Instructions, All Countries, vol. 6, NA.

West and its rising American empire increased American pride as it explained American diplomatic failure.

The administration—really the popular Republican imagination, heavily freighted with anglophobia and national desire—reduced in significance the Napoleonic war and placed at center stage the historic struggle between Great Britain and the United States: England grasping to preserve bloated monopoly; America seeking its rightful chance to continue successfully its revered experiment in economic enterprise and popular institutions. Neutral rights had become the symbol for American society itself. "The English," charged the Tammany Society of New York, "the disturbers and destroyers of nations, burn with infuriated rage toward us and fasten on our neutrality as the pretext for depredation. Already has American enterprise been fettered by the impositions of foreign maritime ascendancy. The stars of the American flag are to become lesser lights in the political heaven, and our countrymen are to share the same fate as our commerce."[83] Such was the Republican fear. Such, especially, was Jefferson's. In 1806 he held back, letting both Congress and the diplomats in London shape policy. But on June 25, 1807, he learned of the outrage committed on the *Chesapeake* off the coast of Norfolk three days before. The American vessel, sailing for the Mediterranean, had been approached by H.M.S. *Leopard* and ordered to submit to a British search for deserters. When the American commander refused, the *Leopard* fired into her, wounding eighteen and killing three. The *Chesapeake* was then boarded, and the British party removed four alleged deserters from the Royal Navy.[84] This British attack in the summer of 1807 dramatized Jefferson's comprehension of the English problem, radicalized his policy preferences, and enlarged his appetite for political control. The year 1807 found Jefferson's emotions involved in the definition of foreign problems and in the formulation of policy as 1806 never did. The *Chesapeake*, it seemed, was never from his thoughts. That "extraordinary occurrence," he wrote a friend, "and the state of things that brings on, really occupy my pen through the day and my thoughts through the

[83] Tammany Society, Columbian Order Number One, New York, to TJ, Jefferson Papers, LC.

[84] Peterson, *Jefferson and the New Nation*, pp. 874–75.

night."[85] During the months between the June attack and the meeting of the Tenth Congress in October, Jefferson strove to shape policy to a greater degree than in any other period, issue, or crisis of his presidency. His preferred policy—war against England—placed him at odds with most of his cabinet and with the prevailing views of the Republican congressional majority.

[85] TJ to Craven Peyton, Aug. 10, 1807, Jefferson Papers, UVa.

3

"TO SETTLE THE OLD AND THE NEW"
Jefferson and the Chesapeake

The President

The *Leopard*'s hostile act pointed toward war. So thought much of
the Washington community during the long *Chesapeake* summer.
Compared to the opinions of his major advisers, however, the president's mood was more angry, more insistent, and strangely ebullient.
As Jefferson contemplated the attack, past and present fused to reveal a frightening pattern. Serving as both a metaphor of British
malevolence and a harsh reminder of British power, "the extraordinary occurrence" merged easily into the larger tangle of commercial
and national rivalry to become, for Jefferson, a genuine and seemingly inescapable cause of war. "Now then," he believed, "is the time
to settle the old and the new."[1]

The cabinet shared neither Jefferson's certainty nor his optimism.
Wanting more to avoid war than to justify it, the president's men
searched for shiftings in Europe's military situation and in England's
impressment and commercial practices to find ground firm enough
to support a diplomatic settlement. Much of this activity merely revealed a compelling desire to escape war, the wish preceding and
shaping the thought. But their attempts to conjure up peace did not
blind them to the severity of the nation's predicament or to the real
possibility of war. And their efforts were grounded in a flexible
awareness that time, events, and levers short of armed power might
yet spare the nation violence. The president, however, was unsympathetic to these hopeful explorations. In August, for example, the
heads of the Navy and Treasury departments suggested that England's recent military setbacks on the Continent explained a noticeable decline in British impressments of American sailors and made

[1] TJ to William Duane, July 20, 1807, Jefferson Papers, LC.

plausible a negotiated settlement of the *Chesapeake* affair. Jefferson disagreed, writing to Robert Smith that he did "not see the probability . . . in the same favorable light with Mr. Gallatin and yourself."[2] Madison also tried to strike a hopeful note with the president. British newspapers and parliamentary debates, he suggested, hinted at a reconsideration of England's American policy. Conceivably, French power in Europe and the threat of American nonimportation might drive England to settle not only the *Chesapeake* but impressments and the colonial trade as well. Jefferson debunked Madison's optimistic reading of British intentions. "I do not give the newspaper and parliamentary scraps the same importance as you do," he replied. In the immediate aftermath of the June incident, Jefferson clearly favored war. His particularly fearful understanding of English hostility, its sources and its goals, created his bellicose spirit.[3]

In Jefferson's mind, England's European difficulties did not explain but only rationalized its mistreatment of American commerce. He was equally convinced that only Napoleon's European strength thwarted the completion of British designs against American economic growth. He also believed that the future course of the European war offered little comfort to the United States, if it stood on the sidelines. Military setbacks would impel England not to negotiate fairly, "but only to temporize with us." British victory in Europe spelled America's commercial defeat worldwide. But if America chose to fight England now, the European war became a blessing. It provided an opportunity that would evaporate with the return of peace, and it made the present moment the proper one for combating the nation's historic enemy. "To do this," Jefferson wrote in October, "we shall never again have so favorable a conjuncture of circumstances." War "can never be in a better time for us," he wrote his navy chief. "A war need cost us very little," he reminded his nephew in July, "and we can take from them [the English] what would be an idemnification for a great deal. For this everything shall be in readiness at the moment it is declared."[4] The emotions of the *Chesapeake* assault awakened in Jefferson an uncharacteristic fondness for strong executive power. It fell to "the executive," he wrote in mid-July, "to

[2] Smith to TJ, Aug. 23, 1807, TJ to Smith, Sept. 3, 1807, ibid.

[3] Madison to TJ, Sept. 3, 1807, TJ to Madison, Sept. 4, 1807, ibid.

[4] TJ to Thomas Paine, Oct. 9, 1807, to Robert Smith, Sept. 3, 1807, to John Wayles Eppes, July 12, 1807, ibid.

direct the whole public force to the best advantage of the nation." In the months between the June outrage and the October session of Congress, Jefferson used this ample understanding of executive power to prepare the United States for war.[5] His decision to postpone the special session until October, a decision opposed by much of his cabinet, was part of a calculated strategy of war. Postponement, of course, prolonged peace. But in July the hope for peace was frail and, for Jefferson, largely unwanted, and in the context of his summer thinking, postponement served a military master. "The postponing of the summons of Congress will aid in avoiding to give too quick an alarm to the adversary," he informed William Duane. "We should procrastinate 3 or 4 months," he wrote John Page, "only to give time to our merchants to get in their vessels, property, and seamen, which are the identical materials with which the war is to be carried on."[6]

The timing of the congressional summons engaged the cabinet in early July. Robert Smith, the secretary of the navy, and Albert Gallatin, the treasury chief, argued for an immediate congressional session, though for different reasons.[7] Shocked by the *Chesapeake* attack and fearing a follow-up British invasion, Gallatin thought the nation's safety demanded a summer congressional meeting. By the end of the month he was still trying to bring the president to his point of view. "We must expect an efficient [English] fleet on our coast late this autumn," he warned Jefferson on July 25, "if the British ministry is possessed of enough energy, and that we have no reason to doubt."[8] Smith's reasons, on the other hand, rested on diplomacy. As a demonstration of genuine American anger, an early session might jolt the English into sincere negotiation.[9] Soon after the attack, Jef-

[5] TJ to John Page, July 9, 17, 1807, to Thomas Cooper, July 9, 1807, to Thomas Mann Randolph, July 13, 20, 1807, to William Duane, July 20, 1807, to William Cabell, July 24, 1807, to John Taylor, Aug. 1, 1807, to John Nicholas, Aug. 18, 1807, ibid.

[6] TJ to Duane, July 20, 1807, TJ to Page, July 9, 1807, ibid.; TJ to Samuel Smith, July 30, 1807, Samuel Smith Papers, UVa.

[7] Albert Gallatin to Hanna Gallatin, July 10, 1807, Gallatin Papers, NYU, reel 14; Robert Smith to Wilson Cary Nicholas, July 20, 1807, Wilson Cary Nicholas Papers, UVa; Robert Smith to Thomas Jefferson, July 17, 1807, Jefferson Papers, LC.

[8] Gallatin to TJ, July 25, 1807, Jefferson Papers, LC.

[9] TJ, Notes on Cabinet Meeting, July 9, 1807, ibid.; Smith to Wilson Cary Nicholas, July 20, 1807, Wilson Cary Nicholas Papers, UVa.

ferson had also considered a prompt congressional session, though he preferred a later one. Had the intelligence reports from Virginia indicated any British intention to heap onto the initial outrage additional acts of violence, the president would have called Congress into session.[10] By the end of the month, however, he was reasonably sure that the British ships off the coasts of Virginia and New York intended to remain quiet until they received different instructions from London.[11] Virginia's governor, William Cabell, reported stability in the Chesapeake, quiet in Norfolk, and British compliance with the presidential proclamation of July 2 that had interdicted all British national vessels from American waters and had allowed communication by flag only. Calm in the Chesapeake and "the diseases of the season" on the Potomac prompted Jefferson to leave for Monticello after the cabinet meeting on July 28. Before he left, he checked postal schedules between New York and Virginia, informed his spy in Lynnhaven inlet to stop his daily intelligence reports to Washington, and ignored Gallatin's eleventh-hour plea for a summer session. Gallatin, a bit angered, thought Jefferson's concern for his own health weighed unduly in the final decision.[12]

Had the Congress met in the summer, it would have given Jefferson the war he wanted, but not at the time he wanted it. Wilson Cary Nicholas, influential Republican congressman from Virginia, styled the June outrage a "fortunate occurrence." It fired the public spirit, made clear the nature of the British threat. "It is impossible that the people can ever be brought to a better temper to give their full support to your government" on the question of war, Nicholas wrote Jefferson. While popular anger burned, while party divisions receded before the imperative of national union, Nicholas advised, Jefferson must call into session the only branch of government constitutionally able to make war. And the war was justified: the *Chesapeake*, "the commercial injuries she [England] is every day dumping on us," and the plain fact of English conspiracy against America's future under-

---

[10]TJ, Notes on Cabinet Meeting, July 4, 1807, TJ to Henry Dearborn, July 7, 1807, Jefferson Papers, LC.

[11]TJ to William Cabell, Aug. 17, 19, 1807, TJ to Gallatin, Aug. 20, 1807, ibid.; TJ to William Cabell, Sept. 18, 1807, Jefferson Papers, UVa.

[12]Cabell to TJ, July 18, 1807, TJ to Cabell, July 27, 1807, TJ to William Tatham, July 28, 1807, Jefferson Papers, LC; Albert Gallatin to Hanna Gallatin, July 10, 1807, Gallatin Papers, NYU, reel 14.

scored a problem that defied diplomatic settlement. Jefferson agreed with Nicholas's gloomy assessment of English aims and shared his belief in the necessity of war. "We differ not in opinion," he replied, but only "as to the time of calling Congress for reasons not attended to generally."[13]

Those reasons rested on the need to avoid war with England while so much American commerce was on the oceans and vulnerable to British capture. By Jefferson's estimate, between twenty and forty thousand sailors were at sea in the summer of 1807.[14] If Congress met and declared war, this tremendous national asset would be an easy mark for British cruisers. And if Congress decided on coercive measures short of war, either war through British declaration or a great increase in impressments and confiscations would ensue. Besides the human resources afloat, the amount of commercial wealth on the oceans was staggering. Samuel Smith, one of Baltimore's leading merchants, estimated that at least 2,500 vessels with a total value in shipping and cargo of over one hundred million dollars were at sea.[15] From the port of Salem, Massachusetts, came indications that much of this maritime wealth was uninsured. Republican merchant Jacob Crowninshield estimated that only $700,000 of Salem's $2,800,000 in ships and cargoes on the ocean at the time of the *Chesapeake* attack was covered.[16] Untimely war would ruin scores of private fortunes and careers. Beyond that, the nation's mercantile community owned the lion's share of the nation's circulating capital. On their private careers depended their ability to lend to the government. And on the health of the insurance companies depended the solvency of the nation's banks; a popular run on the insurance companies would cripple the banking community's ability to lend to the government in the event of war. More important, seamen and ships were vital to the contemplated war effort. "The loss of these to us," Jefferson feared, "would be worth to Great Britain many vic-

[13]Nicholas to TJ, July 7, 1807, Wilson Cary Nicholas Papers, LC; TJ to Nicholas, Aug. 6, 1807, Jefferson Papers, LC.

[14]TJ to Thomas Mann Randolph, July 5, 13, 20, 1807, to John Page, July 9, 17, 1807, to Thomas Cooper, July 9, 1807, to William Cabell, July 16, 1807, to William Duane, July 20, 1807, Jefferson Papers, LC.

[15]J. A. Buchanan to Samuel Smith, Jan. 31, 1808, Madison Papers, LC, reel 10. Smith forwarded these estimates to Madison on the following day.

[16]Crowninshield to Gallatin, Sept. 14, 1807, Gallatin Papers, NYU, reel 14.

tories of the nile and trafalger." So it was that the president wanted
England to think that the United States was doing no more than
waiting on England's next move. In the meantime, he boasted to the
governor of Virginia, "everyday is restoring to us our best means for
carrying it [war] on."[17]

Jefferson's war strategy turned on Great Britain's continuing
European struggles. It fitted nicely between the opportunities provided by that involvement and the fiscal, institutional, and ideological tugs of Republicanism. The war in Europe made unlikely the
possibility of a massive British invasion of the United States. Consequently, seacoast fortifications could protect the nation from whatever force England could spare from the Old World and mount
against the New. Jefferson's faith in the efficacy of gunboats was tai-
lored to this defensive need. He never contemplated that these instruments of coastal defense might be used as offensive weapons of
war.[18]

Offensively, Jefferson's military strategy combined expeditions
into Canada and attacks on British trade and omitted the "ruinous
folly of a navy." The United States could never challenge the royal
fleet. Whatever ships could be built, given the limited resources of
the country, would soon be captured and added to the enemy's
number. Rather than gird for a head-on war, a conflict that Napoleon's armies spared the United States, the nation should call in its
resources, arm its merchant ships, protect its harbors, ports, and seacoast cities, plunder the British trade, and strike, in Jefferson's
words, "quick and deep into Canada." In general, the nation should
pursue what Jefferson described to John Armstrong in July as a
"galling" campaign against areas of British vulnerability.[19]

[17] TJ to John Page, July 17, 1807, to William Cabell, July 16, 1807, Jefferson
Papers, LC.

[18] TJ, Notes on Cabinet Meeting, July 2, 1807, ibid.; TJ to Samuel Smith, July
30, 1807, Samuel Smith Papers, UVa.

[19] Jefferson spoke of the "ruinous folly of a navy" in a letter to Thomas Paine, Sept.
6, 1807 (Jefferson Papers, LC). On the importance of French military victories to
the American war effort, see TJ to John Wayles Eppes, July 12, 1807, to Thomas
Mann Randolph, July 13, 1807 (ibid.). On American merchant vessels becoming a
force of at least "250 privateers," see TJ to John Page, July 17, 1807 (ibid.), to
Samuel Smith, July 30, 1807 (Samuel Smith Papers, UVa), to Gallatin, July 10,
1807 (Gallatin Papers, NYU, reel 14). He called for "quick and deep blows" into
Canada in a letter to John Page, July 17, 1807, reiterated the importance of a Cana-

The cabinet discussed offensive and defensive preparations during a three-day period toward the end of July. On the twenty-sixth, an invasion of Canada was outlined. The planned attack aimed at upper Canada and the upper part of lower Canada to the mouth of the Richelieu River. The key points of attack were Detroit, Niagara, Kingston, Montreal, and certain British islands in Passamaquoddy Bay. By far the most important question decided was the nature of the strike force. A law of the previous congressional session now enabled the national government to "detach" up to 100,000 volunteers from the states for a year of national service. Consequently, all but 100 of a contemplated strike force of 10,200 were to be state militiamen. The cabinet also decided to move men and equipment into the "neighborhood" of the attack points "as fast as the men can be collected and marched." Gallatin was especially anxious to have this process begun.[20]

Why this emphasis on militia? Because the Jeffersonian political and social order had no place for standing armies.[21] Jefferson's bright hopes for his militia-army assumed the implementation of the national volunteer militia act that Congress had passed in February. It was anchored to the republican concepts of volunteerism and the "citizen soldier," and it tried to fashion a national military force with state manpower and national money and equipment. Those who volunteered for the national militia would be liable to a twelve-month service of duty upon being called up or, in the phrase of the law, "detached" by the national government. Once the required number of men had volunteered, formed companies, and elected officers, the national government would arm, uniform, and equip them.

Jefferson believed the February law gave the president the revenue and authorization to create, during the congressional recess, a na-

---

dian invasion to Madison on Aug. 20, 1807, and asked Dearborn on Aug. 12, 1807, to conduct Indian policy in the northwest against the high probability of war against England and invasion of Canada (Jefferson Papers, LC). Jefferson described the combination of privateering and invasion of Canada in a letter to Armstrong, July 17, 1807 (ibid.).

[20] TJ, "Notes on Consultations with Heads of Departments in View of a Possible War with Great Britain," July 5, 7, 26, 27, 28, 1807, Jefferson Papers, LC; Gallatin to TJ, July 25, 1807, Gallatin Papers, NYU, reel 14.

[21] The only full-length treatment of the conflict over a standing army in early national history is Richard H. Kohn, *Eagle and Sword: The Beginnings of the Military Establishment in America* (New York, 1975).

tional fighting force. That is why he thought the postponement of Congress not incompatible with military preparation. "The law for detaching 100,000 militia and the appropriation for that," he wrote in July, "puts all military preparation in our power."[22] The controlling principle of the law, however, was volunteerism, and it could not support a national army. From Virginia, Jefferson learned that the applications for service which had poured in to the state governor in the wake of the *Chesapeake* attack were for the local militia; three months' service, in the state, to protect hearth and home.[23] The republican citizen-soldier had reacted to the British insult in a manner befitting his historical image. He would drop his plow and reach for his sword to protect family and neighborhood. Of such stuff offensive wars are not made.

The shortcomings of the February 1807 law focused administration attention on the regular state militias. The immediate aim was a national fighting force that avoided the pitfalls of both volunteerism and standing armies. This goal meshed with a larger task of classifying and harmonizing all the state militias. A national law that marked a certain portion of the combined state militias for national duty could blend the two goals together.

Secretary of War Henry Dearborn estimated that the state and territorial militias totaled 636,000 men. In "An Outline of a System for Organizing the Militia into Three Classes," Dearborn proposed that 566,000 of the men be classified into three groups. The first class— "all free, white citizens between the ages of 19 and 26"—totaled 185,000 men. In Dearborn's plan, the national government would arm and equip this class, which would be eligible for service in all the states and liable to a term of eight months in a given year. The second class—"free, white male citizens between the ages of 26 and 33"— totaled 174,000 men. They would arm and equip themselves and would not be liable for service beyond their own or adjoining states. The third class—those above the age of 33—would arm themselves and be liable to service only in their own states.[24]

What captured Jefferson's attention, apart from the obvious system

[22] TJ to Thomas Mann Randolph, July 20, 1807, to William Duane, July 20, 1807, Jefferson Papers, LC.

[23] TJ to William Cabell, Aug. 17, 1807, ibid.

[24] Dearborn, War Department, "Outline of a System for Organizing the Militia into Three Classes," Aug. 7, 1807, ibid.

and coherence that would replace the random, differing, and chaotic state militia organizations, was the part of the proposal that permitted the national use of state militiamen. Essentially, Dearborn's proposal incorporated a "draft" for national duty. He had suggested that the final legislation permit the national government to call out one-tenth of the second and third classes for defense of garrisons and forts within the states and one-fourth of the first class for service in the field. Such a draft created out of the first class three armies ranging from 10,000 to 30,000 men each. Jefferson was impressed. "I like it greatly," he wrote Dearborn on August 9.[25]

Militia classification, which Jefferson had long favored, could not create an armed force in the summer of 1807. Its implementation would require executive refinement, extended congressional discussion, and money. Jefferson turned to it in the midst of the summer crisis only because the nation's response to the February law had been so disappointing. With much to commend it as a long-term military reform, neither Dearborn's August proposal nor anything similar could satisfy the immediate needs arising from the *Chesapeake* attack. The creation of a usable national army still awaited the reordering of the American militia establishment and a threat to the nation grave enough to breathe life into the February volunteer militia law.

The administration's inability to enforce state compliance with the volunteer act of 1807 crippled all attempts to place an attack force in position. The states pleaded poverty to all national requests for military matériel. The decision to move men and equipment into position died in the July cabinet meeting. By October none had been moved. As late at August 1808, when Gallatin was again considering war in the wake of the embargo's failure abroad and ruinous effects at home, he complained bitterly to Jefferson about the complete refusal of all the states to honor their militia quotas.[26] From his own Virginia, Jefferson learned that the gratifying response to the governor's re-

[25] TJ to Dearborn, Aug. 9, 1807, ibid. Of Dearborn's system Jefferson wrote to Madison on the same day, "prima facie, I like it well" (Madison Papers, LC, reel 9).

[26] Dearborn to TJ, July 17, Aug. 11, 14, 1807, Dearborn to Samuel Smith, July 2, 1807, Gallatin to TJ, Aug. 9, 1808, TJ to Dearborn, Aug. 15, 18, 1807, Aug. 15, 1808, TJ to William Cabell, Aug. 17, 1807, TJ to John Nicholas, Aug . 18, 1807, TJ to Madison, Sept. 20, 1807, Samuel Smith to TJ, July 23, 1807, Jefferson Papers, LC.

quest for volunteers had not survived the initial enthusiasms of the *Chesapeake* incident.[27]

So difficult was it to create a fighting force, fund it, supply it, and enlist the states in active cooperation that by October 1807 the thought of war thoroughly frightened those most involved in its military and financial preparations, Henry Dearborn and Albert Gallatin. Republican ideology and decentralized government were obstacles to energetic national action. Jeffersonian policy could not evade Jeffersonian philosophy. A large navy was "ruinous folly." A large standing army, centrally controlled and administered, was unimaginable. Core ideals of Republicanism pushed the administration to rely on state militias, voluntary cooperation, and the energizing force of public spirit. Volunteerism, virtue, and cooperation did not facilitate preparation for war in the summer and fall of 1807 any more than they supported the embargo in 1808.

On July 27 the cabinet discussed coastal defenses. It divided the nation's seaports into three priority groups: those requiring no attention, those requiring minor repair, and those requiring major improvement. The priorities were based not only on present condition but on military importance, vulnerability to enemy attack, and commercial importance as registered in tonnage and impost figures. Fourteen ports needed minor physical repair, and seven required extensive expenditures, including New York, Washington-Alexandria, Norfolk, Savannah, and New Orleans. The cost of the contemplated fortifications was staggering; more important, it was largely unappropriated. On July 28 the cabinet decided to use available funds to begin work on New York, Charleston, New Orleans, and Savannah and to "leave the others for future appropriations."[28]

The cabinet also decided to add one hundred gunboats to the coastal fleet. This decision, however, encountered two problems. First, naval appropriations for the present year were spent. Second, the administration could not assume that Congress shared its hatred for ships of the line and its fascination with gunboats. Consequently, the cabinet instructed Robert Smith to purchase material for the gunboats on credit in the expectation that Congress would later honor the purchases. But the administration hedged its bets by ordering Smith to purchase only materials "useful for the navy should

[27] TJ to William Cabell, Aug. 17, 1807, ibid.
[28] TJ, "Notes on Consultations," July 27, 28, 1807, ibid.

Congress not authorize the building of gunboats." The cabinet also decided that Smith should buy on credit five hundred tons of saltpeter and one hundred tons of sulfur "on the assumption that Congress will sanction it." The cabinet also instructed the navy chief to recruit marines for gunboat service.[29]

At the July cabinet meetings, Gallatin presented figures on the potential cost of war and on the necessary increase in the national debt to fund it. Total government expenditures for 1808, assuming war, Gallatin estimated at $18 million. Contemplated revenues, including impost figures (estimated at only $8 million because of war), additional taxes, and land sales amounted to $11 million, leaving a deficit for the first year of $7 million. The figure did not include installments on the public debt that would fall due during the year. All told, Gallatin estimated a need for $7 million in loans for the initial war year and approximately $11 million in annual loans thereafter.[30]

Thus in the *Chesapeake* summer, money was as elusive as manpower. Unable to count on patriotic gifts and loyalty loans at no interest—"People will fight, but they will never give up their money for nothing," Gallatin wrote a senator in July—and realizing that taxation would be difficult and largely unproductive during the first year, the treasury chief was forced to consider several forms of borrowing, all costly. On Jefferson's advice, he scouted the American banking community. The news was mixed. Loans would be available, Gallatin learned, but not to the amount required. Samuel Smith informed him that the insurance companies had first claim on Baltimore's lending capital and that insurance needs to honor wartime property losses would consume most of Baltimore's bank capital in 1808. After that, money would be available for the war effort, but not to the one-half of total bank assets that Gallatin had hoped.[31]

Because of the meager returns expected from taxation and the limited amount of banking assets available for 1808, Gallatin turned to popular and foreign loans. Money from abroad, he was sure,

[29] TJ, "Notes on Consultations," July 28, 1807, ibid.; Gallatin to Samuel Smith, July 27, 1807, Gallatin Papers, NYU, reel 14.

[30] TJ, "Notes on Consultations," July 28, 1807, Jefferson Papers, LC; Gallatin to Samuel Smith, July 17, 1807, Gallatin Papers, NYU, reel 14.

[31] Gallatin to Smith, July 17, 1807, Smith to Gallatin, July 19, 1807, Gallatin Papers, NYU, reel 14.

would come at top dollar; and from the American people, he knew, "we must buy at the market price." To reduce the cost of domestic borrowing, Gallatin pitted his own ingenuity against popular avarice. He broached a rather complicated plan to Samuel Smith—"all this of course is between ourselves," he cautioned—to lower the cost of domestic loans by secret government purchases in the national debt. Secrecy was essential because open purchases would both embarrass the government and drive up the price of foreign loans. Because the "private" purchases would inflate the market value of government paper, the high market price would more than offset the increased interest rates when the government began selling debt certificates (that is, borrowing from the people) and, consequently, lower the real cost of government borrowing. As it turned out, Gallatin's treasury agents did not hide the fact that they were buying government paper at the request of the administration. Gallatin soon learned of their indiscretion and called off the whole operation.[32]

Whenever possible, military and financial preparations were kept secret from the American public in order to conceal them from the British. Few Republicans outside the executive branch were consulted unless, like Samuel Smith, they had either financial expertise or influence in the private banking community. Consequently, many grumbled that the administration's calm was soothing rather than sharpening public anger; that Jefferson's silence, added to his postponement of the congressional session, would "prove fatal" to later attempts to rekindle the popular spirit. "The merchants will begin to calculate," a New York Republican warned Gallatin. "Soon," he added, "considerations of profit and loss" would overwhelm national "resentment" and lock the nation in a pacific stance from which no amount of presidential warnings, pleas, or jeremiads could rouse it.[33]

Jefferson ran a calculated risk that national outrage was sufficiently strong to withstand the dampening effects of the months of silence required to launch military preparations and retrieve maritime property. A bit angered by probings into administration policy and accusations of "do-nothingism," he reminded William Duane, the inquisitive editor of the Philadelphia *Aurora*, that "the time is coming

[32] Gallatin to Smith, July 17, 1807, Gallatin to George Simson, July 18, July 21, 27, 1807, Gallatin to Jonathan Burall, Nov. 23, 1807, Smith to Gallatin, July 17, 27, 1807, Edward Jones to Gallatin, Sept. 1, 1807, ibid.

[33] Joseph Hopper Nicholson to Gallatin, July 14, Sept. 10, 1807, ibid.

when our friends must enable us to hear everything and expect us to say nothing." With one eye on the nation's maritime resources still at sea and the other trained on the Royal Navy, the president believed that "our greatest praise shall be that we appear to be doing nothing." The low profile was a pose. Unable himself to fuel the popular enthusiasm for war, Jefferson asked the editor of this important Republican sheet to act as his surrogate: "The public mind is made up for war," he informed Duane, "I believe [it] should maintain itself at that point."[34]

As the *Aurora* became more bellicose, the public appeared to become less so. Secretary of War Dearborn reported from New York that "fortifications fever" had disappeared with the hot weather. In August, Gallatin informed Madison that New Yorkers were so opposed to war they had convinced themselves it would never happen.[35] Equally convinced was Jefferson's attorney general, Caesar Rodney. So sure was he that the British government would "lower its flag" on the *Chesapeake* that he asked the president, in early October, if he could postpone his return to Washington because of his wife's illness. But Jefferson ordered Rodney back to Washington because, the president wrote, "everything we see and hear leads in my opinion to war."[36] Jefferson intended his October message to Congress to prove the futility of further diplomacy and to underscore the need for war. He intended to ask Congress for a declaration. On the substance and direction of the annual message, the executive branch would finally divide.[37]

The Cabinet

Jefferson sent draft copies of his annual congressional address to the members of the cabinet in the middle of October. In significance, his seventh annual message invites comparison with his first inaugural

[34] TJ to Duane, July 20, 1807, Jefferson Papers, LC.

[35] Dearborn to TJ, Oct. 1, 19, Dec. 29, 1807, ibid.; Gallatin to Madison, Aug. 15, 1807, Madison Papers, LC, reel 9.

[36] Rodney to TJ, Oct. 1, 3, 1807, TJ to Rodney, Oct. 8, 1807, Jefferson Papers, LC.

[37] Dearborn to TJ, Oct. 17, 1807, Robert Smith to TJ, Oct. 19, 1807, Gallatin to TJ, Oct. 21, 1807, ibid.

address. It came in the midst of a foreign crisis as dangerous to the nation as the internal tensions that in 1800 had engulfed and imperiled Jefferson's peaceful election. But while the first inaugural address ("we are all federalists, we are all republicans") obscured Jefferson's true reckoning of the Federalist party, his draft of the 1807 paper illuminated clearly Jefferson's understanding of the Federalist party's patron, Great Britain. As a description of Jefferson's fearful encounter with the Republic's historic enemy, the message, in its original draft, is one of the most revealing he ever wrote.

The president's words amounted to an extended exploration of British arrogance and malice; "a manifesto against the British government," according to one of his cabinet. In it, Jefferson ripped England's recent maritime pretensions from excusable moorings in the Napoleonic wars and relocated them in British jealousy of America's commercial and national aspirations. Not France as it now was but America as it might become triggered and sustained Great Britain's unannounced war against the United States.[38]

Jefferson traced in careful detail the persistence and purpose of British actions. Then came his description of the failure of all reasonable American attempts at accommodation. Building on the two themes of threat and failure, there followed a summary of what the executive branch had done to place the national defenses in order. Finally, Jefferson outlined the additional military preparations that needed congressional approval and appropriations. Little was said of American difficulties with Spain except that "differences remain unsettled." France went unnamed throughout. "With other nations of Europe," the president wrote, "our harmony and friendly intercourse have been maintained on their usual footing."

This seventh annual message resembles not only Jefferson's first inaugural but the Declaration of Independence as well. Obviously, both papers dealt with American difficulties with Great Britain. Both described differences that had passed the point of quiet negotiation. Both justified the legitimate use of force by an aggrieved people. The Declaration had secured the moral right of revolution by distinguishing between transient, accidental grievances and long-practiced conspiracies to deprive the colonists of their liberty. The

[38] TJ, "Draft of Annual Message to the Congress for 1807," Oct. 26, 1807, Robert Smith to TJ, Oct. 19, 1807, ibid.

first situation did not justify war; the second did. Jefferson's 1807 remarks made the same distinction, as his handling of the *Chesapeake* affair shows. Rather than dwelling on the June outrage, the president blended it into the history of prior and contemporary British oppressions. He deliberately attached it "to a long train of injuries and depredations under which our commerce has been afflicted on the high seas for years past."

A cabinet meeting on October 10 foreshadowed Jefferson's difficulties in winning cabinet acceptance both of the message and of the policy that lay within it. In late August, the president had asked Madison to prepare a full record of diplomacy's failure for the annual message. Gallatin, however, disagreed, and the cabinet decided not to include in either the message or any accompanying documentation a discussion of the negotiations with England, which, although unproductive to date, were still pending.[39]

The cabinet members who criticized Jefferson's draft had particular objections and specific suggestions. More important, and as a whole, cabinet strictures added up to a general disagreement with the assumptions and arguments of the paper. All shared a concern with its tone, feeling, and pulse. So carefully written were Jefferson's major state papers that their impact transcended a mere summing of the parts. It was the art of the paper, a wholeness that defied minor revision, that prompted Gallatin to confess to Jefferson that "I have kept your message longer than usual because my objection being less to details than to its general spirit, I was at a loss what alterations to submit to your conideration."[40]

The message ran squarely into cabinet opposition because it conveyed the idea that Jefferson had already decided on war with Great Britain; that its central purpose, as navy chief Robert Smith put it, was "to present to them [Congress] a ground upon which to found . . . war measures." Dearborn insisted on the deletion of provocative and misleading statements on the aims of executive actions during the summer recess. The message "as it stands," he chided Jefferson, "indicates the intention of offensive operations." As Dearborn remembered them, the summer discussions carried no such goal. Plans for offensive war were hypothetical, based, he thought, on the need to

[39] TJ to Madison, Aug. 26, 1807, TJ, "Notes on Cabinet Consultations," Oct. 10, 1807, ibid.
[40] Gallatin to TJ, Oct. 21, 1807, ibid.

guard against the total failure of diplomacy. The *Chesapeake* crisis was ominous, and the executive branch would have been remiss had it not discussed military defense in the privacy of its summer deliberations. But to air the discussions publicly and to portray contingent plans as adopted policy distorted the purpose of the summer meetings and endangered the nation. Jefferson boasted in the message that the state militias "are ordered to be organized and ready at a moment's warning to proceed on any service to which they may be called." The boast obscured the immense difficulties the administration had encountered in prying from the states contributions of men and matériel and in molding the state forces for an organized military effort. Jefferson's militant language, Dearborn feared, would undercut diplomacy with the British and impel the Congress to declare a war the nation was not prepared to fight. "Every preparation within the executive power has been made to insure us the benefit of early exertions," Jefferson had assured. This invitation to "offensive" war Dearborn thought reckless. He urged Jefferson to reword the sentence to assure the Congress and the British that all executive actions during the summer aimed only "to insure some means of prompt defense." In a separate opinion, Gallatin echoed the same demand.[41]

More caustic than Dearborn's criticisms, Robert Smith's brought to a head his long-standing disagreement with Jefferson's policy that began over the timing of the congressional session. Smith's objections centered on the meaning of the *Chesapeake* attack and, by extension, on the precise nature of the British threat. Jefferson had made sense of the June incident by making it part and proof of an accelerating British plot against the United States. The pattern to British activity that Jefferson always saw, Smith feared, would place fatal strains on diplomacy's ability to resolve a specific crisis and thereby avoid war. For Smith, the first sentence of the message shaped its tone and made the whole paper wrong, dangerous, and irresponsible. "Circumstances," Jefferson had written, "which threaten the peace and prosperity of our country have made it a duty to convene you at an earlier period than usual."[42] The president's use of the present tense was not accidental. It described a continuing

[41] Smith to TJ, Oct. 19, 1807, Dearborn to TJ, Oct. 17, 1807, ibid.; Gallatin to TJ, Oct. 21, 1807, Gallatin Papers, NYU, reel 14.

[42] TJ, "Draft of Annual Message to the Congress for 1807," Oct. 26, 1807, Jefferson Papers, LC.

phenomenon; a crisis that was both historic and ongoing, a crisis not of the *Chesapeake* attack, but merely illumined by it.

Smith prudently saw the crisis in its most limited form. It was specifically located in time, in June 1807. Consequently, the message would have the wrong effect on both Congress and the English government. "As peace is our favorite object," he reminded Jefferson, why "excite Congress to a declaration of war"? As there was "at this moment a pending negotiation," why imperil it with "a manifesto against the British government"? The message, then, ignored the real interests of the nation, misrepresented the thinking of the administration, jeopardized the future of diplomacy, and brought closer a war the nation did not want and was not ready for, and one which the nature of the Anglo-American crisis did not require.[43]

Jefferson and Smith were not personally close. Gallatin, however, had been part of Jefferson's intimate political circle from the origins of Republicanism as an organized movement in the 1790s. Gallatin was the man that Jefferson selected to set right the nation's finances. With the exception of Madison, he was Jefferson's closest adviser.[44] But like Smith and Dearborn, Gallatin had serious misgivings about Jefferson's annual congressional message.

His criticisms centered on the direction of administration policy, the drift toward war, the betrayal of diplomacy, and the strength of the nation's adversary. "The message," he wrote on October 21, "appears to me to be rather in the shape of a manifesto issued against the British government on the eve of a war." He tactfully reminded Jefferson that the Federalists could easily distort it "into an eagerness of seeing matters brought to an issue by an appeal to arms." Gallatin was now clearly against war. Long frustrations in military and financial preparations exaggerated his desire to continue negotiations, he wrote the president, "so long as any hope, however weak, remains for an honorable settlement."[45] This advocacy of diplomacy climaxed a summer and autumn odyssey away from his earlier belief that war with England was inevitable.

"War will be a most calamitous event," Gallatin had written his

[43] Robert Smith to TJ, Oct. 19, 1807, ibid.

[44] On Gallatin's career within the Republican party, see Henry Adams, *The Life of Albert Gallatin* (Philadelphia, 1879); Alexander Balinky, *Albert Gallatin: Fiscal Theories and Policies* (New Brunswick, N.J., 1958); Raymond Walters, Jr., *Albert Gallatin: Jeffersonian Financier and Diplomat* (New York, 1957).

[45] Gallatin to TJ, Oct. 21, 1807, Gallatin Papers, NYU, reel 14.

wife, Hanna, on Independence Day, 1807. "Our immense commerce will be destroyed, our progress and improvement retarded, and a thousand fortunes be ruined." Beyond material setbacks loomed disturbing political and social "mischiefs": "the necessary increase in executive power and influence," the door opened to "speculators, contrivers and jobbers," and the "introduction of permanent military and naval establishments." Yet in July, Gallatin had thought war with England quite probable. "British haughtiness," he then feared, made settlement of the *Chesapeake* attack unlikely. Although official England, he was reasonably certain, had not ordered the attack on the government vessel, its failure to make adequate reparations would involve the British government directly in the outrage. The recklessness of an admiral and the arrogance of his government had created a pressing affair of honor that the young nation could not ignore.[46] So while diplomacy sought satisfaction in London, Gallatin had assumed a large share of the financial and military preparations for war that the summer recess had left to the executive branch.

His own search for the tools of war convinced Gallatin that hostilities with England would find the United States dangerously unprepared. Apart from the consequences to the nation of this sovereign fact, the political costs to Republicanism were potentially devastating. "The Administration will do well to be fully prepared," Samuel Smith had warned in midsummer. "If with such warning as we have received they should not be prepared . . . , [they] will not find defenders in Congress." A national canvass was a year away. An ill-timed war would certainly produce enough Federalist victories to alter the Republican ascendancy.[47]

With the passing of summer, therefore, a negotiated settlement became, for Gallatin, America's and the Republican party's salvation. That the English had obeyed the president's July 2 proclamation encouraged him. The British haughtiness that in midsummer he feared would spoil a negotiated settlement became less of a problem in the light of England's post-*Chesapeake* behavior. Unpreparedness imposed the need to avoid both war and diplomatic failure, and these, in turn, placed limits on what the United States could rea-

[46] Albert Gallatin to Hanna Gallatin, July 4, 1807, to Joseph Hopper Nicholson, July 17, 1807, ibid.

[47] Smith to Gallatin, July 17, 1807, Samuel Smith Papers, LC; Gallatin to TJ, Oct. 21, 1807, Gallatin Papers, NYU, reel 14.

sonably demand from the British. To exceed these limits, to embed the *Chesapeake* in the confounding tissue of past humiliations and future rivalry, would only mortgage negotiation to the unattainable and ensure its failure. Specifically, a negotiated settlement rested on the important difference between American merchant ships and public vessels (such as the *Chesapeake*) and on confining the impressment issue to the latter. Only a "madcap," the Republican *Citizen* of New York editorialized, would blur the difference and "be disposed to go to war to support the pretension."[48] Gallatin, Smith, and Dearborn thought the administration's official demands on England (ironed out by the cabinet in early July) honored this vital distinction. Their hopes for settlement and, by extension, their criticism of Jefferson's militance, turned on this belief.

The official instructions that the State Department sent to James Monroe and William Pinkney combined the two kinds of impressments in one general demand, and pegged the peaceful settlement of the June attack to the British renunciation of both.[49] Jefferson and Madison had listened to Dearborn's, Gallatin's, and Robert Smith's arguments at the July 2 cabinet meeting, had agreed to confine the official demand to the issue of boarding, searching, and pressing from American public vessels, and then changed their minds without informing the others. Gallatin wrote his wife three days after the meeting that the administration's position omitted general impressments. Two weeks later, he assured Samuel Smith that "the claims of the parties prior to the attack on the *Chesapeake*," including general impressments, were not included in the scope of the demands. In October, the secretary of the navy reminded the president that "under the *proposed instructions* to our ministers at London, a disavowal of the order of Admiral Berkeley is to be considered an adequate satisfaction for *that* insult." Finally, Jefferson's handwritten notes of the July 2 cabinet meeting confirm that the agreed-upon instructions required only "a disavowal of the act and of the principle of searching a public armed vessel" by Great Britain.[50]

[48] Quoted in Nicholas Biddle to Monroe, Oct. 31, 1807, Monroe Papers, LC, reel 4.

[49] Madison to Monroe and Pinkney, July 6, 1807, Diplomatic Instructions, All Countries, vol. 6, NA.

[50] Albert Gallatin to Hanna Gallatin, July 4, 1807, to Samuel Smith, July 17, 1807, Gallatin Papers, NYU, reel 14; Robert Smith to TJ, Oct. 17, 1807, Robert

Henry Dearborn's anger provides additional proof that Jefferson and Madison departed from an established consensus to leave the general question of merchant impressments to later Anglo-American diplomacy. Shortly after the administration had decided on reparations, the secretary of war left Washington to inspect fortifications in the North. While in New York and still under the illusion, he later wrote, that "no alterations of any considerable importance had been made in the instructions to our ministers," he heard "several gentlemen" upbraid the government for linking the two types of impressments in one general demand. He denied the accusation, and then wrote Jefferson an angry letter explaining his embarrassment when, after giving assurances that "your demand for ratification had been confined to the attack on the Chesapeake and [that] it was not intended to connect that hostile act with any complaints of a former date," he saw in the newspapers that the July 6 instructions had indeed combined all impressments together. Dearborn thought a later meeting had overruled, in his absence, "the first agreement."[51] This is understandable because the official document that went out over Madison's signature changed the demands from what Dearborn had correctly remembered the cabinet had agreed upon. There were only the July 6 instructions, however, and these contained the bloated aims that Dearborn associated with a second, and controlling, set. They also ensured that diplomacy could not resolve the *Chesapeake* crisis. John Randolph believed that Jefferson forced Madison to enlarge the demands. "Your surprise I have no doubt will equal mine," he wrote a friend, "when you hear that the P[resident] peremptorily enjoined upon M[adison] to connect with the demand for reparation of the outrage of the Chesapeake claims *which he had a previous* knowledge would not be conceded by Great Britain, even under the late ministry, thus shutting with his own hand the door to that insulting injury."[52] Randolph's version, supported by Dearborn, Gallatin, Robert Smith, and the president's July 2 notes, is probably correct, for in early July, while Jefferson was contemplating settling

and William Smith Papers, Md. Hist. Soc.; TJ, "Notes on Cabinet Consultations," July 2, 1807, LC (TJ's handwritten notes for this cabinet meeting and others from 1807–8 are located in the 1806 reels [reel 57] of the LC collection).

[51] Dearborn to TJ, Oct. 18, 1807, Jefferson Papers, LC.

[52] Randolph to Joseph Hopper Nicholson, Mar. 28, 1808, Joseph Hopper Nicholson Papers, LC.

old and new scores with Great Britain, he had no interest in a diplomatic resolution of the *Chesapeake* attack. His thoughts were on war. All the administration was demanding, he wrote his son-in-law in late July, was "reparation for the past [and] security for the future." Because the English would never "grant them to the extent required, the probability is for war."[53]

James Monroe was in London to handle the *Chesapeake* diplomacy. Before he received the July 6 instructions, he confidently predicted to Madison complete satisfaction on the "principle" in question. For Monroe, the principle was the limited one: "a ship of war possessed all the people on board and could not be entered or searched for deserters or for any purpose without violating the sovereignty of the nation whose flag she bore." But Monroe made a tactical blunder that would soon add embarrassment to defeat. He outlined what he thought would be his government's position to George Canning, the British foreign secretary, before he had received formal instructions from the secretary of state. He did so because Canning had previously intimated that the nationality of the sailors on board the *Chesapeake* affected the amount of satisfaction that Great Britain might owe to the United States. Not wanting his silence to lend support to Canning's position, he formally complained that "the character of the men have nothing to do" with the validity of the principle, which he then proceeded to outline as he understood it to be.[54] Soon after, Monroe received the instructions that bound him to the broader principle. On this point, the negotiations collapsed.

Monroe blamed his failure on the scope of the American demand. "You ask me whether I am authorized to separate the [*Chesapeake*] incident from the general practice [of impressment] and to treat it as a distinct topic," he wrote Canning on September 29. "A sentiment of candor merits a frank reply. I have to state that my instructions, which are explicit, enjoin me to consider [all impressments] as an entire subject."[55] Monroe's anger deepened with the decision to resume the discussions in Washington between Madison and a special British envoy. Had the American demands been reasonable, he believed he could have wrapped up the discussions in London.[56] "But,"

[53] TJ to Thomas Mann Randolph, July 20, 1807, Jefferson Papers, LC.

[54] Monroe to Madison, Aug. 4, 1807, Monroe Papers, LC, reel 4.

[55] Monroe to George Canning, Sept. 29, 1807, ibid.

[56] Monroe to TJ, Feb. 27, 1808, ibid.

he complained to a friend, "our government . . . found in it a new motive for insisting on the suppression of the general practice of impressment."[57] Monroe overestimated his chances of settling even the specific issue of the *Chesapeake* assault. Canning had already informed him that the presidential proclamation of July 2 was a unilateral act that diminished the amount of reparation the British government was obliged to bestow. Canning would certainly haggle over the nationality of the sailors on board the *Chesapeake* and over the number of British sailors in the American service. Though they did not doom Monroe's diplomacy, the State Department instructions certainly did not help.

Chesapeake diplomacy soon became an issue in presidential politics. While Monroe was still in London, friends wrote him about the foolishness of the administration decision to burden his negotiations with the whole weight of impressments. John Randolph went further, warning him that the instructions were framed to damage Monroe's presidential aspirations and to ensure the Republican nomination of James Madison.[58] None of the stories charging Jefferson and Madison with crass political maneuvering was true, and Jefferson personally denied them all.[59] But the July instructions went beyond the inclinations of the cabinet and harmed the chances for a diplomatic settlement. More important, the opposition to Jefferson's excessive demands that surfaced in the cabinet, newspapers, and among friends and supporters of Monroe better mirrored the mood of Congress and the nation than did the July instructions. It was primarily for this reason—congressional and public opinion—that Albert Gallatin emerged as the cabinet's severest critic of Jefferson's annual message.

"Congress is certainly peaceably disposed," Gallatin wrote his wife in October. "True it is," wrote one congressman, "that many of us

[57] Monroe to James Bowdoin, Oct. 18, 1807, to John Armstrong, Oct. 18, 1807, ibid.

[58] Nicholas Biddle to Monroe, Oct. 31, 1807, Randolph to Monroe, Mar. 22, 1808, ibid.

[59] TJ to Monroe, Feb. 18, Mar. 10, April 11, 1808, Jefferson Papers, LC. The reasons for TJ's handling of the official instructions regarding the *Chesapeake* had nothing to do with the presidential succession, but rested squarely on his intense summer anglophobia. John Taylor spoke the truth when he told Monroe: "Mr. Jefferson is unquestionably your best friend" (Taylor to Monroe, Feb. 22, 1808, Monroe Papers, LC, reel 4).

who have known 'the tug' before are extremely unwilling to try it again, and the nation will not part with the blessings of peace but from the most pressing necessity." "The temper of the legislature is decidedly pacific," Jefferson's secretary noted. "They will not resort to violence unless it shall be forced upon them."[60] Fear of war and a passion for peace led Republican leaders, inevitably, to rein in their anglophobia and to reduce the complex compound of Anglo-American difference to its essential element: the *Chesapeake* attack. "The propriety of insisting at this juncture on the exemption from searching merchant vessels is questioned by many," Nicholas Biddle wrote from Philadelphia, "and the great mass of the nation are, I think, very adverse from making such an exemption an indispensable part of our arrangements with Great Britain." Congressional opinion supported the cabinet voices that had argued against extensive demands. "There was a great error in [Monroe's] instructions," wrote one New England congressman, "which did not permit him to adjust the affair of the *Chesapeake* separate from all other matters in dispute."[61] Fearing war more than it loathed impressments and commercial restrictions, congressional opinion pegged the crisis to the negotiable issue of England's right to stop, search, and press from American ships of war.

Jefferson, however, had pitched his "war manifesto" on the self-evident truth of British malice, on the lingering crisis in Anglo-American affairs that dated to the unfinished business of the American Revolution. The nation and Congress, Gallatin warned him, would not support the war that was implicit in the structure of Jefferson's thought. "Public opinion . . . at home is indispensable," he cautioned, and it demanded the equation of the English crisis with the attack on the *Chesapeake*. "I am confident," he warned, "that we will meet with a most formidable opposition should England do justice on that point, and we should still declare war because she refuses to make the proposed arrangements respecting seamen."[62] Undeniable facts crowded in on Gallatin, facts that Jefferson ignored: mili-

---

[60] Albert Gallatin to Hanna Gallatin, Oct. 30, 1807, Gallatin Papers, NYU, reel 14; Nicholas Gilman to William Eustis, Dec. 14, 1807, William Eustis Papers, LC; Isaac Coles to William Cabell, n.d., 1807, Joseph C. Cabell Papers, UVa.

[61] Biddle to Monroe, Oct. 31, 1807, Monroe Papers, LC, reel 4; Nicholas Gilman to William Eustis, Dec. 14, 1807, William Eustis Papers, LC.

[62] Gallatin to TJ, Oct. 21, 1807, Gallatin Papers, NYU, reel 14.

tary and financial preparations had been slow and uneven; the people did not want war, and their fear of British evasion, boiling in June, had since evaporated; the viewpoint of a sizable portion of Congress ensured that the war debate would be divisive and produce dangerous popular and political opposition even if a declaration should emerge. These were the points of departure for Gallatin's criticism of the message and of Jefferson's perceptions of the English problem that lay beneath it.

The president had loaded his message with examples of British hostility in order to support his belief in British design. Gallatin insisted that all evidence for historical conspiracy be removed; that the paper focus on the present, not the past; on the *Chesapeake* attack, not long-marching conspiracies; and on the practical need for cautious defensive preparations, not the historic need for war.[63]

Nor would the war, if it came, be as neat and safe as Jefferson seemed to believe. Reasons for optimism were available and on the surface plausible, and Jefferson sought them out. French victories, he believed, were America's salvation. His association of the popular mood with his own, and his commitment to the soundness of American political principles convinced him that the nation could create ample military strength and yet preserve its republican future. But it was, finally, the depth of his hatred of the British that shaped Jefferson's stance toward war. A deeply rooted anglophobia linked the *Chesapeake* crisis with the moods, emotions, and unfinished agenda of the Revolutionary epic. It led Jefferson to idealize popular virtue, to dwell on British weakness and wink at British strength, and to transform England's rational desires to defeat Napoleon and to defend its commercial empire into a cruel obsession with America's death.

Gallatin's criticisms dashed the hopeful military strategy that Jefferson had hammered out during the summer. England would have sufficient time to fortify Canada and to scuttle America's offensive plans. England would plunder the American wealth still at sea—$20 million in the China trade alone, much of it uninsured and not expected home until March 1808.[64] And how safe was the nation from English "attacks on our most exposed seaports," asked Gallatin. The fortifications at New York were largely incomplete, those in the

[63] Ibid.
[64] Gallatin to TJ, Aug. 26, 1807, Gallatin Papers, NYU, reel 14.

South no better, and appropriations not yet made for any port cities except New York, Charleston, Savannah, and New Orleans. A congressional declaration, or even discussion of war, might unleash the British squadrons in American waters, regardless of orders from England. New York could easily fall before winter. "Great would be the disgrace attaching to such a disaster," Gallatin warned. "The executive especially would be particularly liable to censure for having urged immediate war whilst so unprepared against the attack." The losers in such a policy would be the Republican party and the nation; the winners, England and Federalist "anglomen."[65]

Prudence, Not Passion

President Jefferson often compared popular outrage over the *Chesapeake* attack to the "spirit of Lexington and Concord."[66] His attitudes toward the English, the Federalist party, and the mass of republican citizenry indicate that he was almost reliving the crusade of an earlier generation. Indeed, the most striking element in Jefferson's encounter with nineteenth-century English problems was its déjà vu quality. He had never escaped the emotional tugs of the earlier battle against Great Britain. The past shaped the present, and in both Jefferson saw an unreasonable and outrageous English crusade against the Republic's future. The image of the patriotic citizen-soldier from Lexington and Concord also crowded his perception, and in it was no room for the peace-loving merchants and entrepreneurs of Richmond, Boston, and Philadelphia. He saw the heroic imagery he desperately wanted to see and missed the national desire for peace and the inglorious urge to continue, uninterrupted, wartime profit taking. This urge was too petty for Jefferson, and from it he diverted his regard.

The message that the president sent to Congress on October 26 bore marks of extensive revision. From a change of verb tense in the first sentence, Jefferson softened and toned down. The *Chesapeake* attack became the raison d'être for the early summons. Both defensive preparations and continuing diplomacy were stressed.

---

[65] Gallatin to TJ, Oct. 21, 1807, ibid.

[66] TJ to Pierre Samuel Dupont de Nemours, July 14, 1807, Jefferson Papers, LC.

Throughout, Jefferson obeyed Gallatin's major request, that of "per-severing in that caution of language and action which may give us some more time and is best calculated to preserve the remaining chance of peace and is most consistent with the general system of your Administration." In a rare moment of self-congratulation Galla-tin confided to his wife that "the President's speech was originally more warlike than was necessary but I succeeded in getting it neu-tralized. This between us."[67]

Jefferson's revised address did not involve Congress in his true perceptions of the English crisis. Free to interpret the shape of things for itself, Congress located the danger in the dimensions of the June outrage and thus rendered it capable of diplomatic settlement. Con-sequently, congressmen talked about defensive preparations, placed their faith in negotiation, and breathed sighs of relief. A month of the special session passed without progress on any military or financial bill. "It seems to be understood," Wilson Cary Nicholas observed, "that everything should be suspended until we hear from our minis-ters" in London. "I know you would be glad to hear what is expected to be done in relation to Great Britain," Congressman Nathaniel Macon from North Carolina wrote a friend in New York, "and I sincerely wish I could tell you the opinion of any of our leading men. But I cannot. All of them are waiting for the arrival of" foreign news. "Little is being done except to make speeches."[68]

Jefferson was bitter about the whole turn of events. On the day he sent his message to Congress, he wrote his son-in-law that the law-makers were foolishly disposed toward peace; that they were letting slip a chance to fight England with its back against the European wall. The fight would come, he assured Thomas Mann Randolph, but at Great Britain's choosing, and when it was freed of its Old World adversary. Then the nation would pay for its timidity. Nor was Jefferson at all sanguine about economic coercion as a substitute for war. "Non-importation will end in war and give her [Great

[67] TJ, Annual Message, Oct. 26, 1807, *Annals*, 10th Cong., 1st sess., pp. 14–18; Gallatin to TJ, Oct. 21, 1807, to Hanna Gallatin, Oct. 30, 1807, Gallatin Papers, NYU, reel 14.

[68] Wilson Cary Nicholas to William Cabell, Nov. 20, 1807, Wilson Cary Nicholas Papers, LC; Nathaniel Macon to Joseph Hopper Nicholson, Nov. 22, 1807, Joseph Hopper Nicholson Papers, LC.

Britain] the choice of the moment of declaring it," he promised. "I think it well that our constituents should know what is probable."[69]

By the opening of the special congressional session, American policy was mired in contradictions. With divisions in his cabinet, desires in Congress to postpone policy decisions and wait upon a diplomatic miracle, a pacific temper abroad in the nation, time needed to retrieve seamen and commercial property, and glaring inadequacies in military preparation, Jefferson could not exhort the nation to war. At the same time, the government's excessive *Chesapeake* demands imperiled a negotiated settlement while the softened annual message reinforced congressional inattention to military planning. The president had no doubts on the outcome of Monroe's efforts in London. Although the administration had not received his dispatches on the results of his discussions with Canning, David Erskine, England's minister in the United States, had received letters from Canning, and these he showed to Madison and Jefferson. They were "proud," "unfriendly," and "harsh," the president thought. They showed no desire to go beyond a mere disavowal of the act, "and little concern to avoid war."[70] With the outcome of the *Chesapeake* diplomacy settled in fact if not in form, Jefferson was more concerned with rumors circulating in Washington that both England and France intended to tighten the commercial vise.

Jefferson reacted predictably to these rumors. Those about France had been cut from whole cloth by Boston Federalists to confuse Congress and the people.[71] More English oppressions, however, were "probable" because of England's "known principles" and beneficial because of their potential impact on an overly pacific Congress. They "would produce an immediate declaration here," he confided to his son-in-law, they "are the only thing[s] that will." Until the confirmation of the rumor, there was little to do but wait.[72] Although Jefferson's war policy had not withstood Gallatin's stern facts, his war spirit clearly survived the collapse of his policy within the cabinet and lingered until unwanted facts from France dissolved the anglophobic

---

[69] TJ to Randolph, Oct. 26, 1807, Jefferson Papers, LC.

[70] TJ to Thomas Mann Randolph, Nov. 30, 1807, ibid.

[71] TJ to John Minor, Nov. 25, 1807, ibid.

[72] TJ to William Short, Nov. 15, 1807, to Thomas Mann Randolph, Nov. 16, 30, 1807, ibid.

emotions and naive assumptions that had fueled his summer militance in the acidic realities of European power and American weakness.

The fear (and hope) of new levels of British hostility led Jefferson to consider a temporary defensive embargo. In early December he solicited Gallatin's opinion. The president wanted only the discretionary power to impose an embargo on American shipping "during the [present] session of Congress" if the oceans became too dangerous. The measure's relevance depended on the direction of foreign intelligence, and its passage, Jefferson. thought, should not deflect Congress's attention from military preparation.[73] Nor did he expect it to raise serious objections within the mercantile community. That many of the nation's merchants had ceased their foreign commerce in the aftermath of the *Chesapeake* attack suggested a fund of popular support for a temporary presidential ban on shipping based on the hard data of British intentions and the need to protect maritime property for the future war effort.[74] This embargo, then, was defensive, non-coercive, and in no way a substitute for war. As cool as Jefferson was to the nonviolent policy of economic sanctions in the summer and fall of 1807, when he considered that type of policy, he thought in terms of the American market, not American ships.

At any rate, the issue became moot when Gallatin convinced the president that Congress would never vest such discretionary power in the executive branch. For the next several days, the two bandied about alternative policies that attained neither's favor. Since war was unthinkable, the secretary of the treasury suggested a complete ban on English imports (a selective ban was scheduled to become law on December 14). Although this policy had deep roots in the history of Republican statecraft, Gallatin knew its pitfalls and never endorsed the policy that he suggested. Jefferson was distinctly cool toward an experiment in economic coercion. Because it did not touch American shipping, it could not promote the return of American men and property or keep vital resources at home in the event of a dangerous escalation of British confiscations. Quite probably the English would

[73] Gallatin to TJ, Dec. 2, 1807, ibid.

[74] TJ to James Bowdoin, July 10, 1807, TJ to Thomas Leghorn, July 9, 1807, Jacob Crowninshield to Caesar Rodney, Aug. 3, 1807, ibid.

regard it as pro-French and perhaps declare war while America was so ill-prepared.[75]

All that seemed proper was for Congress to address squarely and steadily the business of preparedness. It was in this context that Jefferson countered Gallatin's ideas with a seemingly contradictory policy: another congressional suspension of the partial nonimportation act. Unable to get from the Congress a discretionary embargo for military purposes, the president did not mind letting the law die stillborn because he did not think any amount of nonimportation equal to the English crisis. On the positive side, suspension might postpone war until America was better prepared.

Suspension, however, had its disadvantages. Daily Jefferson expected Monroe's dispatches and hoped their accounts of English arrogance and the failure of the *Chesapeake* diplomacy would spur congressional preparedness legislation. To suggest another suspension would create false hopes, contradict the pessimism Monroe's dispatches were to foster, and confuse Congress on the urgency of military matters. On the horns of a dilemma, Jefferson lost interest in the whole stratagem. Perhaps the best policy was no policy at all. He decided only to send to the legislature the results of Monroe's efforts and to allow the official record of British haughtiness to convince Congress to strengthen the nation.[76] This posture of quiet waiting did not survive the autumn. Mid-December foreign intelligence prompted Jefferson to request an embargo and launched the administration into unintended relationships with the European powers and the American people.

[75] Gallatin to TJ, Dec. 2, 1807, TJ to Gallatin, Dec. 3, 1807, ibid.; Gallatin to TJ, Dec. 5, 1807, Gallatin Papers, NYU, reel 15.

[76] TJ, "Message to the Senate and the House of Representatives of the United States," Dec. 7, 1807, Jefferson Papers, LC.

4

"A GREAT MADHOUSE"

The Embargo and America's Search for a Manageable War

Jefferson's Embargo

On Tuesday, December 15, 1807, the president sent a short note to Gallatin. "Will you be so good," Jefferson asked, "as to meet the heads of departments here tomorrow to consult on our foreign affairs."[1] The news from Europe, received the day before, was all bad. A royal proclamation promised more impressments. From Paris, Jefferson learned that Napoleon intended to apply the Berlin Decree rigidly to the ocean-borne commerce of the United States. Rumors also continued to mount that Great Britain had already announced a more oppressive order-in-council.[2] The vise was tightening. The British intelligence confirmed Jefferson's long-standing fears. The gloomy news from Paris transformed the fear itself. The French intelligence altered the focus of Jefferson's thinking by blurring the image of English villainy into a larger, more threatening picture of European sickness. When it became increasingly difficult to distinguish French from British high-handedness, when an intimidating fear of European madness overwhelmed the liberating fear of English malice, an instinct to withdraw overwhelmed a desire to fight. From this powerful urge to remain safe in the New World, to keep American ships and sailors—the nation really—out of "harm's way," Jefferson's embargo was born.[3]

[1] TJ to Gallatin, Dec. 15, 1807, Jefferson Papers, LC.

[2] TJ to Gideon Granger, Jan. 22, 1808, TJ to U.S. Senate and House of Representatives, Feb. 2, 26, 1808, ibid.; Nathaniel Macon to Joseph Hopper Nicholson, Feb. 20, 1808, Joseph Hopper Nicholson Papers, LC; *American State Papers: Foreign Relations*, 3:25–26; Dumas Malone, *Jefferson the President, the Second Term* (Boston, 1974), p. 481.

[3] TJ to William Cabell, Mar. 13, 1808, Jefferson Papers, LC.

Before December, an obsessive anglophobia had shaped Jefferson's view of the nation's dilemma and its salvation. England was the contemporary culprit and the historic enemy; English power threatened American independence and thwarted the nation's legitimate commercial ambitions. It was England's desire for world mastery and the resulting strains on English military resources that placed within American reach an armed defense of commerce, seamen, and reputation. During the *Chesapeake* summer, Jefferson had reduced policy to the question of war's timing: before or after England had freed itself from continental war. He welcomed new examples of British hostility to awaken a disturbingly quiet Congress.[4] Many in Washington commented on Jefferson's militant attitude. "The aspect [with England] is portentous," wrote Congressman Nicholas Gilman. "The man in the stone house is of the opinion that the die is cast." But after mid-December, Jefferson constantly spoke of the European dimension of American travail. Europe had finally succumbed. It was "a great madhouse," "truly in an awful state," convulsing in "a paroxysm of insanity." Europe at the dawn of the new century "was displaying the vandalism of the fifth." In short, Europe, as Jefferson now viewed it, was "a maniac."[5]

This European capitulation to "vandalism" pushed Jefferson toward escape and isolation, but not completely so. The nation might postpone its European reckoning; it could not ignore it. Nor could it deny that war was still likely.[6] Both considerations shaped Jefferson's embargo proposal, ironed out in cabinet on December 16 and forwarded to Congress on December 18. He asked the legislature to impose a temporary ban on all American foreign shipping. Only half of a comprehensive proposal that embraced military preparation as

[4] TJ to Thomas Mann Randolph, Oct. 26, 1807, ibid.

[5] Gilman to William Eustis, Dec. 14, 1807, William Eustis Papers, LC; TJ to Gideon Granger, Jan. 22, 1808, to Tammany Society of New York, Feb. 29, 1808, to Charles Pinckney, Mar. 30, 1808, to Pierre Samuel Dupont de Nemours, May 2, 1808, to Gen. Thaddeus Kosciusko, May 2, 1808, to David Baille Warden, July 16, 1808, to Ketochton Baptist Association, Oct. 18, 1808, Jefferson Papers, LC.

[6] TJ to John Taylor, Jan. 6, 1808, Jefferson Papers, LC; Wilson Cary Nicholas to [?], Dec. 22, 1807, Wilson Cary Nicholas to Col. Lindsay, Jan. 31, 1808, John Nicholas to Wilson Cary Nicholas, Feb. 1, 1808, Wilson Cary Nicholas Papers, LC. One week after the embargo was passed, Henry Dearborn submitted his resignation to Jefferson because he felt his talents unequal to the task "in the event of a war such as we now contemplate" (Dearborn to TJ, Dec. 29, 1807, Jefferson Papers, LC).

well as temporary commercial isolation, the embargo shared equal billing with a presidential request to set the nation's military house in order. Jefferson's penciled draft of the December 18 message better revealed his thinking than did the actual message because it clearly blended temporary embargo into the larger purpose of preparedness. "I am persuaded," his own draft began, "that [you] will be induced to prosecute with greater energy all the preparations which may be necessary for whatever events grow out of the present crisis, but [you] doubtless perceive all the advantages which may be expected from an immediate prohibition of the departure of our vessels from the ports of the U[nited] States." Madison revised Jefferson's one long sentence into two, with the first calling for the embargo, and the second encouraging military preparation, thereby creating an impression of two policy proposals and obscuring somewhat the intimate connection that Jefferson saw between a temporary ban on foreign shipping and the development of an effective military capability.[7]

Congress quickly complied with the president's embargo request. The Senate suspended its normal rules and passed the embargo on the same day it received the message. The House followed suit three days later. The final law, signed by Jefferson on December 22, prohibited all American vessels, except those "under the immediate direction of the president of the United States," from sailing to foreign ports. Foreign-bound vessels that wished to engage in the American coastal trade were further required to post bond equal to double the value of ship and cargo that they would not sail to foreign ports, "dangers of the sea excepted." The law also allowed foreign-owned ships in American ports to sail away with the cargoes they currently had on board.[8] Both Jefferson's proposal and the congressional law were remarkably simple. The coasting trade and penalties and punishments for illegalities were not mentioned. No administrative machinery was established. The reason is as simple as the legislation. The embargo, in Gallatin's words, was "hastily adopted on the first

[7] TJ, "Message to the U.S. Senate and House of Representatives Proposing an Embargo on the Belligerent Powers of Europe," penciled draft corrected by Madison, Dec. 17, 1807, and TJ, Embargo Message to the Congress, Dec. 18, 1807, Jefferson Papers, LC.

[8] The embargo law, Dec. 22, 1807, J. B. Varnum, Speaker of the House, Geo. Clinton, President of the Senate, Gallatin Papers, NYU, reel 15.

view of our foreign intelligence." Neither Congress nor the cabinet anticipated that a long and principled episode in economic warfare was beginning. In the context of recent foreign news, the December 18 request was not a shocking and far-reaching proposal. The president remembered that in the aftermath of the *Chesapeake* assault the previous June, many commercial men had asked for similar protection. The December embargo's expedient and obvious relationship to harsh international facts explains its origins, its simplicity, and its prompt passage.[9]

"The great objects of the embargo," Jefferson informed the governor of Virginia in March, "are keeping our ships and seamen out of harm's way." Until the early spring, all of Jefferson's public words and private letters elaborated this defensive, isolationist theme. The embargo, he wrote Gideon Granger in January, was a precaution imposed on the United States by the rapid deterioration of European respect for international law. The equation was quite simple. Trade now spelled certain captures, and for these, Jefferson feared, "we must have gone to war to avenge the wrong." They would also precipitate war at the worst possible time for the United States: defensive fortifications were painfully incomplete, state and national militias were undermanned and disorganized, the amount of commercial wealth at sea and vulnerable to capture was still sizable.[10] The new spate of European oppression obscured Jefferson's aggressive memories of America's eighteenth-century English epic in the harsh realities of Europe's nineteenth-century war. With a sincere belief that "there is no bravery in fighting a maniac," he cleared an emotional path for the nation to sit on the sidelines, protected in the short run by isolation and by the slim hope that Europe might right itself before it dragged the United States into war.[11] The embargo was "salutary," Jefferson believed, because "it postpones war, gives time, and the benefit of events which that time may produce, especially peace in Europe, which will postpone the differences until the

[9] Gallatin to TJ, Dec. 18, 1807, Gallatin Papers, NYU, reel 15; TJ to Thomas Leghorn, July 9, 1807, to James Bowdoin, July 10, 1807, Jefferson Papers, LC.

[10] TJ to William Cabell, Mar. 13, 1808, to Granger, Jan. 22, 1808, Jefferson Papers, LC; William Hollins to Wilson Cary Nicholas, Jan. 8, 1808, Wilson Cary Nicholas Papers, LC; Samuel Smith to Madison, Feb. 1, 1808, Madison Papers, MS, LC.

[11] TJ to David Baille Warden, June 16, 1808, Jefferson Papers, LC.

next [European] war." And then, in the future where Jefferson was always confident of the nation's possibilities, the United States, liberated from debt, stronger and more populous, would be equal to any European challenge.[12]

Although this isolationist theme of easy and final escape from European distress shaped Jefferson's early thinking about the embargo, it never completely dominated because it involved amounts of time that the economic appetites of the American people would not grant. These appetites directed that the embargo be above all else temporary. They precluded economic isolation as both a quixotic goal and a commercial weapon in the peaceable coercion of offending nations. For most of the embargo's career, Jefferson understood and acted within these limitations. His original proposal merely afforded a temporary reprieve from difficult policy choices imposed on the young nation by Europe's refusal to accept American definitions of neutral rights and by America's refusal to abandon the legal assertions that supported its prosperous neutrality. His embargo was simply an expedient, "an intervening period" Jefferson called it, a means toward a yet unknown and elusive end.[13] The international setting had changed drastically. Time was the nation's best friend: time to catch its breath, to husband its resources, to take new readings of the European scene, and to fashion new policies, diplomatic and military, that reflected the nation's worsened predicament. The embargo anticipated no more than the protection of sailors, ships, and property, procrastination, and the temporary avoidance of a commerce that, given the competing tyrannies of France and England, must surely result in ill-timed war with all of Europe.[14]

Although it was anchored firmly to defensive needs and military preparation, the embargo affected the European economies because it kept American ships at home. But potentially unsettling consequences do not prove a coercive purpose. The Jeffersonians had long championed economic retaliation as a valuable weapon of commercial diplomacy, but the president had never touted a complete ban on American shipping. Jefferson's mercantilism, like the European variety it warred against, was market oriented and rested on the im-

[12] TJ to Benjamin Rush, Jan. 3, 1808, to John Taylor, Jan. 6, 1808, to Charles Thomson, Jan. 11, 1808, to Thomas Leiper, May 24, 1808, ibid.

[13] TJ to Madison, Mar. 11, 1808, Madison Papers, LC, ser. 2, reel 25.

[14] TJ to Levi Lincoln, Mar. 23, 1808, Jefferson Papers, LC.

portance of American purchasing power to European prosperity. But because colonial patterns of trade, common language and business practices, English manufacturing ability and credit arrangements, and American taste gave to Great Britain the lion's share of America's foreign trade, a mercantilist policy conceived on a European scale became, in Jefferson's hands, primarily an anti-English weapon.[15] American dependence on Great Britain, looked at another way, Jefferson's way, became English dependence on America. From this angle, Jeffersonian theory saw an opportunity to counter English prejudice with American power. And if English pride hardened English prejudice beyond redemption, Jefferson's theory still anticipated compensatory benefits. To prohibit British vessels from entering American ports helped the nation's merchant marine. To boycott the importation of British goods encouraged trading relationships with other European nations, spurred domestic household manufactures, and reduced America's debilitating addiction to English luxuries. A complete embargo on American shipping honored none of these precepts of Jeffersonian economic coercion. It destroyed much of the foreign market for American agriculture. It supported England's quest for monopoly of the world's carrying trade. When one considered whom it rewarded and whom it punished, the embargo caricatured the Republican tradition of economic retaliation.

Yet the idea of coercion surfaced immediately when the cabinet discussed an embargo in mid-December. No notes survive the meetings, nor do the private letters of the cabinet members shed conclusive light on their respective positions. But one member championed the embargo's coercive potential at the December 16 meeting. Such, at least, is the implication of a long letter Gallatin wrote Jefferson on December 18.

The bulk of Gallatin's letter dwelt on the defensive goals of a temporary embargo. He supported this prudent bow to the realities of European power, but with minor reservations. To prevent increasing dangers to American vessels still at sea, he suggested allowing foreign vessels the right to leave American ports in ballast or with the cargoes they presently had on board. To clarify the embargo's defensive purpose to both the European belligerents and the American people, he also suggested a six-month time limit. The treasury chief

[15] See Peterson, "Thomas Jefferson and Commercial Policy, 1783–1793," Peterson, ed., *Thomas Jefferson, a Profile*, pp. 104–34.

completely opposed a coercive embargo, "permanent embargo" Gallatin called it, a dangerous mix of two dissimilar traditions. "In every point of view," he warned Jefferson, "privations, sufferings, revenue, effect on the enemy [and] politics at home, I prefer war to a permanent embargo." An embargo could not compose American differences with Great Britain. "As to the hope that it may have an effect on our negotiations with Mr. Rose [the British envoy just arrived to continue the *Chesapeake* discussions], or induce England to treat us better, I think it entirely groundless." It seems, given the sternness of Gallatin's remarks, that he was trying to dissuade Jefferson from a line of policy that had been strenuously advocated in cabinet session. Gallatin did not identify the cabinet exponent of coercive or permanent embargo. Several factors, however, suggest that Secretary of State Madison was the administration's early advocate of the embargo as a peaceful weapon of economic war.[16]

Jefferson's outgoing correspondence in December, January, and February weighs against coercion counting for much in his original conception of the embargo. Silent on coercive hopes, his correspondence amply documents the defensive and precautionary goals of the policy. More important, an honest trial for economic coercion demanded an open-ended expenditure of time that Jefferson neither anticipated nor endorsed. Bounded by temporal limits that he himself imposed on it, the embargo, he wrote numerous correspondents, must perform its mission by the beginning of the next session of Congress in the fall of 1808.[17] "Should [European] peace be made [before then]," he hoped, "we shall have safely rode out the storm in peace and prosperity."[18] A year off the ocean might witness the return of European peace. While waiting on the outcome of Europe's struggle, a realistic appraisal of European politics and American eco-

---

[16] Gallatin to TJ, Dec. 18, 1807, Jefferson Papers, LC.

[17] In a host of letters, Jefferson located the embargo's end at the beginning of the next Congress, then to be followed by either war or peace and trade. See TJ to Thomas Mann Randolph, Jan. 26, 1808, to Joseph Eggleston, Mar. 7, 1808, to Levi Lincoln, Mar. 23, June 22, 1808, to Charles Pinckney, Mar. 30, 1808, to John Strode, April 3, 1808, to Thomas Worthington, April 24, 1808, to William Lyman, April 30, 1808, to Benjamin Smith, May 20, 1808, to James Bowdoin, May 29, 1808, to Thomas Paine, July 17, 1808, to William Pinkney, July 18, 1808, to William Bibb, July 28, 1808, to New Hampshire Legislature, Aug. 2, 1808, Jefferson Papers, LC.

[18] TJ to Charles Pinckney, Mar. 30, 1808, ibid.

nomics demanded stern attention to national defense and military preparation because, failing the miracle of peace, Jefferson knew that war must follow the temporary embargo, and soon. As he apprised Levi Lincoln, the embargo was America's "last card" short of war.[19]

Other matters of content as well as the style of Gallatin's letter point away from Jefferson's advocacy of economic coercion in the cabinet meeting. Gallatin wrote "as to the hope," not "as to your hope." Second, the tone of the criticism is abrupt, almost condescending. When disagreements on public policy had surfaced between Gallatin and Jefferson earlier, Gallatin's corrections or suggestions had had more the flavor of helpful admonishment than sharp rebuke.[20] Gallatin's strictures also married a coercive embargo to the second round of the *Chesapeake* diplomacy, soon scheduled to begin in Washington, and from which Jefferson expected little. Even before the president learned the British envoy's name, he expected only procrastination, a development ideally suited to the defensive goals of the embargo. The new discussions would yield proposals and counterproposals. Their crossing and recrossing the Atlantic would consume months during which events in Europe might take a favorable turn. By January, Jefferson had not departed from this pragmatic assessment: "Mr. Rose stays on board his ship at Hampton. We know not why. If he is seeking time, we may indulge him. Time prepares us for defense. Time may produce peace in Europe. That removes the ground of differences with England till another war and that may find our revenues liberated by the discharge of our national debt, our wealth and numbers increased, our friendship and our enmity more important to every nation."[21]

That Secretary of State Madison would conduct the actual negotiations increases the probability that he voiced in the cabinet meeting the coercive rationale for the embargo that Gallatin found troubling enough to challenge. Other factors point to the same conclusion. Madison's historic fascination with the economic weapons of war rivaled Jefferson's. In December an anonymous author extolled the

---

[19] TJ to Levi Lincoln, Mar. 23, 1808, ibid.

[20] Compare Gallatin's frank dismissal of the coercive power of the embargo on Dec. 18, 1807, with his long and tactful dissection of Jefferson's 1807 annual message in Gallatin to TJ, Oct. 21, 1807, Gallatin Papers, NYU, reel 14.

[21] TJ to John Page, Nov. 30, 1807, TJ to Charles Thomson, Jan. 11, 1808, Jefferson Papers, LC.

coercive power of the embargo in the pages of the *National Intelligencer*, a Jeffersonian newspaper. The letter is in Madison's style, and his foremost biographer attributes it to him. And where Jefferson's private correspondence in the first two and one-half months of the embargo's run is silent on the idea of coercion, Madison's, though far less extensive, is not. So when Gallatin cautioned the president against wedding the embargo to economic war, it is likely that he warned against the false hopes of the secretary of state.[22]

Several Republicans in Congress soon embraced Madison's coercive interpretation of the embargo. They realized, however, that a mere prohibition on American foreign shipping was an empty gun. To enlist the nation's export sector on behalf of foreign policy goals required a boycott on the international sale of American produce as well. Nathaniel Macon of North Carolina and others spoke immediately for such a ban because they believed that the aim of the law was "to keep within the limits of the United States everything which would sustain life." Since the purpose of the original law (Macon believed) was to test whether Congress could "produce an effect on the Powers of Europe," the North Carolinian opposed the foreign sale of American "provisions or supplies of any kind" until Europe relented.[23] The Congress included a ban on American exports in foreign vessels in its December legislation. But more than coercion shaped the policy, for to allow American exports in European bottoms ensured domestic inequities, bias against France, and inglorious reward for England's abuse of American commerce.

To equalize the burden of economic suffering between the nation's merchants and its farmers demanded a comprehensive ban on American exports. Otherwise, the mercantile interest would wither while the agricultural interest, floated by European ships, prospered. And simply to clear the oceans of American vessels unfairly aided England's military war against France and foolishly supported its commercial war against the United States. The disparity between the English and French navies, without a counterbalancing ban on exports, guaranteed American food and cotton to English bellies and machines, denied them to France, and created a mocking scene perfectly suited to the British: continued access to the American market

[22] Irving Brant, *James Madison, Secretary of State* (Indianapolis, 1953), pp. 399–403.

[23] Macon, *Annals*, 10th Cong., 1st sess., p. 1245.

and American resources while America's commercial challenge died of self-inflicted wounds. So it was that the pressures of domestic equity, a fair neutrality, and a desire not to play England's fool combined with a yearning to strike back at British abuse to endow a precautionary policy with coercive muscle. Throughout 1808, coercion would challenge, equal, and finally overwhelm the prudent defensive and time-bound goals that lay behind Jefferson's original recommendation. A congressional urge to avoid all unpleasantness, the momentum of established policy, traditions of Republican statecraft, and diplomatic failure, beginning with the collapse of the second round of the *Chesapeake* negotiations, all contributed to the transformation of the embargo.

Diplomatic Failure

The administration learned in early December 1807 that the British government was sending George Rose to Washington to continue the discussions that Monroe and Canning had been unable to conclude in London. At first, word of the Rose mission disappointed Jefferson. He had hoped that Monroe's failure would influence congressional deliberations toward military preparation. New discussions, the president feared, would build false hopes and encourage a congressional tendency to dawdle on preparedness legislation. But the mid-December intelligence from Europe dampened Jefferson's war spirits, reshaped his understanding of American problems and, consequently, led him to see positive benefits from continued *Chesapeake* diplomacy. Like the embargo, it would give what the United States most needed: time.[24] But the Rose mission went worse than Jefferson had expected. Sensing that the general practice of impressment would be swept under the rug, he did not anticipate the insulting preconditions that England attached to the mere discussion of reparations for the June 1807 assault.

The extent of American demands had contributed to Monroe's failure in London. Now that the administration was anxious to avoid untimely war, it decided to settle the *Chesapeake* incident alone and to leave for later general impressments. Clued by Monroe's dis-

---

[24] TJ to Benjamin Rush, Jan. 3, 1808, Jefferson Papers, LC.

patches that England might demand an American revocation of the July 2 presidential proclamation before it would discuss reparations, the administration decided to compromise in the interests of settlement. If Rose unofficially outlined acceptable reparations, "a repeal of the proclamation," in Madison's words, "and the act of reparation might be done at the same time."[25] But Rose's demands were more extensive than the Jeffersonians had imagined, and insulting as well, because they carried the offensive idea that the United States was partly to blame for the British attack on the *Chesapeake*.

On February 7 Rose informed Madison that he could not discuss reparations until, Madison noted in a journal he kept of the talks, there was "some disavowal on the part of the U.S. as to the conduct of their agents in encouraging, harboring and retaining deserters natural born subjects of his Britannic Majesty." Madison was shocked by "this new and unlooked for . . . ultimatum," and he asked Rose to put it in writing "so there might be no possible misconception." Rose presented the written ultimatum on February 8. Its precise wording divided the responsibility for the attack between England and America. Worse yet, it required an American disavowal of enticement activities before Rose would even outline the reparations England intended to offer. As Madison interpreted it, the English position argued that if the United States apologized for causing the *Chesapeake* affair, Great Britain might make amends for concluding it.[26]

Although the Rose ultimatum seemingly jeopardized a settlement, it also gave Madison a chance to sneak general impressments into the discussions, and he seized it. He asked Rose if England would renounce its right to press American citizens from public and private vessels alike if the United States promised to protect bona fide British citizens from enticement into the American service. Difficulties abounded on this issue. The English government never claimed the right to take American sailors, just British sailors serving illegally on American ships. Unfortunately, English and American definitions of citizenship differed, and these differences were the heart of the impressment problem. Although Madison recognized the difficulties inherent in a full discussion of impressments, both from the Ameri-

[25] George Canning to Monroe, July 25, 1807, Monroe Papers, LC, reel 4; Madison to Monroe, Mar. 18, 1808, Madison Papers, LC, reel 10.

[26] Madison, "Notes on Meetings with George Rose," Feb. 7, 9, 1808, Madison Papers, LC, reel 10.

can and English point of view, he was willing finally to confront American complicity in English desertions if that was the price of getting the whole business onto the negotiating table.

Madison won his point but lost the game. Logically, he was on sure ground. Rose's own ultimatum had broadened the negotiations. If they continued on the wider track, there must be reciprocity. On the defensive, Rose lamely suggested that in exchange for an American disavowal of enticement, Great Britain would accept in the final settlement a provision that reserved to the American government "a right to claim from G.B. a like disavowal." But, Madison quickly parried, "between an actual disavowal and a right to ask a disavowal" there was no reciprocity whatever. With the talks at a dead end, Madison brought them back to the *Chesapeake* itself.[27] Rose continued to insist that an American repeal of the July 2 proclamation precede any British discussions of reparations. On this point, the diplomacy collapsed.[28]

Although the administration did not expect much, England offered less. Long months of negotiation in London and Washington had produced nothing on the *Chesapeake*, on impressments, on commercial abuse. Not tremendously important by itself, Madison's failure with George Rose closed a story of total diplomatic frustration. "We are where we were," Secretary of War Dearborn noted on March 19, "and Congress (after receiving a full statement of the whole business) will determine what is next to be done."[29]

Confusion and New Directions

The administration had also to consider "what is next to be done." In the aftermath of the Rose mission, it moved forward on several fronts and considered, in Madison's phrase, "provisions of different kinds" to handle the European problem.[30] War was still quite likely. To that end, Jefferson sent Congress proposals to fortify the nation's seacoast,

[27] Madison, "Notes," Feb. 9, 14, 16, 1808, ibid.

[28] Madison to Monroe, Mar. 18, 1808, ibid.; John Nicholas to Wilson Cary Nicholas, Feb. 9, 1808, Wilson Cary Nicholas Papers, LC; TJ, "Public Report to Congress on the Result of the Rose Mission," Mar. 22, 1808, Jefferson Papers, LC.

[29] Dearborn to William Eustis, Mar. 19, 1808, William Eustis Papers, LC.

[30] Madison to William Pinkney, Mar. 30, 1808, Diplomatic Instructions, All Countries, vol. 6, NA.

build and man gunboats, classify the militia, protect the frontiers, and augment the army. Paltry appropriations doomed much of this effort.[31] To the president's keen disappointment, the proposals to classify the militia and to lure frontier forces to New Orleans with land bounties failed to gain congressional approval before the summer 1808 recess.[32] On April 12 Congress did create "for a limited time" a regular army of eight divisions. But the law did not create a military staff, and this omission prompted Samuel Smith to observe that he was "almost tired of public life."[33] Because maritime property and seamen were essential to any contemplated war effort and because the need to avoid war until military preparations were further along demanded calm in America's external relations, the administration continued to expect and to exact obedience to the December 1807 embargo. Therefore, Gallatin, in late February, sent Congress a second group of proposals to block loopholes and strengthen the enforcement apparatus on the coastline and the frontiers and in the port cities. The February proposals built on the first wave of embargo reform which Gallatin had suggested to the president on December 22 and Congress had made law in early January. These had aimed at the most glaring failures in the original law: the absence of penalties on coasting vessels that sailed illegally to foreign ports and the smallness of the penalties on vessels licensed for foreign trade that sailed without clearance papers.[34] But the February proposals differed from the earlier amendments because they touched the nation's economic relations with foreign territory separated from the United States by lines on a map, not by water. Although the December legislation had banned American exports in foreign bottoms, equity at home and abroad as well as punitive desires contributed to the prohibition. The

[31] Robert Smith to TJ, Jan. 13, 1808, TJ to Gallatin, Jan. 14, 1808, TJ to Robert Smith, Jan. 14, 1808, Jefferson Papers, LC. Legislation concerning marine militia, army, navy, and defensive fortifications were all stalled in Congress; see TJ to Cornelia Jefferson Randolph, April 5, 1808, ibid. John Adams chalked up the inaction to Republican frugality (John Adams to John Quincy Adams, April 12, 1808, Adams Family Papers, Massachusetts Historical Society [MHS], microfilm, reel 406). Nathaniel Macon located the problem in Republican politicking (Macon to Joseph Hopper Nicholson, Mar. 29, April 6, 1808, Joseph Hopper Nicholson Papers, LC).

[32] TJ to Gallatin, April 25, 1808, Jefferson Papers, LC.

[33] Smith to William Eustis, April 23, 1808, William Eustis Papers, LC.

[34] Gallatin to TJ, Dec. 22, 1807, Jefferson Papers, LC.

March 12 amendment betrayed a more explicit congressional commitment to economic warfare. Under the pressure of events, the administration's conception of the embargo was changing. Now challenging defensive needs were coercive dreams. The change did not go unnoticed, either by the Federalists or among the party faithful.

In the fourth section of the March 12 legislation, Congress banned exports to foreign nations by land (to Canada in the north and to Spanish territory in the south). Federalist Congressman Barent Gardenier from New York triumphantly noted the disparity between the president's announced goal of protecting essential maritime property from dangerous voyages and the new request to stop the flow of American goods over Canadian and Spanish borders. "I ask the intelligent and candid men of this House," Gardenier harangued on February 20, "whether to prevent the farmers of Vermont of selling their pigs in Canada is calculated to increase or diminish our essential resources?" For Gardenier, the new legislation branded Jefferson a liar and revealed a steady administration intention, dating from the embargo's beginning, to strangle all foreign commerce in a reckless attempt to punish Great Britain. Why so monstrous an attempt to lay waste the commercial prosperity of the United States? Why, demanded Gardenier, "wherever we espy a hole if it be no bigger than a wheat straw, at which the industry and the enterprise of our country can find vent, [are] all our powers called into requisition to stop it up"? Gardenier's answer lay in Jefferson's anglophobia and francophilia. "There is an unseen hand, which is guiding us to the most dreadful destinies—unseen, because it cannot endure the light." Napoleon had cast a spell on Jefferson, and Jefferson on Congress. "Darkness and mystery overshadow this House and this whole nation," the Federalist accused. "We sit here as mere automata; we legislate without knowing, ... without wishing to know, why or wherefore. We are told what to do, and the Council of Five Hundred do it."[35]

Gardenier's attacks on the integrity of the president and the Republican majority earned him stern rebukes from members of the national legislature.[36] Perhaps Gardenier's language was stock political abuse. Perhaps, as Ezekiel Bacon observed, the New Yorker's

---

[35] Gardenier, *Annals*, 10th Cong., 1st sess., pp. 1653–6.
[36] Ibid., pp. 1657–66.

performance was a "rapsody of 'melancholy madness,'" the venom of
a man so possessed by the idea of Jefferson's wickedness that no
crime, including truckling to Napoleon, was too awful to be true.[37]
But whether the charges stemmed from political opportunism or political pathology, or whether they said more about Gardenier's
Federalism than about Jefferson's Republicanism, the New Yorker's
wild rantings touched on something valid about the embargo: the
coercion of Great Britain was gaining importance in the cluster of
goals which underlay the policy.

Virginia Republican John Taylor's misgivings about the embargo's changing focus echoed Federalist disbelief. He thought the
original law "a short and not . . . a long piece of policy." As such it
had his support and, he was sure, the nation's. But a lengthy experiment in coercion, he was equally convinced, would squander public
approval, encourage smuggling (thereby "losing the ships and sailors
[the embargo] was meant to save"), and produce enough domestic
suffering to threaten the Republican ascendancy. Although he said it
more politely, a long coercive embargo was madness. It would "im-
poverish the agriculturalists," enrich "the lawless, drive our seamen
and shipping into foreign service, drain the treasury, expel our
money, break our banks, and fail to achieve a better treaty" with
England. "Was it prudent," Taylor wondered, to wager so much on a
policy that in the end must surely "lose."[38]

Gardenier's public attack and Taylor's private analysis came from
different ends of the American political spectrum, expressed the unrelated feelings of partisan hatred and loyalist doubt, yet shared a
common concern with the future of a policy that was clearly changing. Both took their intensity from changes in presidential perception. Quietly, but with gathering momentum, Jefferson was transforming his embargo into an economic weapon of war. So much encouraged the change. Because coercion offered national vindication
without bloodshed, it had always claimed his attentions. Because it
elevated the American economy to a significant position in the world

[37] Ibid., p. 1657. Two recent works that ably chart Federalist attitudes toward
Jefferson and the Republican movement are James M. Banner, *To the Hartford Con-
vention: The Federalists and the Origins of Party Politics in Massachusetts, 1789–1815*
(New York, 1971); and Linda Kerber, *Federalists in Dissent* (Ithaca, N.Y., 1970).

[38] Taylor to Wilson Cary Nicholas, May 10, 1808, Edgehill-Randolph Collection,
acc. no. 1397, UVa.

marketplace, it fueled Jefferson's pride in American institutions and power. Federalist sniping angered him, domestic smuggling and the abortive discussions with George Rose sharpened the bitterness, and all combined to exaggerate his faith in the embargo's coercive capacity. "That nothing for sale shall be exported," he reminded Gallatin in March, "is as much the object of the law" as the protection of our maritime property. "The intention of the legislature," he reiterated in April, "was to keep our seamen and property from capture and to starve the offending nations." And in May he applauded the fullest use of congressionally sanctioned executive power to enforce the embargo, even though an ample interpretation of the law worked hardships on the legal coasting trade, especially North Carolina's, because, he wrote Gallatin, the embargo was "the first experiment" at peaceful coercion and "it is of great importance to know its full effect."[39]

In anger Jefferson had fashioned a new purpose for the embargo that departed from his earlier understanding of it, ignored important realities which posed insurmountable obstacles to success, and pulled and tore at the policy until, a year later, it lay in tatters. Although politics and emotion reduced these obstacles in Jefferson's mind to Federalist "maneuvers" and "intrigues," more than these doomed a coercive embargo to failure, indeed compromised this "first experiment" from almost the moment Jefferson began to laud it.[40] Put simply, coercive embargo was flawed by a massive contradiction between the time required to put it to a fair test and the time the American people could be expected to endure it. This disparity produced expectations more naive than wise because they rested on the delusion that a policy predicated on an unlimited expenditure of time

[39] TJ to Gallatin, Mar. 23, April 8, May 20, 1808, Jefferson Papers, LC. See also TJ to Gallatin, May 15, 1808, "I place immense value in the experiment being fully made [to see] how far an embargo may be an effective weapon in the future as well as on this occasion," and TJ to Gallatin, May 27, 1808, "I set down the exercise of commerce, merely for profit, as nothing when it carries with it danger of defeating the objects of the embargo" (ibid.). Gallatin warned Jefferson about the embargo's imposition on North Carolina's legal coasting trade in mid-May, and the cabinet decided at the end of June to adopt Gallatin's proposals to relieve the pressure. The decision, Jefferson wrote, "has a special view to the relief of North Carolina that her corn and lumber may be sent coastwise" (Gallatin to TJ, May 16, 1808, TJ, Notes on Cabinet Meeting, June 30, 1808, ibid.).

[40] TJ to Daniel Brent, June 24, 1808, to James Sullivan, Aug. 12, 1808, ibid.

could achieve miraculous results within the span of a few months. Nor is this a retrospective judgment. Against Jefferson's occasional and understandable celebrations of a coercive tradition that reached deeply into Republican soil, we must weigh his own appreciation that domestic economic appetites placed the embargo on a short tether, robbed it of time, and therefore spoiled the dream of coercion through isolation. Until November 1808, Jefferson never imagined that it might go beyond "the fall or beginning of winter."[41] "Whatsoever the belligerent powers mean to do, must be done before that time," he wrote in July, "as on the state of things then existing and known to us, Congress will have to act."[42] Not only did the president share these thoughts with countless correspondents but, at his insistence, American diplomats shared them with England and France.[43] A logical question intrudes. How could an economic weapon accomplish its anticipated good works when its complete and short duration was spelled out clearly and in advance to the intended victims? The conflicting sources of the embargo's potential strength, one resting on economics and an ample investment of time, the other bound to the promise of war in the very near future, suggest an answer.

A welter of confusions pressed on both the president and his policy at midyear 1808. Beginning to champion the embargo as a grand experiment in peaceful war and a contribution to a more humane type of world statecraft, he constantly dwelt on the partisan sources of its anticipated failure while he seemingly ignored the real reasons for pessimism—the domestic economic factor—that had impelled him to confine the embargo in a narrow compass and reject the goal of coercion in the first place. This produced the embargo's irony. When Jefferson thought and acted within these ironic limits, the policy resembled a realistic foreign policy weapon. The embargo's success, defined only by the transformation of English policy, depended not on its indeterminate continuation and the economic pain it inflicted on Europe, but on the very thing that marred it as a weapon of economic war: the refusal of the American people to support it very long. This was always its chief strength. To broadcast

[41] TJ to Madison, Mar. 11, 1808, ibid.

[42] TJ to William B. Bibb, July 28, 1808, ibid.

[43] Madison to Pinkney, July 18, 1808, to Armstrong, July 18, 1808, Diplomatic Instructions, All Countries, vol. 7, NA.

this fact to England, to assure the English government that the embargo must soon be abandoned and that also, in Jefferson's words, "if this is before the repeal of the orders in council, we must abandon it only for a state of war," [44] only this could overturn the English system. It was not economic power implied in a lengthy withdrawal from the world's marketplace, but rather the promise of war that was implicit in the embargo's necessarily speedy repeal that sustained the president's pursuit of peace. To compound the irony, both Jefferson and the Federalists accepted the time limits imposed on the embargo by the economic desires of the American people. Both paraded this American weakness before the English. The Federalists' variation on the theme implied retreat. "They are endeavoring to convince England that we suffer more by the embargo than they do, and that if they but hold out a while, we must abandon it." [45] This is what angered Jefferson the most. His own variation promised war, and on this promise, American policy rested. Traditional modes of international force still dominated the president's thinking well into the embargo's career as a much compromised and very complicated alternative to war.

The Embargo and the European Powers: The Search for a Manageable War

In April 1808 Congress passed into law an administration request to allow the executive, under certain conditions, to remove the embargo against one or both European belligerents during the summer and autumn legislative recess. [46] Almost two months before Congress passed this suspension bill, the president had determined the goals and tactics of a diplomatic strategy that reflected the economic desires of the American people and the realities of the European war and that would occupy the administration until the news of its final failure in November 1808. "I take it to be an universal opinion," Jefferson wrote Madison on March 11, " . . . that war will become

[44] TJ to Thomas Cooper, June 21, 1808, Jefferson Papers, LC.

[45] TJ to Gallatin, June 22, 1808, ibid.

[46] Madison considered this act the most important outcome of the first session of the Tenth Congress (Madison to Pinkney, April 4, 1808, to Armstrong, May 2, 1808, Diplomatic Instructions, All Countries, vol. 6, NA).

preferable to a continuation of the embargo after a certain period of time. Should we not then avail ourselves of the intervening period to procure a retraction of the obnoxious decrees peaceably if possible?" "I wish you to consider therefore the following course of proceeding." Jefferson continued. "To instruct our ministers at Paris and London, by the next packet, to propose . . . that these decrees and orders shall no longer be extended to vessels of the United States in which case we shall remain faithfully neutral. But without assuming the air of menace, to let them both perceive that if they do not withdraw these orders and decrees there will arive a time when our interests will render war preferable to a continuance of the embargo, and then when this time arrives, if one has withdrawn and the other not, we must declare war against that other [and] if neither shall have withdrawn, we must take our choice of enemies between them." In this revealing correspondence with his secretary of state, Jefferson placed the embargo in its most valid context. It simply provided "an intervening period." By itself, the embargo could not and was never intended to solve the nation's dilemma. Only through creative and forceful diplomacy might the nation find redress. Second, Jefferson stated the complete length of the embargo's run, from December 1807 to November 1808. As he further explained to Madison: "It will be our duty to have ascertained [the results of the new diplomatic offensive] by the time Congress shall meet in the fall or beginning of winter, so that taking off the embargo, they may decide whether war must be declared and against whom." [47] Throughout the spring and summer Jefferson maintained his conviction that the embargo must be repealed by December 1808, simply because the American people would not support it beyond that time. The State Department insisted on complete information from its ministers abroad. There could be no mistakes. Madison even instructed Armstrong in Paris and Pinkney in London to double-check the schedules of all American dispatch vessels in European waters to ensure that the results of the summer diplomacy arrived in Washington well before the first day of the new Congress. "It is extremely important," he informed Pinkney, "and the president is particularly anxious that the communications to Congress on the meeting which takes place in the first Monday in November shall embrace the fullest and most au-

[47] TJ to Madison, Mar. 11, 1808, Jefferson Papers, LC.

thentic view of our foreign affairs. I must request your particular exertions to enable the present dispatch vessel to return in due time with all the materials you can contribute for that purpose."[48] By Jefferson's own reckoning, the next congressional session would see the embargo's end. If European commercial harassment continued, the United States would fight.

Until the early spring of 1808, Jefferson's hopes for the embargo rested primarily on the resources it saved and the realities it escaped, on precaution and isolation. But now, added to these rather passive and frightened hopes was a grand strategy to use aggressively the embargo's remaining months to solve or at least make manageable the nation's predicament. The rationales behind the new bout of diplomacy were two. The president now realized that the web of European commercial abuse was spun from the larger tangle of European war, and he appreciated the marginal power of any American policy that did not threaten to involve the United States in the European struggle and thereby affect its outcome. Second was the degree of economic sacrifice that the administration could reasonably anticipate from the American people. One rendered economic coercion ineffectual; the other made it dangerous. Jefferson was not yet wedded to the coercive aims of the embargo. Nor was his ongoing struggle to affirm the courage, virtue, and the public spirit of his countrymen yet fixed to their obedience to the policy. His certainty that they would face another war in the spirit of "Lexington and Concord" meant for him that the nation's honor was still intact. His encounter with embargo violations was more pragmatic and understanding than it would be at year's end. He was in almost daily correspondence with Gallatin, and Gallatin with the customs collectors in America's port cities. The accumulating information and data charted a long and difficult career ahead in embargo enforcement. Not only from Federalist Boston, but from New York, Philadelphia, Providence, Baltimore, Richmond, Alexandria, indeed from most of the nation's port cities, came the news, beginning in December 1807, of fraud, evasion, and merchant ingenuity in ignoring what the commercially active class considered nothing more than an impediment—like rough seas and bad weather—to trade and profit. The

[48] Madison to Pinkney, July 18, 1808, Diplomatic Instructions, All Countries, vol. 7, NA.

violations that Jefferson anticipated and confronted both shaped his understanding of the embargo's strengths and limits and precluded its continuation beyond the autumn. He hoped that the new diplomacy would unravel all belligerent commercial restrictions. If one belligerent recanted while the other persisted, the United States would declare war against the still offending nation. But if the diplomacy completely failed, Jefferson was determined to remove the embargo and to "take our choice of enemies . . . by the time Congress shall meet in the fall."[49]

But without some diplomatic relief, the task of choosing one enemy would not be easy. Clearly, the president never considered asking Congress for a declaration of war against France. Great Britain was still the prime commercial enemy, the author of innumerable impressment outrages and of the *Chesapeake* attack. Yet a declaration of war against England while the French decrees still operated against the United States would elicit from the Federalists loud cries of francophilia and bias, enmesh the war debates in partisan politics, and strike at American unity when it was most needed. For the sake of manageable war against a single enemy, then, the administration made it easier for France than for England to avoid war with the United States and to regain its valuable trade.

James Madison was confident of France's cooperation because he knew how little the administration had really asked from Napoleon.[50] Although the United States offered ostensibly the same package to each belligerent—revocation of its maritime restrictions in exchange for American trade and American cooperation in the European war—the offers were quite unequal in fact because their maritime emphasis threatened England's entire apparatus of commercial war but left unchallenged the heart of Napoleon's commercial system, his control of the European continent. The administration demanded that Great Britain repeal all its restrictions that interfered with American neutral trade on the oceans. The awesome power of the Royal Navy supported these restrictions, and they worked hardships on both the French military effort and American commer-

[49] TJ to Madison, Mar. 11, 1808, Jefferson Papers, LC. For the cabinet discussion of British and French actions required to regain American trade, see TJ, Notes on Cabinet Meeting, July 6, 1808, Jefferson Papers, LC.

[50] Madison to Pinkney, April 30, 1808, to Armstrong, May 2, 1808, Diplomatic Instructions, All Countries, vol. 6, NA.

cial ambitions. But in keeping with its maritime focus, the administration divided the French decrees into two broad categories: municipal regulations ("vigorously legal, tho not friendly," Jefferson called them) and illegal maritime restrictions. The French control of the continent of Europe made the municipal, or port, regulations significant indeed, and they worked great hardships on both British commerce and the neutral nations that tried to breach Napoleon's Continental System. The second category, the French maritime restrictions, was powerful on paper, but the Royal Navy had reduced them to impotence in practice. In effect, then, the administration demanded that France revoke only the part of its apparatus of economic warfare it was powerless to enforce. Madison told Armstrong to emphasize that what the United States demanded of France "would . . . immaterially diminish its operations against the British commerce, that operation being so completely in the power of France on land, and so little in her power on the high seas."[51]

The two goals of peace and limited war did not run on the same line, and the Jeffersonians knew that the pursuit of limited war foreclosed any chance for peace, however slim, because Great Britain would never equalize French and British power on the ocean while Napoleon maintained his dominance over the port cities of Europe. The manageable war strategy guaranteed war. This the Jeffersonians tried to ignore but finally could not.[52] Consequently, Madison instructed Armstrong to preserve whatever hope for peace remained by pressing the French negotiators to repeal the municipal regulations as well. But so small was this hope, and so large was the need for at least some European relief, that Madison also told Armstrong not to demand the full repeal he suggested. The explicit design of the

[51] TJ to Robert Livingston, Oct. 15, 1808, Jefferson Papers, LC; Madison to Armstrong, May 2, 1808, Diplomatic Instructions, All Countries, vol. 6, NA.

[52] As Pinkney in London pointed out, "If they [the British government] should repeal their orders, France will repeal her decrees *so far as they are purely maritime* and no further. But the maritime provisions of those decrees, whatever may have been pretended to the contrary, were never considered here as of the least importance. It is the *territorial* branch (adopted by Holland and the other connexions and dependencies of France) which has pinched them by excluding their productions and trade from the continent. No british object would be gained therefore by such a repeal of the French decrees as would likely follow the recall of their orders" (Pinkney to Madison, Dec. 25, 1808, Dispatches, Great Britain, Pinkney, vol. 15, NA).

American offer tempted France to believe it could not lose. By re-
voking its maritime decrees France would not jeopardize its strength
in Europe. If Great Britain followed the French lead, that action
"would restore to France the full benefit of neutral trade which she
needs." And if England "persevere[d] in her obnoxious orders,"
France would then achieve American participation in the European
war because English persistence (Madison instructed Armstrong to
hammer this home) "would render collisions with the United States
inevitable."[53]

A diplomatic stance tilted toward France was the understandable
result of long frustrations with Great Britain. Not only commercial
abuse but impressments and the *Chesapeake* had defied settlement.
So when the new diplomacy made it easier for France to deal with
the United States, the bias reflected a lingering anglophobia that
defined Republicanism itself and the obvious fact that British oppression was greater, more insulting, and of a longer run. But more importantly, the inequality spun from the pragmatic need to wipe clean
the slate of French abuse, even if this meant winking at the restrictive
municipal decrees, and to recreate for Congress and the nation what
existed immediately after the *Chesapeake* affair and before the French
decrees Europeanized America's foreign problems: one single enemy,
the English nation. But although a realistic view of European politics
and power pointed American diplomacy toward France, hopes still
pointed to England. Weighed against the Jeffersonians' passion for
peace, the prospect of limited war counted for little. So it was that
William Pinkney's impossible negotiations with the British became
more important to the overall Jeffersonian aims than was John
Armstrong's more plausible mission in France.

With the return of James Monroe to the United States in the fall of
1807, William Pinkney of Maryland became the resident American
minister in London. Before he received detailed instructions from
Madison in June, Pinkney expected his continued presence in England to accomplish little. Occasionally he wrote optimistically to
Washington, but usually after he had read of or heard opposition
criticism of the government's policy toward American trade. His
promptings were toward negotiation, but from George Canning he

[53] Madison to Armstrong, May 2, 1808, Diplomatic Instructions, All Countries,
vol. 6, NA.

expected little. England would not precipitate a war, his advice ran, but neither would it budge from its unfair maritime policies. Counting on America's fear of war, on the continuing deterioration of Franco-American relations, and on its own ability to make its commercial tyranny palatable with niggling concessions, England intended no major changes.[54] Nor did it seem to mind the embargo. In the short run, the embargo hurt France more than England, inflicted pleasant wounds on American commercial enterprise, and was violated enough by American smugglers to ensure an adequate stream of trade. And from England's point of view, there would be no long run. Soon American cupidity would overwhelm American patriotism and force the Jeffersonians to retreat.

More chilling were Pinkney's springtime observations on the purpose behind the British commercial system and on England's attitude toward another American war. The British system aimed more at the American economic challenge than at Napoleon's armies and Continental System. The French decrees were only the "pretext" for the larger crusade. If France repealed them, England might fiddle with its system, but it would not tamper with the main lines of a policy that underwrote its maritime ascendancy. Before it removed the commercial orders that protected its monopolistic dominion from the American challenge, Great Britain would fight. "Although they did not wish and would not seek a war with the United States," Pinkney warned, "yet, if we made such a war necessary, they would perhaps not much regret it; as a check on our maritime growth was becoming indispensible."[55]

Pinkney's gloomy hypothesis supported a Jeffersonian view that had long suspected an ulterior anti-American purpose to the British orders-in-council. His Federalism lent credence to his observations. Jefferson's England was "a bloated omnipotence." Its avarice warred against American interest and ideology, against the growth of American commerce and the flowering of a free and competitive international maritime order. The girth of British ambition mortified

[54] Pinkney to Madison, Dec. 7, 14, 29, 31, 1807, Jan. 7, Feb. 6, 10, 17, 22, May 10, 1808, William Pinkney Letterbooks, Vols. 1–2, Md. Hist. Soc.; Pinkney to Madison, "private," Feb. 18, 1808, Madison Papers, LC, reel 10; Pinkney to Madison, Mar. 11, 1808, Dispatches, Great Britain, Pinkney, vol. 15, NA.

[55] Pinkney to Madison, Jan. 24, Feb. 17, May 10, 1808, Dispatches, Great Britain, Pinkney, vol. 15, NA.

and exasperated Jefferson. The English think "they can oblige all nations to carry all their produce to their island as an entrepot," he wrote in July, "to pay them a tax on it, and to receive their license to carry it to its ultimate market. It is indeed a desperate throw."[56] The British system aimed at "destroy[ing] American rivalship," Madison noted in September; it aimed at "usurpation" and "monopoly," he had written in March.[57] These fears created the futile ambience that enveloped the Jeffersonian encounter with the British negotiations. The British system grew from a set of assumptions and goals that bore no relation to either the French decrees or the American embargo. Consequently, American policy makers expected no change from England yet still hoped for miracles and the avoidance of war. But Pinkney's efforts, as Washington viewed them, were not without importance. They had a particular relevance that at least fitted neatly in the domestic political dimension of manageable war. "If [England] has nothing more in view than it is willing to avow," Madison wrote America's negotiator, "it cannot refuse to concur in an arrangement rescinding on her part the orders in council, and on ours, the embargo."[58] The unspoken but assumed necessity was the simultaneous French repeal of its maritime restrictions. Faced with that and an American promise to abandon the embargo, England's continued refusal to dismantle its unfair system would reveal its anti-American core and unite the American people against English hostility. What Madison forgot in his analysis were the important differences in what America demanded of France and of England.

By the first of June, the State Department had not heard, in Jefferson's phrase, "one word interesting" from Pinkney.[59] The American diplomat did not have the power to produce any interesting words. He had not yet received the April 30 instructions and did not know he could promise the resumption of American trade and, depending on the French diplomacy, pledges of American military cooperation against France in exchange for the revocation of the British orders. The spring was a lonely time for Pinkney in London; his presence

[56] TJ to Pinkney, July 18, 1808, Jefferson Papers, LC.

[57] Madison to TJ, Sept. 21, 1808, ibid.; Madison to Pinkney, Mar. 18, 1808, Diplomatic Instructions, All Countries, vol. 6, NA.

[58] Madison to Pinkney, July 18, 1808, Diplomatic Instructions, All Countries, vol. 7, NA.

[59] TJ to Dearborn, Aug. 9, 1808, Jefferson Papers, LC.

was only as relevant as he chose to make it. Canning never initiated discussions; diplomatic meetings depended on Pinkney's asking for them. Finally, in early June he requested an exploratory and informal discussion over the whole range of outstanding issues: impressments, the *Chesapeake*, the orders-in-council. He promised Madison that he would "press by every argument in my power the justice of the American position," but he was not optimistic. "If I cannot make things better than they are," he wrote the secretary of state, "I will not make them worse."[60] A dreary appraisal. Madison was struck by its pessimism, and by a host of other developments that augured ill for the future. He counted them off in a litany of grief to the president: Pinkney had requested the interview; the parliamentary opposition had not taken the government to task for the failure of the Rose mission; the change in Spanish policy opened new markets, colonial and continental, to Great Britain; England preferred diplomatic stalemate so that the embargo would keep American trade away from this "new commercial prospect"; England was stalling so that domestic dissatisfaction with the embargo would rout the Republicans in the next presidential canvass, thrust the Federalists into power, and the United States into war against France.[61]

Armed with the April 30 instructions, Pinkney met with Canning on three occasions between June 29 and July 29, 1808. He quickly outlined the American offer to the British foreign secretary. Rather than waste time in the usual appeal to international law and fair play, Pinkney went straight to the heart of the matter. If England revoked its orders, the United States would repeal the embargo as it applied to Great Britain. If France did not follow the British lead, the United States would "combat French irregularities," with war between France and America the probable result. But if France revoked its decrees and England did not, the United States would remove the embargo against France, resume trade with Napoleon, and combat the British commercial system. Pinkney thought Canning noncom-

---

[60] Pinkney to Madison, Feb. 23, Mar. 11, April 16, 1808, William Pinkney Letterbooks, vol. 1, Md. Hist. Soc.; Pinkney to Madison, June 5, 1808, Dispatches, Great Britain, Pinkney, vol. 15, NA.

[61] Madison to TJ, Aug. 14, 17, 1808, Jefferson Papers, LC. On the probable impact of Spanish developments on English policy toward America, TJ wrote: "The turn in Spanish affairs may mount them on their stilts again. . . . It is a government of no faith" (TJ to Thomas Digges, Aug. 10, 1808, ibid.).

mital but receptive to the American position. Jefferson was far less sanguine. "A letter from Mr. Pinkney," he wrote in September, "expresses a hope that the British government will repeal their orders on his engagement that we will repeal our embargo. He *infers* this from a conversation with Mr. Canning, but I have little faith in diplomatic *inferences*, and less in Canning's good faith."[62]

Jefferson's premonitions proved finally correct, but Pinkney had expressed his optimism very cautiously. He believed that the future of the negotiation rested on the central purpose of the British system. If it aimed at the French decrees and "at anything short of the establishment and practical support of an exclusive dominion over the seas," Great Britain might respond favorably to the American offer.[63] Pinkney's reasoning, and Jefferson's, anchored the British response to larger questions of honesty and liberality. Thus, a favorable British response rooted the orders in the necessities of European war. But England's refusal equaled a confession that the system had little to do with the European war, with France, or with the needs of belligerency, but rather took its shape from the American commercial challenge. As did his superiors, Pinkney ignored the bias in the American offers to the two belligerents and the impact this distortion must surely have on the British reply. The administration knew full well that the limited redress demanded of France almost ensured the failure of its English diplomacy; this, indeed, was the exasperating cost of manageable war. Pinkney in London and the Jeffersonians in Washington obscured this unwanted fact in their images of British malice and instead located probable diplomatic failure in the ironically comforting folds of an English crusade against American national growth.

Flirtatious in June, Canning was ice cold in July. Throughout the negotiation, he had deceived Pinkney. Canning thought the American offer so trivial that he never mentioned it to the king.[64] But until the end of the month he feigned interest and strung the Ameri-

---

[62] Pinkney to Madison, June 29, 1808, William Pinkney Letterbooks, vol. 2, Md. Hist. Soc.; Pinkney to Madison, Aug. 4, 1808, Dispatches, Great Britain, Pinkney, vol. 16, NA; TJ to John Wayles Eppes, Sept. 20, 1808, Jefferson Papers, LC.

[63] Pinkney to Madison, Aug. 4, 1808, Dispatches, Great Britain, Pinkney, vol. 16, NA; Pinkney to Madison, "private," Aug. 3, 1808, Madison Papers, LC, reel 10.

[64] Perkins, *Prologue*, p. 205.

can along. Pinkney knew that perplexing difficulties crowded in: English power and pride, its image of republican government, the resolve of the American people, and the discrepancy between the American offers to France and England. Expecting difficulty, he also expected candor. Knowing that his tasks were herculean, he did not know that he had become an American Sisyphus. To the very end he clung to a slim chance for success. Well after the hand was really over, he wrote Madison that the need to balance American goals against the needs and pride of Great Britain made the formal offer he was drafting for Canning, already rendered meaningless by events, the most difficult correspondence he had ever written.[65]

Pinkney's and America's failure began on July 22, when Canning asked him to put in writing the American position. Pinkney demurred because, he said on the spot, a loose and informal approach would produce better results. Actually, Pinkney objected to written communications because he knew they would kill the negotiations. Any written statement must clearly express the orders' illegality and fix responsibility for the embargo on them. With so much working against his efforts, he did not want to burden the discussions with stabs at British pride. This, of course, went unsaid. Canning's reaction to Pinkney's rejection of written communication confused the American. The foreign secretary reiterated his demand for a written statement but volunteered that Pinkney might want to know British thinking on the various issues before reducing his offer to paper. Canning then scheduled another meeting for the following week. Now thinking that serious discussions would soon begin, Pinkney left the July 22 interview more hopeful than he had been all summer.[66]

The July 29 discussions crushed Pinkney's brief optimism. Canning suddenly announced a need for "caution" and "circumspection." He told Pinkney that "difficulties" beset the whole business, but he would not explain them. He backed off from his generous offer of the previous week and informed the American that discussions would not begin until Canning had the American written offer in hand. He threatened the negotiations by announcing that if the American

---

[65] Pinkney to Madison, "private," Aug. 3, 1808, Madison Papers, LC, reel 10.
[66] Pinkney to Madison, "private," Aug. 4, 1808, ibid.

statement characterized the orders-in-council as illegal or responsible for the December 22 embargo, the British government would disregard it totally. Canning then announced that he, and his government, were largely uninterested in seeing the American offer. But if Pinkney wished to write a letter that England might not even consider, he was free to do it at his own discretion. The end was quick, and for Pinkney, humiliating.[67]

After Canning's abrupt remarks, the rest of the meeting was unnecessary, but Pinkney continued the futile charade. Ignoring the wreckage that lay about him, he scurried back to his previous arguments against written communication. But now he told Canning what he had feared to mention a few days before; that in a formal note the United States would have to fix responsibility for the embargo on the British orders-in-council. "And where would this end?" he almost begged of Canning. "To what wholesome end could it lead?" The foreign secretary was uninterested. Unwilling to let his own silence terminate the negotiations, Pinkney finally put the American position in writing. But, he advised Madison after his frosty meeting with Canning, "if any other consequence than mere discussion should follow the receipt of my note, it would be at a great distance."[68]

The American diplomat sent the note on August 23, waited a month, and received Canning's caustic reply on September 23.[69] Although August and September were lean months in accomplishment, Pinkney made them rich in observation and analysis. In a series of private letters to Madison and Jefferson and official dispatches to the State Department, he discussed the underpinnings of British policy, the options available to the United States, and the victory that would surely reward the pursuit of economic coercion. He did not conclude the summer diplomacy on a note of despair. Rather he gave an administration struggling to find a viable policy

[67] Pinkney to Madison, Aug. 4, 1808, to Armstrong, Aug. 5, 1808, William Pinkney Letterbooks, vol. 2, Md. Hist. Soc.

[68] Pinkney to Madison, Aug. 4, 1808, Dispatches, Great Britain, Pinkney, vol. 16, NA.

[69] Pinkney worked on the note from Aug. 8 to Aug. 23 and delivered it in person to Canning. On Sept. 12 and Sept. 13 he went again to Canning's office and was told that the foreign secretary was in the country. Ten days later, Pinkney received Canning's reply (Pinkney to Madison, Sept. 6, 12, 13, 1808, Canning to Pinkney, Sept. 23, 1808, Pinkney to Madison, Sept. 24, 1808, William Pinkney Letterbooks, vol. 2, Md. Hist. Soc.).

in the wake of diplomacy's failure a set of arguments that comprehended the setback and encouraged a total commitment to economic coercion.

"A Rigorous Execution of the Embargo"

Pinkney's extended analysis assumed that British aspirations doomed all reasonable American attempts at diplomatic accommodation. "The spirit of monopoly has seized the government and the people of this country," he wrote on September 21. "We shall not under any circumstances be tolerated as *rivals* in navigation and trade. It is vain to hope that Great Britain will voluntarily foster the naval means of the United States."[70] Such was Pinkney's central observation of British motivation, elaborated and refined in all his correspondence of the late summer and autumn.

England aimed at commercial monopoly, and the orders spoke to that anti-American purpose. Great Britain never intended to unravel the tangle of commercial restrictions that kept the United States in economic "dependence." That the Jeffersonians required France to repeal only its maritime edicts, he now argued, gave England a convenient excuse to continue the orders, just as the promulgation of the French edicts gave the British orders their initial pretext and obscured their true motivation. Nor should the United States be duped by English theatrics, Pinkney warned. Periodically they might revise the orders, but only in "subordinate provisions," only to make them "more palatable" without imperiling their central purpose.[71]

Not only was British policy anti-American by design, but the English banked on success because of American weakness. Pinkney was certain that England's belief that the United States lacked the courage to fight, combined with "the notion that we cannot much longer maintain the embargo," shaped British policy. Greed and cowardice were the chief components of the British image of the United States. England's America cared little for national honor, a lot about trade, and feared war. Before the embargo hurt the English economy, American discontent would spill into politics and force either the

[70] Pinkney to Madison, Sept. 21, 1808, ibid.
[71] Pinkney to Madison, Sept. 7, 1808, ibid.

embargo's repeal or a change in national administration. "I am mistaken," Pinkney wrote Madison, "if the [British] government has not felt inclined to calculate upon that discontent, and at least give it a fair trial."[72]

British character amply explained the failure of the summer diplomacy. But because embargo violations fed the British image of American weakness and cupidity, they contributed to English intransigence. "That the embargo pinches here is certain," he told Madison on September 7. "There is undoubtedly room for alarm on the score of provisions (corn and flour) and it is confessed they feel severely the want of our trade." The embargo had not defeated the English system because "the numerous evasions" supported the British hope that ultimately England could have both its monopoly and American trade as well.[73]

Policy was at a crossroads, and economic interest and national honor demanded a "rigorous execution of the embargo." Such was Pinkney's central contention, understandably given from his English vantage point, but an invitation to suicide in the context of American politics and economic expectations. Its only alternatives, Pinkney reasoned, were national humiliation, permanent economic harm, or war. Conceivably the United States could diffuse domestic pressure by opening a trade with Spain and Portugal, as these nations were temporarily out of Napoleon's Continental System, and keep the embargo in force against England and France. But a breach in the embargo wall would surely result in a "circuitous" trade with Great Britain and its colonial possessions. The United States could not mask a trade with England by calling it a trade with Spain, and if America traded with England in fact, it should do so in form as well. Only then could it reap the full economic benefit from the sacrifice of its honor and economic future. But the rewards were nothing compared to the costs: an unfair neutrality, war with France, and economic vassalage to Great Britain. "We throw ourselves," Pinkney warned, "bound hand and foot upon the generosity of a government that has hitherto refused us justice, and all this when the affair of the *Chesapeake* and a host of other wrongs are unredressed, and when Great Britain has just rejected an overture which she must have accepted with eagerness if her views were not such as it became us to

[72] Ibid.
[73] Ibid.

suspect and guard against." Great Britain would be "a jealous ally" and a dangerous friend. And after the misshapen Anglo-American alliance lost the thin connecting tissue of a common enemy, Pinkney concluded, "it would be endless to enumerate in detail the evils which would cling to us in this new career of vassalage and meanness, and tedious to pursue our backward course toward" colonial dependence. In Pinkney's hands, the Revolutionary epic itself hung on the enforcement of the embargo. A complete repeal of the embargo would better serve the United States. Though as fatal to American economic independence as a partial repeal which excluded France, at least complete submission to European power honored the requirements of a fair neutrality and perhaps might spare war.[74]

A powerful statement of support for the embargo followed Pinkney's grim analysis of the other alternatives. It would yet pry justice from Great Britain. "The embargo and the loss of our trade," he informed the State Department, "are deeply felt here, and will be felt with more severity every day. The discontents among their manufacturers are only quieted for the moment by temporary causes. Cotton is rising and will soon be scarce. Unfavorable events on the continent will subdue the temper, unfriendly to wisdom and justice, which now prevails here. Our measures have not been without effect. They have not been decisive because we have not been thought capable of persevering in self-denial." In the final analysis, the embargo's failure owed more to execution than to conception. If the Jeffersonians could handle disrespect for the law at home, the embargo could yet topple England's unfair commercial system.[75]

Albeit unconsciously, Pinkney's bleak history of British policy and motivation underscored the necessity for war, and not the wisdom of further embargo enforcement. By his own accounting, the British commercial system was so intimately connected with monopolistic economic goals and an anti-American orientation that economic coercion was likely to have little impact on official decisions even if it had significant effect on the lives of British workers and the prosperity of England's manufacturing. The embargo encouraged domestic evasion, not domestic support. Its success abroad hung on the outcome of an administration battle against the economic aspirations of the American people. That battle raised implications that Pinkney

[74] Pinkney to Madison, Sept. 21, 1808, ibid.
[75] Ibid.

completely ignored. The embargo's future, even assuming sufficient domestic support, was mortaged to a host of uncontrollable international factors. Pinkney struggled to interpret these imponderables in ways favorable to the embargo. He branded the changes in Spain that opened colonial and continental markets to English commerce as only "temporary." He assumed that inevitable English reverses on the Continent would "subdue England's temper" and push its American policy toward "wisdom and justice." But what if Latin American markets and raw materials remained available to the British? Since Pinkney connected changes in Spain to the embargo's success, his unstated conclusion was that the embargo, regardless of the support given by or coerced from the American people, would fail in England if Napoleon failed in Spain.[76]

In March 1808 the president had suggested and defined the tactics and goals of the summer diplomacy. He then saw it as a last attempt to clear the slate of foreign abuse without a war, or, more probably, to provide the nation with a clear and manageable single enemy. The strategy accepted the gravity of the European crisis and therefore assumed the possibility of war; hence the dissimilarity between the English and French demands. Shaping the entire venture was the knowledge that the American people would not support an embargo on their livelihood beyond a year's time. Throughout the spring and summer Jefferson had emphasized the importance of knowing the outcome before the next meeting of Congress so that the nation's legislators could remove the embargo, decide on war if necessary, and determine against whom it would be waged. If the enterprise failed completely, then Jefferson expected Congress to take its choice of enemies. A war against all of Europe was never anticipated; neither was a lengthy experiment in economic coercion.[77]

The diplomacy completely failed. France and England ignored the American offers and continued their respective crusades against

[76] Ibid.

[77] Caesar Rodney tried to call Madison back to the goals and obligations of the summer diplomatic offensive. War against both belligerents was out of the question. So too was indefinite embargo. "England is our old and inveterate enemy. She has done us more injury. The impressment of our seamen alone is worse than all we have sustained from France. She is vulnerable by land and water. Her provinces we can conquer and . . . her commerce will become a prey to our privateers" (Rodney to Madison, Jan. 16, 1809, Madison Papers, LC, ser. 2, reel 25).

American commerce. To make matters worse, Napoleon issued the Bayonne Decree which insultingly proclaimed a French commitment to the success of the embargo by promising to capture all American merchant vessels, obviously British ships in American disguise, both on the high seas and in European ports. The Bayonne Decree galled Madison. The administration had made it so easy for the French to accommodate America and to gain a resumption of its trade. "It would seem," he wrote Armstrong in exasperation, "as if the Imperial cabinet had never paid sufficient attention to the smallness of the sacrifice" the United States had requested.[78] Attorney General Rodney could not understand how the manageable war strategy had failed. "England and France have both played a foolish game in relation to this country," he wrote Madison. "Either of them, by withdrawing their arbitrary orders or decrees, might have involved us in a war with the other. They have acted as if they were blind."[79]

France's failure to revoke its maritime decrees made it difficult, but not impossible, for the administration to go to war against Great Britain. There was still the unsettled *Chesapeake* affair, still the general practice of impressment, still the arguable point that the French decrees aimed at the British while the British orders aimed at the United States. The State Department received Armstrong's and Pinkney's grim dispatches in November. Jefferson's mood controlled his response. Of no small importance, the news of the final diplomatic defeat came on the eve of a presidential election and Jefferson's retirement from almost a half century in public life. His thoughts were increasingly on retirement, wandering amidst the happy tasks of family, farms, and books and the unpleasant realities of private debt. Jefferson was incapable of ending a public career committed to individual happiness and national growth with a call to combat; incapable of bequeathing to his countrymen, in his final acts, the horrors of war. The harsh realities that he had perceived in the spring and summer (concerning war, international politics and rivalry, domestic politics and economic hopes) dissolved in his personal longing to escape office with the nation still at peace.

[78] Madison to Armstrong, July 22, 1808, Diplomatic Instructions, All Countries, vol. 6, NA.

[79] Rodney to Madison, Jan. 16, 1809, Madison Papers, ser. 2, reel 25, LC.

By the end of 1808 Pinkney had become the administration's strongest advocate of coercive embargo. Unable to face the clear implications of diplomatic failure that he had charted in the spring, Jefferson now saw in Pinkney's many letters and dispatches what he desperately wished to see. The embargo was having an effect; but for the malcontents in the midst of a virtuous people, but for the "rank growth" of fraud, evasion, and disrespect for law, the embargo would succeed. Pinkney's analysis came at a time when the president craved manageable explanations for the embargo's failure and alternatives to war or submission. The diplomat's advice helped the coercive hopes that were always embedded in Jefferson's understanding of the policy to triumph finally over the prudent conceptions that had initially tied the embargo securely to defensive purposes, diplomatic strategy, the constraints of time and economic desires, and the possibility of war. Yet the newfound importance of economic coercion was only part of the embargo's refashioned meaning. It had become bound up in the redemption of the American economy and the protection of the social and political legacy of 1800. Pervading and dramatizing all these concerns was Jefferson's sense of guilty involvement in the nation's departure from the economic traditions of its founding "as a great agricultural country."[80]

[80] TJ to Thomas Leiper, Jan. 21, 1809, Jefferson Papers, LC.

5

A RUDDERLESS SHIP
Policy and the Presidential Succession

"Waiting on Events"

Josiah Quincy, Jr., a Federalist congressman from Massachusetts, had little love for President Jefferson and none for the embargo. He thought the nation should rid itself of the foolish policy, strengthen the army and navy, resume trade in a dignified manner, and enjoy "the rich harvest of neutrality" that awaited the United States when its government replaced diplomatic whispers and economic self-destruction with a more manly policy. "But how can such a dish of skim milk as now stands . . . at the head of the nation be stirred to so mighty an action?" Quincy asked for all of Federalist New England in December 1808. "Fear of responsibility and love of popularity are now [Jefferson's] master passions and regulate all the movements," Quincy believed. Jefferson was temporizing. His policy was "to keep things as they are and wait for European events" and for his own retirement. And "then away to Monticello and let the —— take the hindmost. Not a whit deeper project than this fills the august mind of your successor," Quincy wrote John Adams, unless it be the premeditated ruin of "mercantile enterprize" and "New England."[1]

Quincy's charge touched most of the components in the traditional Federalist litany against Thomas Jefferson: unmanly, indecisive, demagogic, governed by the heart (feminine-Republican) and not by the head (masculine-Federalist). It was a chorus that had rolled through the corridors of Federalist abuse since Alexander Hamilton had coupled "French" with "womanish" and joined them both to

---

[1] Quincy to Adams, Dec. 14, 1808, Jan. 17, 1809, Adams Family Papers, MHS, reels 406, 407.

Jefferson in 1792.[2] Distorted by regional and political hatreds, dwelling on irresponsibility, cowardice, and the uncharitable notion that Jefferson was insensitive to the nation's plight, Quincy's view was more caricature than honest portrait. That the president's commercial diplomacy since 1803 had taken him well beyond his southern roots and southern constituency made little difference to Quincy. But despite its transparent political motivation, the New Englander's appraisal touched on certain troublesome aspects of Jefferson's final encounter with America's foreign problems. Men who held the president in high regard—Albert Gallatin, John Quincy Adams, and Wilson Cary Nicholas to name three—fretted over the paralysis that afflicted Jefferson in the fall of 1808.[3]

The president was waiting on events, trusting to "the chapter of accidents," and clinging desperately to the embargo. So oppressive had the thought of war become to him that, despite the failure of the summer diplomacy, and despite his own premonition that within a year from inception the embargo would lose popular support and unleash divisions and disharmonies within American politics and society, Jefferson could contemplate no other policy. "I think one war enough for the life of one man," the president wrote New Hampshire's governor, John Langdon, on August 2, 1808, "and you and I have gone through one which at least may lessen our impatience to embark on another." Although Jefferson added that if war came, he and his fellow Revolutionary compatriots would meet it—"like men, old men indeed, but yet good for something"[4] —one can ignore the bitterness and error in the Federalist image of Jefferson and still appreciate how large was his desire to avoid war in his remaining months of public service, and how much this desire fed Jefferson's persistence in national economic withdrawal well beyond the time limit he had earlier imposed on it.[5] Jefferson's attachment to the embargo was now total. Orchard Cook, a leading Republican congressman from Massachusetts, "freely conversed" with Jefferson in

[2] Hamilton to Col. Edward Carrington, July 25, 1792, Richard B. Morris, ed., *Alexander Hamilton and the Founding of the Nation* (New York, 1969), p. 52.

[3] Gallatin to TJ, Nov. 3, 8, 1808, Jefferson Papers, LC; Adams to William Branch Giles, Nov. 15, 1808, Adams Family Papers, MHS, reel 135; Nicholas to TJ, Dec. 22, 1808, Wilson Cary Nicholas Papers, LC; Nicholas to Joseph C. Cabell, Dec. 23, 1808, Joseph C. Cabell Papers, UVa.

[4] TJ to Langdon, Aug. 2, 1808, Jefferson Papers, LC.

[5] TJ to Thomas Mann Randolph, Jan. 26, 1808, to Joseph Eggleston, Mar. 7,

December 1808 and later reported to John Quincy Adams how frantic rather than positive that attachment was. Cook told Adams that Jefferson could "think of no other alternative but such as involves war." And rather than go to war, the president, Cook thought, was "incline[d] to hug the embargo and die in its embrace."[6]

By early autumn, dissatisfaction with the embargo was growing within both Jefferson's cabinet and the congressional Republican majority. Wilson Cary Nicholas, the sponsor of the resolution that culminated in the embargo's repeal in February 1809, dated his opposition to the continued pursuit of coercion at the failure of the summer diplomacy.[7] As early as December 18, 1807, two days after the administration decided on an embargo, Gallatin registered his strong protest against piling on it a coercive purpose and begged Jefferson never to allow coercion to become the controlling rationale of the embargo legislation.[8] Throughout the fifteen-month experiment the secretary of the treasury was both a constant critic and a dutiful enforcer. He doubted that the government could ever make the embargo watertight, or even that its perfect enforcement could unravel the British system of commercial restrictions. "The navy of Great Britain is hardly sufficient to prevent smuggling," he warned Jefferson in July 1808, "and you recollect," he further advised, "the army of employees and the sanguinary code of France [are] hardly adequate to guard their land frontiers [against smuggling]." The enterprising nature of the American people and the democratic bedrock of their governmental system warred against the scope of enforcement the measure required.[9] Archibald Stuart wrote much the same thing to Jefferson when he noted in December 1808 that the embargo "does not appear adapted either to the nature of our government or the genius and character of our people."[10]

Doubting whether the administration could support the embargo

---

1808, to Madison, Mar. 11, 1808, to Levi Lincoln, Mar. 23, 1808, to Charles Pinckney, Mar. 30, 1808, to John Strode, April 3, 1808, to Thomas Worthington, April 24, 1808, to William Lyman, April 30, 1808, to Thomas Paine, July 17, 1808, to William Pinkney, July 18, 1808, to William B. Bibb, July 27, 1808, ibid.

[6] Cook to Adams, Jan. 1, 1809, Adams Family Papers, MHS, reel 407.

[7] Nicholas to Joseph C. Cabell, Dec. 10, 23, 1808, Joseph C. Cabell Papers, UVa.

[8] Gallatin to TJ, Dec. 18, 1807, Gallatin Papers, NYU, reel 15.

[9] Gallatin to TJ, July 29, Sept. 30, 1808, Jefferson Papers, LC.

[10] Stuart to TJ, Dec. 23, 1808, ibid.

at home and if domestic support even mattered abroad, Gallatin also feared that the attempt to force compliance with the unpopular law would erode Republican strength and diminish the effectiveness of Congress and the resolve of the people in the face of unremitting foreign threats. "Government prohibitions do always more mischief than had been calculated," Gallatin had reminded Jefferson at the embargo's onset, "and it is not without much hesitation that a states-man should hazard to regulate the concerns of individuals as if he could do it better than themselves."[11] At a quieter time, Jefferson understood the sovereign power of public opinion and the special "genius and character" of the American people. When asked in the first year of his presidency why he was not moving energetically to implement the Republican platform, he responded that he would do things differently "were I free to do whatever I thought best. But when we reflect on the great machine of society, how impossible to advance the notions of a whole people suddenly to ideal right, we see the wisdom of Solon's remark, that no more good must be attempted than the nation can bear."[12]

Gallatin's great fear centered on Jefferson's disregard of Solon and the consequences of misplaced idealism. The most horrible mischief that Gallatin imagined was the likelihood that rigorous embargo en-forcement would leave Congress and the nation confused, divided, and "perplexed." As early as July 1808, Gallatin's worse fears were coming true. The whole tissue of commercial restraints—"orders in council, decrees, embargo"—he told Jefferson, was blurring in the popular mind into one monstrous assault on economic enterprise. Lacking "a single object which might rouse their patriotism and af-fections," helped along by "the criminal party rage" of the "federalists and tories," the people were fast viewing the embargo as of a piece with European restrictions and beginning to group Jefferson with Napoleon and George III as enemies of American commercial free-dom.[13] In the summer of 1808 Gallatin worried that the embargo might jeopardize both Madison's election and Congress's ability to respond to the foreign crisis in a way compatible with the national interest.

The summer of 1808, then, found the administration on the horns

[11] Gallatin to TJ, Dec. 18, 1807, Gallatin Papers, NYU, reel 15.
[12] TJ to Dr. Walter Jones, Mar. 31, 1801, Lipscomb and Bergh, 10:256.
[13] Gallatin to TJ, July 29, 1808, Jefferson Papers, LC.

of a terrible dilemma. Gallatin warned Jefferson that the embargo's slim chance to change British policy was being destroyed by domestic evasions; yet to render the embargo equal to the task of prohibiting foreign trade required types of legislation that would create different sets of problems in their own right. So it was that beginning in July, Gallatin tried to shake Jefferson's commitment to the embargo.

Based on the "experience of the summer," Gallatin wrote Jefferson on July 29, "congress must either invest the executive with the most arbitrary power and sufficient force to carry the embargo into effect, or give it up altogether." "And in the last case," Gallatin continued, "I see no alternative but war." Although the secretary of the treasury listed both embargo enforcement and war as two potential policies, he was clearly losing faith in the former and attempting to build a case with the president for the latter. He neither asked for nor endorsed further enforcement apparatus. He styled the policies necessary to enforce the embargo against a restive people as "odious and arbitrary" to impress on Jefferson just how dangerous and costly the embargo had become. Having done that, having, he thought, relegated the embargo to the past, he then told the president that the major issue confronting the nation in midsummer was "war" and "with whom." It had become the "duty of the executive to contemplate that result as probable, and to proceed accordingly." On August 6 Gallatin continued the argument he had begun a week earlier. He made no reference, as he had on July 29, to the need for arbitrary measures of enforcement, but spoke of the embargo as a dead policy. "Circumstance is the strongest argument that can be brought against the measure." The embargo was having an "inconsiderable effect" on Great Britain while it "threaten[ed] to destroy the Republican interest" at home. The government had tried to protect the nation's interests without war, but the attempt had failed. "The consciousness of having done what was right" justified the experiment, but it did not justify its suicidal continuation.[14]

Gallatin's summer plea had no effect on the president's understanding of the policy needs of the nation and the political needs of the Republican party. If anything, Gallatin's mention of the "criminal party rage" of the "federalists and tories" that was aiding the embargo's failure angered Jefferson and deepened his emotional com-

[14]Gallatin to TJ, July 29, Aug. 6, 1808, ibid.

mitment to the policy. Federalist opposition to the government and its laws was "open" and "rank," no better than treason, Jefferson thought. The embargo was both Republican law and national policy, and Congress, Jefferson replied, "must legalize all means which may be necessary to obtain its end."[15]

Although Jefferson wrote to Gallatin that he was "satisfied with you" that the legislature must legalize any and all means to secure the embargo, his hatred of Federalism blinded him to the purpose of Gallatin's appraisal. Gallatin had not requested oppressive enforcement measures. Although Jefferson maintained the ritual that he was only approving policy, he was, more accurately, making the decision to draw up the enforcement proposals. And his angry fixation on treasonous activity shows how, by mid-summer, Federalist plotting and Republican principles were challenging English power and foreign problems for control of the embargo's rationale and future. These new concerns held no meaning for Gallatin. Rejecting both Jefferson's symbolism and coercive embargo, he asked the president to consider war as probable, and to direct executive actions accordingly. No doubt his view was toward the next congressional session. His advice entailed preparing the nation militarily and psychologically for war, even though the universal American passion was for peace. Behind Gallatin's summer objections to the embargo were his fears that the Republican majority would either abandon the measure before it faced the stark truth that repeal implied war or humiliation or that it would consume itself in an inflexible adherence to the policy.[16]

The desire to avoid all unpleasantness—war, embargo, submission—was common currency in the nation's capital during the second session of the Tenth Congress, and Jefferson was not alone in raising procrastination and faith to policy and in clinging to the embargo because both war and submission were intolerable. But the president's posture was more important because it reinforced and even legitimated congressional fears of war until finally fears of a different sort overwhelmed the embargo policy late in the session. At the commencement of the second session, for example, Wilson Cary

[15] TJ to Gallatin, Aug. 11, 1808, ibid.
[16] Gallatin to TJ, Nov. 15, 1808, to Joseph Hopper Nicholson, Dec. 29, 1808, Gallatin Papers, NYU, reels 16, 18; Gallatin to Joseph Hopper Nicholson, Oct. 18, 1808, Joseph Hopper Nicholson Papers, LC.

Nicholas fully understood the folly of too long a pursuit of economic coercion, and yet he did not publicly condemn the policy, despite its failure abroad and its ruinous implications at home, until it was too late in the session to replace the embargo with anything but disguised capitulation to English power. In December 1808 he confided to Joseph Cabell, the brother of the governor of Virginia, that he had lost "all faith" in economic coercion, that his initial support for the embargo had rested on its sound defensive goals and its short-term diplomatic strategy, and that "no one has yet explained satisfactorily why an appeal to arms never came" after the summer diplomacy had failed. But Nicholas also pleaded with Cabell not to broadcast his opposition to the embargo. Although the Virginia congressman preferred war, his closeness to Jefferson channeled his opposition into private letters to Republican friends. "You will see the delicacy of my situation and will avoid committing me," he requested of Cabell.[17]

Nicholas's desire not to offend the president explained the contradiction between his policy instincts and his public posture and reflected both the tugs of personal friendship and the political needs of the increasingly besieged Republican majority. But misplaced loyalty to president and party only increased congressional polarization and ineffectiveness and eventually took a high cost in poorly developed public policy. Jefferson's quiet but persistent attachment to the embargo stilled the voices of loyal Republicans and thereby left the whole field of congressional criticism to the partisan enemies of the administration. When the Republicans recovered their voices at the end of the session, the harsh abuse that the Federalists were heaping on the embargo, on Jefferson, and, by implication, on the Republican party led congressional Republicans, in a fit of anger, to defend, support, and amend to the point of domestic oppression a measure in which they had largely ceased to believe. To compound the irony, three weeks later they partially in law and totally in fact repealed the embargo. The incompatibility between these two congressional actions did not go unnoticed by contemporary observers. "You set higher and there is no doubt but you must see further," Thomas Leiper of Pennsylvania wrote Jefferson on February 12, "but we who must judge from what we see cannot be reconciled to

---

[17] Nicholas to Cabell, Dec. 23, 1808, Joseph C. Cabell Papers, UVa.

the proceedings at Washington a month ago and those of the present day." Draconian enforcement measures followed so quickly by the embargo's repeal shrouded congressional actions in hazy mystery. "It is impossible in the nature of things [that] both can be right." [18] By "right," of course, Leiper meant logical. If the congressional about-face was not logical, it was very understandable when placed in the powerful contexts of emotion, politics, and fatigue. And because congressional Federalists opposed both the enforcement amendments and the repeal, the explanations of this curious behavior lay exclusively in the dynamics of the Republican party, especially in the relationship between the Republican president and the Republican congressional majority.

Gallatin read the congressional breezes more accurately than did Jefferson. Beginning in November, the treasury secretary was a steady critic of the president's refusal to confront the Republican legislators with harsh realities before the domestic storm broke and Congress retreated in the face of domestic dangers, real or imagined. Jefferson's leadership in the first two months of the session, then, was the single most important variable in the equation that ultimately determined the nation's response to the European crisis. And powerfully affecting Jefferson's policy and his congressional relations was his impending retirement.

"Away to Monticello"

"I am now so near the moment of retiring," Jefferson wrote James Monroe and many others toward the end of his presidency, "that I take no part in affairs beyond the expression of opinion. I think it fair that my successor should now originate those measures of which he will be charged with the execution and responsibility." [19] Thus Jefferson outlined a potential impediment to new policy directions. The foreign crisis did not adhere to the temporal compartmentalization of national elections. Basic to Republican belief was a generational separation of power. Neither generations nor presidential administrations had the right to bind the hands of their successors. Death was a

[18] Leiper to TJ, Feb. 12, 1809, Jefferson Papers, LC.

[19] TJ to Levi Lincoln, Nov. 13, 1808, to George Logan, Dec. 27, 1808, to Joel Barlow, Jan. 24, 1809, to Monroe, Jan. 29, 1809, ibid.

requirement of both human progress and political reform. Many years after his presidency, Jefferson wrote Abigail Adams that the only unforgivable act of her husband's public life was his midnight appointments to the national judiciary, offensive because they deprived the new administration of its right to staff the national judiciary with appointees who reflected the values of the political revolution of 1800.[20]

No doubt an honest belief that he should not compromise the independence of Madison's presidency helped make Jefferson, after November 1808, as much an observer as a participant in the creation of policy. Several factors, however, require additional explanation. That the personnel of Madison's administration would greatly resemble Jefferson's was common knowledge. Second, the transition from Jefferson to Madison bore no real resemblance to the change from Federalism to Republicanism in 1801. It was not a transition from one political party to another, with each defined by rigorous and antithetical policies and beliefs. Power and leadership were to remain within the social and political fraternity of Republican patriot-citizens. Beneath Jefferson's philosophical commitment to inaction was a division between himself, key cabinet members, and much of the congressional Republican majority on public policy. Jefferson wanted to continue the embargo until the European powers accepted American neutrality on American terms. Albert Gallatin, Robert Smith, and to a lesser extent, James Madison, recognized that the domestic scene no longer permitted such a course, and they wanted to honor the implications of the summer diplomatic defeat by complementing the embargo with other measures that approached war and that might, because of their clear message to the belligerents, avoid both war and domestic turmoil as the embargo alone clearly had not.[21] But the embargo had become Jefferson's quixotic weapon of peace, and he could not blend it into any strategy that contemplated violence. Only at its end, when it lay discredited by events, did the embargo express a naive and heroic pacifism.

[20] Peterson, *Thomas Jefferson and the New Nation*, p. 953.
[21] Gallatin to TJ, Nov. 15, 1808, Jefferson Papers, LC; undated memo, "other plans," Gallatin Papers, NYU, reel 18; undated memo, "Repeal of the embargo and commensing hostilities at a given time to be the object contemplated," Gallatin Papers, LC; Smith to TJ, Nov. 1, 1808, Jefferson Papers, LC; Brant, *James Madison, Secretary of State*, p. 469.

The imminence of his final withdrawal from public life trained Jefferson's thoughts on a host of episodes and values dating back to the American Revolution, the emotional touchstone of Jefferson's political and social ideology. He dwelt on the primacy of virtue and disinterestedness in all political transactions, on Federalist apostasy reaching back to the domestic toryism of the imperial crisis and extending into the Federalism of Hamilton and his cohorts, and on his own role in the founding and unfolding of the nation's republican experiment. He was still a public figure, but increasingly he saw his own future apart from the nation's, and in the pursuit of private tasks and hopes. These memories and desires bound his last public months to both the past and the future and generated Jefferson's absolute commitment to the embargo, his insistence on its total obedience or total enforcement, and his opposition to different policies that might bring war closer.

A persistent ambivalence tore at Jefferson all his adult life.[22] The turbulence of politics and the calm of domestic life each had a claim on his affections. In the fall of 1808 the ambivalence ended in Jefferson's gladness to be done, finally, with public affairs. His private correspondence charts in happy detail his irreversible withdrawal. Canceling newspaper subscriptions; instructing agents to ship wine and books to Monticello; refusing all pleas for financial support from civic groups centered in Washington; penning a steady stream of letters to family and friends about the education of children, the delights of private conversation, and the horrors of private debt: all these activities document Jefferson's concern with his private future and his longing "for the scenes of tranquility amidst my family and friends after which my soul is panting."[23]

[22] Fawn Brodie believes that his wife's death "altered the whole rhythm and direction of Jefferson's life" and largely ended the contrary tugs of domesticity and politics (*Thomas Jefferson, an Intimate History* [Boston, 1974], p. 172); Merrill Peterson thinks the ambivalence more lasting, entitling each of two large chapters of his biography "Withdrawal and Return" (*Thomas Jefferson and the New Nation*).

[23] For a sampling of the scores of letters that Jefferson wrote about "those scenes of rural retirement after which my soul is panting," see TJ to John Vaughan, June 22, 1808, to Thomas Appleton, July 28, 1808, to American Philosophical Society, Nov. 30, 1808, to Washington, D.C., Committee on Manufactures, Dec. 26, 1808, to Maria Beckley, Jan. 1, 1809, to Robert Livingston, Jan. 3, 1809, to Charles Willson Peale, Jan. 7, Feb. 6, 1809, to Thomas Mann Randolph, Jan. 17, 31, Feb. 28, 1809, to Abraham Venable, Jan. 23, 1809, to Joel Barlow, Jan. 24, 1809, to Monroe, Jan.

The nearness of retirement, because it unleashed such pleasant thoughts of private life, prohibited a realistic engagement with the grim implications of the past summer's diplomatic failure. So too, by turning Jefferson's thoughts to the purposes of the national founding, the aims of the Revolution, and to his own role in the creation and history of the Republic, did the final withdrawal preclude candid thought on America's future in a world at war. The goals of the founding were in Jefferson's mind enlightened goals. Much more than power and greatness, they were liberty, happiness, and growth. Indeed, Jefferson's own life and his intellectual and mundane interests were a constant celebration of multitudinous varieties of growth: of political freedom, knowledge, languages, mammals, flowers, and trees. In tedious delight he recorded the first and final flowerings of the vegetation surrounding his home.[24] His observation that the earth belongs to the living glorified and placed at the center of human and American purpose the higher claims of the living over the dead and proclaimed the inalienable right of living things to the full measure of their naturally allotted growth and improvement.[25] His stand on behalf of the living, an antitraditionalism that lay at the heart of his philosophical differences with Federalism,[26] made aversion to war an organic part of Jefferson's natural rights philosophy. By the end of his public run, this Revolutionary obligation to avoid war and honor the living became an obsession. This highly charged emotional pacifism represented a mighty departure from Jefferson's equally emotional belief of a year earlier in the need for, and the rightness of, a second war with Great Britain. Then a mushrooming growth of English mistreatments had involved him in the powerful dialectic of American nationalism and British oppression, in the memories of Lexington and Concord. Not only did the antagonism between English malevolence and American innocence frame Jefferson's thinking in 1807 and early 1808; it also seemed to hang the

---

28, 1809, to Col. Henry B. Livingston, Feb. 8, 1809, to Madame Palivae de Corny, Mar. 2, 1809, to Pierre Samuel Dupont de Nemours, Mar. 2, 1809, Jefferson Papers, LC; TJ to Craven Peyton, Jan. 24, 1809, TJ to James Wallace, Feb. 28, 1809, Jefferson Papers, UVa.

[24] See Edwin Morris Betts, ed., *Thomas Jefferson's Garden Book, 1766–1824, with Commentary and Relevant Extracts from Other Writings* (Philadelphia, 1944).

[25] Brodie, *Thomas Jefferson*, pp. 243–45.

[26] For a very sensitive elaboration of this theme, see Merrill D. Peterson, *Adams and Jefferson, a Revolutionary Dialogue* (Athens, Ga., 1976), pp. 62–93.

fulfillment of America's Revolutionary epic on a second war with the British enemy. But by the end of his presidency the romantic nationalism that had led Jefferson to contemplate violence and war became a force less powerful than the obligation to fulfill the nation's humanistic destiny. Honoring its experiment in peaceful nationhood was doubly important because of the exhilarating and oppressive fact that America was a unique human adventure, and yet an important event in the history of the world. To avoid war because "its evils are great in their endurance and leave a long reckoning for ages to come" had now become for Jefferson the heroic duty of a besieged nation that was simultaneously a special place and a universal country.[27]

Like Adams and Hamilton before him, Thomas Jefferson was concerned with fame and reputation.[28] In 1806 he began setting the groundwork for a Republican history of his administration. He hoped Joel Barlow would write it. In July, Jefferson scoured Monticello for available documents, "pack[ing] up large boxes containing between 70 and 80 volumes of newspapers, [and] pamphlets to be forwarded to [Washington]." He also promised Barlow that all his own "manuscript material" as well as "Mr. Madison's materials and all the offices will be opened to you." Jefferson wanted Barlow to begin immediately "while the papers are yet within our power." He hoped that the Republican historian would "put" the materials into "the most judicious form to convey useful information to the nation and posterity."[29]

The desire for a Republican history of his administration expressed the importance that Jefferson attached to the future's reckoning of his own place in the founding and unfolding of the nation's past. Greatly concerned with his departure, Jefferson wanted desperately that nothing should spoil the nation's view of his steady commitment to the public good and the disinterested and patriotic qualities that

[27] TJ to Young Republican Society of Pittsburgh, Pa., Dec. 2, 1808, Jefferson Papers, LC.

[28] See Douglass Adair and John A. Schutz, eds., *The Spur of Fame: Dialogues of John Adams and Benjamin Rush, 1805–1813* (San Marino, Calif., 1966); Trevor Colbourn, ed., *Fame and the Founding Fathers: Essays by Douglass Adair* (New York, 1974), esp. chap. 1, "Fame and the Founding Fathers," pp. 3–26; Gerald Stourzh, *Alexander Hamilton and the Idea of Republican Government* (Stanford, Calif., 1970), esp. chap. 3, "The Springs of Republican Government, Private Passions, Public Interest, and the Love of Fame," pp. 76–125.

[29] TJ to Barlow, July 9, 1806, Jefferson Papers, LC.

marked his participation in public life. A revealing correspondence between Jefferson and a private citizen from Rhode Island illustrates this concern with historical reputation. Samuel Hawkins had sent the president a small gift to thank him for his sacrifices and contributions. Jefferson felt obliged to return "the very elegant ivory staff of which," he wrote Hawkins, "you wished my acceptance." He refused because the traffic between public servants and private citizens in gifts "of sensible value, however innocently offered in the first examples may grow at length into abuse for which I wish not to furnish a precedent." But the prevention of future abuse was not as important in the context of approaching retirement as was Jefferson's fervent desire to know, for himself, that to the end he did not abuse his office in the smallest way for private gain. Jefferson was finishing a public odyssey; of this he was fully conscious. Toward the end, things of small consequence became important in Jefferson's comprehension of his own place in the nation's history. He returned the staff, he told his Rhode Island admirer, "to retain the consciousness of a disinterested administration of the public trusts which is essential to perfect tranquility of [my] mind."[30] Similarly, Jefferson wrote with pride that he was leaving nearly a half century of public service poorer in the world's goods than when he entered upon it. And in his last annual message he asked Congress and the American people to weigh his place in their affections and their history not only against his accomplishments but against his intentions and character. "In the transaction of their business," he wrote, "I cannot have escaped error. It is incident to our imperfect nature. But I may say with truth [that] my errors have been of the understanding, not of intention, and that the advancement of their rights and interests has been the constant motive for every measure."[31] When Jefferson asked the nation to judge his career with a kind look to his intentions, he revealed his deep urges to be done with public life four months before the final retirement. The rest of the message revealed his mood and concerns on the eve of his last Congress. It clung to the embargo for the same reason that Jefferson returned the ivory cane. Both actions were rooted in the Revolutionary republican imperatives of peace, virtue, and productive enterprise. The president could not in his final public

[30] TJ to Hawkins, Nov. 30, 1808, ibid.
[31] TJ, "Annual Message to Senate and House of Representatives of the United States," Nov. 8, 1808, ibid.

words set in motion a train of events that might collapse the nation into war.

Jefferson's last annual message detailed the summer failure to force the repeal of the French and British commercial restrictions. France had not officially rejected the American offer, but it had not, he told the congressmen, given "any indication that the requisite change in her decrees is contemplated." And by Great Britain, he went on, "the arrangement . . . has been explicitly rejected." Summing up past failure, the president offered no new policy for the future. He merely informed Congress that France's and England's rejections had left the embargo in full force. He then catalogued the positive benefits the embargo had produced. Aside from its healthy effect on the American economy, it had demonstrated "the patriotism of our fellow citizens" and "the moderation and fairness which govern our councils," it had educated the republican citizenry in "the necessity of uniting in support of the laws and rights of their country," it had saved "our mariners and our vast mercantile property," it had purchased time "for prosecuting the defensive and provisional measures called for by the occasion," it had saved national honor, and it had avoided war.

The embargo's compendium of good works broke down into four broad categories: the nation's economy, the moral qualities of America's leadership and its people, the defensive goals outlined in the December 1807 message, and peace. But missing in Jefferson's summation of the purposes and accomplishments of the embargo was any claim that it had become a weapon of commercial warfare or that economic retaliation, if persisted in, held a reasonable chance for success. Pinkney had sent from London optimistic predictions on the impact of the embargo on Great Britain. It had hurt the English manufacturing interest. England's lucky fortune in Spain could not indefinitely accommodate the loss of the American market and American resources. English food shortages were great, the price of cotton was rising, the discontent of the laboring classes growing, and political opposition to the government's American policy mounting.[32] None of this information found its way into Jefferson's last annual message. Although it asked for the embargo's continuation, it

---

[32] Pinkney to Madison, Sept. 6, 7, 13, 21, 1808, Dispatches, Great Britain, Pinkney, vol. 16, NA. Pinkney's dispatches had arrived in Washington before the last annual message (Madison to Pinkney, Nov. 9, 1808, Madison Papers, LC, ser. 2, reel 25).

did not build a case in the necessity, the pain, and the utility of economic coercion. Nor did Jefferson point out that though the condition of the world imposed a large measure of suffering on the American people, compared to war, as John Quincy Adams observed, the embargo was "no more than the bite of a flea to the bite of a rattlesnake."[33] On one level, the level that his advisers most responded to, Jefferson's last message merely asserted the continuation of stagnation and courted political and economic disaster. Indeed, the president seemingly offered the nation only a choice between two bleak alternatives: national humiliation or an indefinite hiatus in commercial activity. Giving preference to neither policy, Jefferson maintained that "it will rest with the wisdom of congress to decide on the course best adopted to such a state of things." John Quincy Adams called the message "gloomy." Albert Gallatin thought it bordered on "complaint" and "despondency."[34] With regard to policy and present predicaments, these critics were on the mark. But on another level, on the level of Jefferson's republican concerns, they were wide of the truth. His final message was positive and sharply directed: it was a celebration of economic redemption, of the Revolution of 1800, and of the embargo's vital connections to these republican enterprises. Only these matters, not foreign policy or economic coercion, can explain Jefferson's encounter, in his last several months in office, with the embargo, its violations, and its enforcement.

Although these matters would shape Jefferson's thinking about the embargo after November 1808, they did not answer the needs of policy or qualify his untimely abdication to the congressional Republican majority. It was the likely consequences of this abdication that Albert Gallatin most feared. Difficult decisions awaited the nation. The American people and their legislators wanted what an intractable world simply would not yield: an answer to foreign oppression that entailed neither war nor painful economic suffering. Without the prod of executive leadership, Gallatin feared, Congress, loathing both war and embargo enforcement, would disguise a submission to the Old World with a watered-down coercive policy that would only dot the oceans with American ships. In the transaction, of course, the

---

[33] Adams to Orchard Cook, Aug. [?], 1808, Adams Family Papers, MHS, reel 135.

[34] Adams to William Branch Giles, Nov. 15, 1808, ibid.; Gallatin to TJ, Nov. 3, 1808, Jefferson Papers, LC.

nation would forfeit the good works the embargo had performed at so high a domestic cost.

The nation's past and its expectations complicated its present predicament. "We have been too happy and too prosperous," Gallatin confessed to his wife in June 1808, "and we consider as great misfortunes some privations and a share in the general calumnies of the world. Compared with other nations, our share is indeed very small." But weighed in the scales against the nation's dreams, the share was too large. "Americans," John Quincy Adams brooded, "have grown fat on prosperity." To Wilson Cary Nicholas, "our people, at this moment, exhibit a rare spectacle to the world. We are insulted and abused by England and France, [and] are our own people indignant at it? One portion of them are ready to crucify their rulers for not submitting to it, and another are pursuing after the lucrative trade." Republicans north and south sensed their regions opposed both war and embargo. Senator Samuel Mitchill from New York was "sadly afraid that our nation will prefer a licensed and huckstering trade to a valiant support of its rights by war, or a resolute retirement from the reach of the belligerents." The American people, thought Archibald Stuart of Virginia, were "avaricious, enterprising, and impatient of restraint." They will, he assured Jefferson in December 1808, "compel the govt. to depart from the prudent measures" it had adopted.[35]

The president's last annual message disappointed the heads of state, treasury, and navy. Robert Smith found it too meek in the wake of recent foreign intelligence. Nor should the nation merely continue the embargo. That policy, "a mischief-making busybody" that would soon spawn domestic "monsters," Smith had been anxious to "call in" since August. Now he was the cabinet's loudest advocate for sterner measures. "The honorable and manly feelings of the American people will require that we advance a few steps," he advised Jefferson on November 1. He suggested the immediate recall of Armstrong and Pinkney from Paris and London, a congressional nonintercourse act against both the belligerents, the repeal of the embargo, and the

---

[35] Albert Gallatin to Hanna Gallatin, July 30, 1808, Gallatin Papers, NYU, reel 17; Adams to Orchard Cook, Nov. 25, 1808, Adams Family Papers, MHS, reel 135; Nicholas to TJ, Dec. 22, 1808, Wilson Cary Nicholas Papers, LC; Mitchill to John Quincy Adams, Jan. 30, 1809, Adams Family Papers, MHS, reel 407; Stuart to TJ, Dec. 23, 1808, Jefferson Papers, LC.

legal authorization "of all the necessary arrangements preparatory to war."[36]

Although more wedded to the coercive purposes of the embargo than any other cabinet member, James Madison now thought "a spirit of independence and indignation" must "reinforce the past measures." At the least, Congress should complement the embargo with total nonintercourse against the belligerents to "give a severity to the contest of privations." He welcomed the November 22 House resolution that called for increased military spending because he thought the last chance to avert war was, paradoxically, to move toward it. In his autumn dealings with England's minister to the United States, Madison tried to convey both a desire to settle differences amicably and a willingness to embrace war if necessary.[37]

At the beginning of the congressional session, Jefferson and his cabinet both saw policy narrowed to embargo or war. "All further retreat [is] impracticable," the president wrote Levi Lincoln on November 13.[38] But Jefferson seemed not to realize that the whole future of policy rested on a critical mass of congressional and popular opinion that might at any time reject both embargo and military solutions. Not as sensitive to the popular mood and the escapist tendencies of Congress as was Gallatin, Jefferson still held to a basic policy of procrastination. He recognized that "there will be some division . . . among the republicans" on tactics and strategy, but he innocently believed that all Republican differences lay within the realm of "honest" alternatives, thereby ensuring the continuation of honorable policy.[39] With his view toward the future anchored firmly to congressional Republicanism, nothing warred against postponing the final decision to a summer session. In the interim, the nation could make "another effort" at settlement; in short, at replaying the past summer's diplomacy.[40]

[36] Smith to Gallatin, Aug. 1, 1808, Gallatin Papers, NYU, reel 17; Smith to TJ, Nov. 1, 1808, Jefferson Papers, LC.

[37] Brant, *James Madison, Secretary of State*, p. 469; Madison to Pinkney, Nov. 9, 1808, Diplomatic Instructions, All Countries, vol. 7, NA; Madison to Pinkney, Dec. 5, 1808, Jan. 3, 1809, Madison Papers, LC, ser. 2, reel 25.

[38] TJ to Lincoln, Nov. 13, 1808, Jefferson Papers, LC.

[39] TJ to Charles Pickney, Nov. 8, 1808, to Levi Lincoln, Nov. 13, 1808, ibid.

[40] TJ to Thomas Mann Randolph, Nov. 22, 1808, to Dr. George Logan, Dec. 27, 1808, ibid.

Gallatin was the major critic of Jefferson's escapism. He thought the recent message lacked what Jefferson's 1807 draft had contained in dangerous abundance: strong executive leadership. But the events of 1808 had changed the whole mix of foreign and domestic facts. Both Great Britain and France had added wholesale commercial assaults to the old problems of the *Chesapeake* and impressments. The embargo had struck more at domestic unity than at foreign oppression. The nation was mired "in the languor and indecision incident to free and commercial governments."[41] The "great confusion and perplexity that reigns in Congress" was troubling; combined with executive drift, it became dangerous. On November 15 Gallatin warned that "the temper of the legislature" required immediate executive attention. He spoke on Madison's behalf as well. They strongly suggested another cabinet meeting to discuss the relationship between executive power and the future of congressional policy. The matter was urgent. "The sooner" another cabinet meeting, Gallatin pleaded, "the better."[42]

Needed was a clear and public statement of presidential policy. Although the annual message had supported the embargo's continuation until the removal of the British orders and French decrees, it did not state that the embargo was Jefferson's desired policy, that it aimed at defeating foreign oppression in a commercial war, that it would be costly, and that, because it was preferable to war, it would be enforced with energy by Congress and the executive. Although by November Gallatin questioned whether the embargo could succeed abroad and whether the American people would support it long enough to give it a fair test, the propriety of war or embargo was not at issue so much as the vigor of Jefferson's commitment to any policy and the probable impact Jefferson's indecision would have on a Congress longing to escape all unpleasantness.[43] "We must (or rather you must)," Gallatin implored, "decide the question absolutely so that we may point out a decisive course either way to our friends."[44]

[41] Samuel Mitchill to John Quincy Adams, Jan. 30, 1809, Adams Family Papers, MHS, reel 407.

[42] Gallatin to Joseph Hopper Nicholson, Dec. 29, 1808, Gallatin Papers, NYU, reel 18; Gallatin to TJ, Nov. 15, 1808, Jefferson Papers, LC.

[43] Samuel Smith to William Eustis, Dec. 4, 1808, William Eustis Papers, LC; Nathaniel Macon to Joseph Hopper Nicholson, Dec. 4, 1808, Joseph Hopper Nicholson Papers, LC.

[44] Gallatin to TJ, Nov. 15, 1808, Jefferson Papers, LC.

Jefferson did not convene another cabinet meeting. It soon became public knowledge that "the president," as Nathaniel Macon of North Carolina put it, "gives no opinion as to the measures that ought to be adopted."[45] Jefferson's decision to stay on the sidelines greatly weakened executive control over congressional deliberations and made the stormy legislature the center of policy making. This triumph of Jeffersonian political theory insufficiently compensated for the loss of coherent and realistic policy. As best he could, however, Gallatin used his political friendships and his official duties to shape the efforts of the Republican majority in the national legislature.

[45] Macon to Joseph Hopper Nicholson, Dec. 4, 1808, Joseph Hopper Nicholson Papers, LC.

6

THIS "MISCHIEF-MAKING BUSYBODY"
The Embargo and the American People

Gallatin, Jefferson, and the Embargo Laws

Soon after Jefferson had sent his annual message to Congress, the chairman of the Senate Foreign Relations Committee asked the secretary of the treasury to devise methods to increase the effectiveness of the embargo and to diminish its harsh impact on the American people. William Branch Giles's naive request deepened Gallatin's concern with congressional "confusion" and "perplexity." He knew that even to maintain existing levels of enforcement promised more hardships for the American economy. Rather than contrive additional methods of enforcing the unpopular law, he preferred to let the public's knowledge that war was imminent, that the embargo was reaching the end of its run, and that its only remaining purpose was the preservation of the defensive accomplishments of the past year provide a fund of good will for the existing enforcement apparatus. The day after he received Giles's request, he begged Jefferson for another cabinet meeting. He also postponed responding to the Senate inquiry. But when the president ignored Gallatin's plea for new policy discussions (Jefferson replied to his November 15 letter with a question about the sale of federal lands in the nation's capital), the secretary of the treasury reluctantly sent the Senate committee a comprehensive report that formed the basis of the final embargo law, "the fatal act" as the customs collector from Providence, Rhode Island, called it.[1]

---

[1] Giles to Gallatin, Nov. 14, 1808, Gallatin to Giles, Nov. 24, 1808, Gallatin Papers, NY, reel 18; Gallatin to TJ, Nov. 15, 17, 1808, TJ to Gallatin, Nov. 16, 17, 1808, Jefferson Papers, LC; Jeremiah Olney to Gallatin, Jan. 25, 1809, Providence, Correspondence of the Secretary of the Treasury with Collectors of Customs, 1789–1833, RG 56, M178, NA, reel 28.

Gallatin's authorship of the draconian enforcement law of January 1809 presents an irony. He did everything in his power to dissuade Congress from embarking on the legislation that his report outlined. His methods, he warned, could not withstand a Republican interpretation of the Constitution. Their only defense was Hamiltonian principle, the right of the government to force compliance with unpopular law.[2] Contemporary Republican jurists reached the same conclusion. The end justified the means, Spencer Roane of Virginia argued, even if the means appeared unconstitutional when set against the criterion of "reasonable" congressional powers in "ordinary" times.[3] Roane's logic even surpassed Hamilton's defense of implied powers because he reposed in Congress the power to establish which criteria, normal or abnormal, shaped its legal authority. Although constitutional propriety troubled Gallatin, it was not his chief worry or his major argument against his own proposals. They would cripple legal maritime activity, destroy the embargo's remaining support, ensure its untimely repeal, forfeit its sound defensive accomplishments, and bring on war with the nation again vulnerable to military and commercial havoc.

Gallatin's enforcement proposals derived from the experience of the past year and his reading of the future. They were not his alone. Suggestions from Jefferson, other cabinet members, and the collectors in the field made them an administration project.[4] But they reflected more Gallatin's approach than Jefferson's. Throughout 1808 the president's favorite remedy for embargo violations was

[2] Gallatin to Giles, Nov. 24, 1808, Gallatin Papers, NYU, reel 18; Gallatin to Madison, Sept. 9, 1808, Madison Papers, LC, ser. 2, reel 25.

[3] Roane to Wilson Cary Nicholas, Jan. 5, 1809, Wilson Cary Nicholas Papers, LC.

[4] The collectors in the field were very knowledgeable in the ways of merchant ingenuity. They immediately brought to Gallatin's attention the use of fraudulent proofs and the dangerous practice of exchanging licenses for foreign registers. They were also quick to point out the greatest dangers to the embargo—violations of the coasting trade and sailing without clearance. See Charles Simms to Gallatin, Jan. 5, Jan. 9, Feb. 29, Mar. 30, 1808, Alexandria, RG 56, M178, NA, reel 1; Gabriel Christie to Gallatin, Dec. 24, 1807, Feb. 11, 1808, John Brice to Gallatin, Jan. 2, 12, Feb. 11, 14, 1808, McCulloch to Gallatin, April 23, 1808, Baltimore, ibid., reel 3; John Shore to Gallatin, Jan. 11, Feb. 22, 1808, Petersburg, ibid., reel 19; John Shee to Gallatin, Dec. 28, 29, 31, 1807, Jan. 13, April 15, 1808, Philadelphia, ibid., reel 22.

naval or military power.[5] Gallatin's new proposals banked more on preventing economic activity at the customshouses than on capturing clandestine ships on the rivers, bays, and oceans. Although the final embargo law reflected this approach, Jefferson was not a silent partner in the venture. Particular measures that Gallatin found unimportant, Jefferson thought vital, and these found their way into the final legislation. Throughout the past year, Jefferson had read most of Gallatin's rulings before their promulgation, had advised on the many collectors' referrals concerning the detention of suspicious vessels, and had sometimes vetoed Gallatin's suggestions. When confronted with evidence of mounting evasions, he reacted angrily, assuming the persona of a man betrayed. Then he would command the process of enforcement; but when the anger ebbed, so too did Jefferson's involvement.

The president reacted more emotionally and violently to evasions of the law. He blamed the embargo's travail on merchant sharpsters and Federalist politicians, "parracides" he called them, who were no better than "unprincipled adventurers."[6] His encounter with national character was more hopeful, more romantic, and more naive than was Gallatin's. Expecting more from the American people, he was more easily disappointed and outraged. But Gallatin never forgot the value a dollar had to Americans. He knew that the nation's love for the main chance piled massive obstacles in the path of both embargo enforcement and war preparation. In 1807 popular love of money had forced him to manipulate the securities market to cheapen the price of government loans. Economic aspiration was the dominant strain in the national chorus, Gallatin believed, and statesmen who disregarded this sovereign fact in the formulation of policy threatened the harmony of public life.[7]

[5] The following passage is typical of countless letters that Jefferson wrote Gallatin in both tone and solution: "I hope you will spare no pains or expense to bring the rascals of Passamaquoddy to justice, and if more force be necessary, agree on the subject with General Dearborn or Mr. Smith as to any aid they can spare and let it go without waiting to consult me" (May 20, 1808, Jefferson Papers, LC). See also TJ to Gallatin, Dec. 24, 1807, Gallatin Papers, NYU, reel 15; TJ to Gallatin, April 19, May 20, 27, July 12, 1808, to Robert Smith, Feb. 14, July 16, 1808, to Dearborn, Aug. 1, 1808, Jefferson Papers, LC.

[6] TJ to Governors of Orleans, Georgia, South Carolina, Massachusetts, and New Hampshire, May 6, 1808, to Dearborn, Aug. 1, 1808, to Thomas Lehre, Nov. 8, 1808, Jefferson Papers, LC.

[7] Gallatin to TJ, Dec. 18, 1807, Gallatin Papers, NYU, reel 15.

But Jefferson refused to believe that "the darling Self-Advantage" had seduced his countrymen. Denying that his virtuous Americans were New World entrepreneurs and unable to accept the truth of Senator Samuel Mitchill's observation that "Montesquieu would have been more correct if he had made *jealousy* and not virtue the principle of a republic," the president protected his image of the nation by heaping on the shoulders of avaricious merchants and vindictive Federalists—generally the same people—the sins of the country. Refusing to believe that more than a small percentage of the American people—"the ill tempered and rascally part of our country"— would oppose the embargo if left to their own instincts, Jefferson was forced by his hopes for the character of the nation to repose in that small minority awesome powers. The greedy and the partisan, navigating from loophole to loophole and sowing tares among the patriotic and obedient, were destroying the whole embargo system, and the fabric of republican law as well. With sophistry and the lawyer mentality, the enemies of the embargo turned the law inside out and against itself. Their actions weakened the embargo's impact, and their scandalous behavior forced the patriot to suffer while he observed the corrupt prosper. The whole seamy business confused and angered the obedient citizen and turned his anger against the law. Those who defeated the embargo with blatant illegality— smuggling in the dead of night—did not pose threats as grave as did those who used the law to beat the law. They imperiled not only the embargo but the legal foundations of the Republic.[8] The reforms on which Jefferson personally insisted in the final embargo bill were not the most essential to its success. But they best revealed his temper and concerns. His demands disallowed broad categories of evidence that could be used in a courtroom to avoid conviction and absolutely halted the fraudulent use of legal permission to evade the embargo that had plagued the policy since its inception.

Although the administration had always worked toward a fair and equitable operation of the embargo laws at home, this goal normally meant the equalization of hardship, not its mitigation.[9] Congress

[8] Samuel Harrison to TJ, May 28, 1808, Jefferson Papers, LC; Mitchill to John Quincy Adams, Jan. 30, 1809, Adams Family Papers, MHS, reel 407; TJ to Madison, Aug. 5, 1808, Madison Papers, LC, reel 10.

[9] To an acquaintance who complained of embargo-caused suffering, Jefferson wrote: "However gratifying it might be to our private feelings to indulge these dispensations in particular cases, yet for the mass of society, the doctrine of an equal

more often tried to have its cake and eat it too; tried to make the embargo oppressive on Europe and yet gentle on the American people. Giles's November request culminated this congressional innocence that had its origins in the embargo reforms of the previous spring.[10] At that time Congress bowed to merchant pressure and created a category of legal sailings that jeopardized the embargo, overwhelmed the administration in bureaucratic paper, and offended President Jefferson.[11]

The American mercantile community worried about the future of its money and property in foreign lands and thought that the embargo should not inhibit its right to retrieve them. Within days of the embargo's December 1807 passage, applications for special permission to sail for this purpose were already pouring in on Treasury. The applicants based their demands on a part of the December 22 law that gave the president the right to "exempt" from the congressional prohibition "vessels under the immediate direction of the President of the United States." The merchants imaginatively reasoned that since the embargo placed all American vessels under the ostensible direction of the president, he could exempt those he chose. Jefferson thought otherwise. The process of sorting the legitimate requests from the fraudulent intentions would confound the administration and threaten the embargo; "so extensive a power of dispensation" risked such "great abuse" that it could not have been Congress's intent. Jefferson tried to squash the whole problem by instructing Gallatin to put in the newspapers a clarification that limited executive discretion to only those private vessels necessary to carry on the government's public business. Any wider interpretation, he wrote Gallatin, "will overwhelm us with applications." But still they came. Although he was aware of the sizable merchant stake in foreign-based property, Jefferson was loath to risk the embargo because of this particular economic interest.[12]

---

measure to all is of unquestionable value and I am sure will be approved by your good understanding and disinterested justice" (TJ to Mrs. Catherine Cruger, Dec. 15, 1808, Jefferson Papers, LC).

[10] William Branch Giles to Gallatin, Nov. 14, 1808, Gallatin Papers, NYU, reel 18.

[11] The permissions clause was part of the Mar. 12, 1808, law.

[12] Gallatin to TJ, Jan. 1, 1808, TJ to Gallatin, Feb. 10, Jan. 7, 14, 1808, Jefferson Papers, LC.

Congress finally wilted and on March 12 passed what Jefferson called "an invidious clause" that gave the merchants the right to retrieve their property with executive permission.[13] He tried to undo the damage by bending language to desire. Did the law, he asked Gallatin, obligate the president to grant permission to sail upon the presentation of suitable proof that the foreign property existed, or did Congress allow the president discretion in the matter? The March 12 law stated that "the president of the United States be, and is hereby authorized, if he shall be satisfied by a statement of accounts current, on oath or affirmation, of any citizen of the United States, and such other proof as the nature of the case shall admit or the President may require . . . to grant permissions." Discretion or obligation seemed to hang on the meaning of the phrase "is authorized." Did it mean *may*, or did it mean *shall*? Jefferson argued that the phrase clearly meant *may*. "With respect to the construction of the act," he wrote Gallatin on March 17, "there are cases in the books where the word 'may' has been adjudged equivalent to 'shall,' but the term 'is authorized' unless followed by 'and required' was I think never so considered. On the contrary, I believe it is the very term which Congress always uses toward the executive when they mean to give a power to him, and leave him the use of it at his discretion." [14]

Jefferson used constitutional and linguistic weapons to fight a law he thought wrong in principle and dangerous in practice. The merchants would get their lawyers and their fabricated proofs. The certain abuses of the permissions clause would demonstrate to the country that the law was small barrier to the crafty and quick-witted. A "construction" of obligation, he feared, "puts it in the power of the individual to defeat the embargo in a great measure." A construction of discretion allowed the administration "to combine a due regard to the object of the law with the interest of individuals." Gallatin advised that the vague wording created "an imperative" on the executive to grant the permissions.[15] The president acquiesced, and the administration shouldered the task of judging every request against the requirements of proof and the hazy question of intent.

The March 12 law created one of the most vexing, frustrating, and

[13] TJ to William Cabell, Mar. 12, 1808, ibid.
[14] TJ to Gallatin, Mar. 17, 1808, ibid.
[15] Gallatin to TJ, Mar. 16, 1808, ibid.

time-consuming chores of the whole experiment in embargo enforcement. Gallatin and Jefferson pondered countless requests for permission to sail.[16] So personally oppressive was the task that Jefferson imposed an August 1 deadline on the law after he noted Congress's failure to mandate it for the life of the embargo. The time limit did not end the annoyance. After August 1, merchants still wrote letters, and when the answers from Treasury displeased them, they called on Jefferson. He found "these personal solicitations very embarrassing." Characteristically, he was unable to say no directly and usually promised further consideration and another "written answer." In December 1808 he asked Gallatin to include "in your amendments to the law . . . a repeal of the power to give permissions to go for property." By then, the importance of this ban paled before the stern medicine that the embargo required.[17] It escaped Gallatin's attention, but Jefferson had also asked John Wayles Eppes to make the proposal from the floor of the Congress. The last embargo law repealed the section of the March 12 legislation that had created the whole problem.

Although the special permissions annoyed Jefferson, the high incidence of judicial acquittal for embargo crimes angered and exasperated him. Since its inception, the embargo had spawned a teeming traffic in bogus proofs. "Fabrications of proof," Jefferson noted bitterly, "are a regular part of the systems of infractions of the embargo." Forged "oaths" attesting to "leaky ships," bad weather, accident at sea, distress, and capture were "a regular merchandise in every port" and, worse still, the legal bases of countless acquittals in courts of law. "We must therefore consider them nothing," he instructed Gallatin, and legislate "that the act of entering a foreign port and selling the cargo is decisive evidence of an intentional breach of the embargo." This "rule will not lead us wrong once in a hundred times."[18] Gallatin's final recommendations incorporated Jefferson's suggestions and his anger. The president wanted to go even further by attaching the denial of requests for legal coasting voyages to vague and punitive indices of illegal intention. He wished to refuse permission for these voyages, the only maritime activity allowed to Ameri-

[16] In three letters that Gallatin wrote Jefferson between April 14 and June 29, 1808, he included 149 separate requests for permission to retrieve foreign property.

[17] TJ to Gallatin, Aug. 15, Oct. 19, Dec. 7, 22, 1808, Jefferson Papers, LC.

[18] TJ to Gallatin, Dec. 7, 22, 1808, ibid.

cans by the embargo, if a prior violation could be traced to anyone involved in either the ownership or operation of the vessel. The stigmatizing act need only be asserted by a customs agent; unnecessary, in Jefferson's scheme, was "the formality of its being found by a jury." Citizens who lived in places which were stamped "by a general disobedience to the laws" were themselves guilty until proved innocent. These inhabitants of "tainted towns" had to produce "positive proof" that they "had never said or done anything . . . to countenance the spirit of" illegality. If the collector had already refused individual permission because of municipal reputation, then, according to Jefferson's plan, "the first cause of refusal was sufficient" and "an enquiry into [personal] character and conduct [was] unnecessary."[19]

Because of his views on the American people, New England, merchants, and Federalism, Jefferson dwelt on particular kinds of evasions and neither confronted the breadth of opposition to the law nor fashioned a comprehensive plan to effect its enforcement. This work was left to Gallatin. His goals were three: to sanitize the coasting trade, to prevent outright smuggling by ships licensed for the foreign trade, and to ensure the cooperation of the customs collectors by protecting them from private suits and state legal and judicial interference and intimidation.

The Coasting Trade and the Caribbean

Although not the major worry of the administration, the abuse of the legal coasting trade was a running sore throughout the life of the embargo. The December 22, 1807, law complicated the problem because it placed no restraints on the coasting trade. As a result, shipmasters who had registered their vessels for the foreign trade flocked to the customs officers to exchange foreign registers for coasting licenses.[20] The implications of this merchant trick were devastating. Conceivably, the entire American merchant marine could

[19] TJ to Gallatin, Nov. 13, 1808, ibid.

[20] Gabriel Christie to Gallatin, Dec. 24, 1807, John Brice to Gallatin, Dec. 28, 1807, Baltimore, RG 56, M178, NA, reel 3; John Shee to Gallatin, Dec. 28, 29, 31, 1807, Philadelphia, ibid., reel 22; Gallatin to Gabriel Christie, Dec. 25, 1807, Baltimore, Gallatin Papers, NYU, reel 15; Caesar Rodney to Madison, Jan. 7, 1808, Madison Papers, LC, reel 10.

license itself for the coasting trade and render the embargo on foreign-bound ships a dead letter. On December 25 Gallatin warned the customs collectors who had complained of the practice to use caution in exchanging registers for licenses and to refer all doubtful cases to the Treasury Department. A week later, he prohibited the exchange outright and ordered his men to detain suspicious vessels "ostensibly bound coastwise." [21]

Gallatin's December 31 circular launched the administration on the difficult task of distinguishing between honest and fraudulent coasting voyages. It was a hopeless task. Initially the treasury chief thought detention a temporary protection until Congress penalized coasting violations. This Congress did on January 9 when it required all coasting vessels to post bond equal to twice the value of ship and cargo and specified that violations forfeited the bond and carried both a fine up to $20,000 for each offense and the future loss of credit privileges on import duties. [22]

Gallatin hoped the January 9 embargo law superseded the December 31 circular with its stress on detention. [23] Had the congressional law intimidated the merchant community, the administration would have been spared one of its largest headaches. Such was not the case. The high price of American produce in the Caribbean in early 1808 transformed the penalties to mere operating expenses for American entrepreneurs. [24] They also banked on pleas of bad weather and accidents at sea to exonerate them before sympathetic juries. Often the clandestine traffic eluded detection. Americans transferred cargoes to British vessels waiting at sea and then continued to American ports with no one the wiser. [25] The administra-

[21] Gallatin to TJ, Dec. 31, 1807, Jefferson Papers, LC; Gallatin to David Gelston, New York, to Gabriel Christie, Baltimore, Dec. 25, 1807, Gallatin, Treasury Department Circular, Dec. 31, 1807, Gallatin Papers, NYU, reel 15; Gallatin to Christie, Dec. 28, 1807, Baltimore, RG 59, M178, reel 3.

[22] Public Acts of the Congress, Jan. 9, 1808, *Annals*, 10th Cong., 1st sess., pp. 2815–17; Gallatin, Treasury Department Circular, Jan. 9, 1808, Gallatin Papers, NYU, reel 15.

[23] Gallatin to David Gelston, New York, to Charles Simms, Alexandria, Jan. 11, 1808, Gallatin Papers, NYU, reel 15.

[24] Rodney to TJ, April 22, 1808, Jefferson Papers, LC.

[25] Isaac Ogden to William Duane, Feb. 18, 1808, Madison Papers, LC, reel 10; Joseph Warner Rose to Madison, Jan. 29, 1808, Antigua, T. Tufts to Madison, April 25, 1808, Surinam, Dispatches from Consular Officers, MS, NA. To the ad-

tion soon fell back on the detention of suspicious cargoes. The difficulties were legion, and the customs collectors' understandable hesitation to exercise the power on what was vague legal authority compounded the problem.

According to law, customs collectors were liable to private suits for their public conduct, and the general language of the December embargo law did not afford them adequate protection against civil proceedings. When the administration rediscovered the importance of detention, it sought their legal protection. But the April 1808 law created as many problems as it solved. According to its terms, the executive branch could only suggest nonbinding criteria for detention. The collectors were free to make the final decisions, and they varied from place to place in rhythm with the diligence and courage of the collector, his political persuasion, and the extent of popular opposition to the embargo laws. Potentially workable, the system was often ineffectual and inequitable. And as the embargo wore on, as popular opposition increased and foreign prices rose, the collectors often ignored the Treasury suggestions and responded more directly, as the commissioners of the stamps had done a generation before, to their local situation. Finally, the congressional authorization doubled the bureaucratic load because the administration had to check all the detentions to ensure that the collectors were being both vigorous and fair.[26]

Gallatin was never really pleased with the system the administration had patched together in the first half of 1808 to police the coasting trade, but it worked tolerably well. "We begin with the help of my last circular to do better with the embargo," he wrote Jefferson on May 28, but the system would never be adequate, he warned, "unless an absolute and general rule be given to the collectors." The summer had witnessed impressive success against illegal coasting voyages. "No evasions can now take place worthy of notice under colour of the coasting trade," Gallatin boasted on August 6. Yet the very success of the summer's efforts had raised the prices of American

---

ministration's dismay, much of this trade was in "masts and ship timber" for the Royal Navy. England received more of these vital materials from the United States, the embargo notwithstanding, than from Canada (Gallatin to TJ, Feb. 13, 1808, Jefferson Papers, LC).

[26] Gallatin to TJ, May 5, 28, 1808, TJ to Gallatin, July 12, 1808, Jefferson Papers, LC.

produce in the Caribbean to levels that ensured future violations unless the administration embraced measures whose severity would imperil all legal maritime activity. To make matters worse, the winter and spring difficulties that preceded the summer success combined with the particular shape of the embargo's impact on the Caribbean economy to reduce the coercive impact of the embargo's hard-won summer gains. Because of the islands' proximity to American ports, the coasting problem blended into the larger danger of illegal American-Caribbean trade.[27]

The initial ineffectiveness of the embargo on voyages to the British West Indies owed in part to the Jeffersonian desire to guarantee an adequate supply of food for the American people. This goal of minimal domestic discomfort created the chore of determining which regions supplied their own needs and which imported food and grain from other parts of the country. Then came the work of devising a system to ensure the necessary interregional trade without endangering the goals of the embargo. In the early going, these tasks confounded the administration.

On Jefferson's suggestion, the administration allowed the various governors to determine the food needs of their states and to issue certificates that legalized the necessary importations. Gallatin opposed the plan because he knew the embargo risked abuse when the power to allow ships to sail was taken out of the network of president, Treasury, and customs. And abuse there was, especially in Massachusetts, but in other states as well. The governors' certificates became a laughingstock, a common circulating currency in most port towns, "granted without discretion," Gallatin knew, "and for districts where flour is not wanted." The legitimated flour imports into Massachusetts alone well exceeded local needs and found their way, via Halifax, New Brunswick, British ships, or American smugglers into the British islands.[28]

Treasury Department rulings and congressional embargo legislation buttressed the shaky certificate plan and finally gave the administration a workable method of policing the Caribbean trade and reducing significantly the flow of produce to the West Indies. The ad-

[27] Gallatin to TJ, May 28, Aug. 6, 1808, Jefferson Papers, LC.

[28] Gallatin to TJ, May 20, 23, 28, July 15, Aug. 6, Sept. 18, Oct. 15, 1808, Gallatin, "Memorandum of Certificates of Governor Sullivan for Importation of Flour into Massachusetts," Sept. 20, 1808, TJ to Gallatin, May 23, Oct. 14, 1808, TJ to Levi Lincoln, Nov. 13, 1808, ibid.

ministration adopted a rule which allowed the portion of provisions and other "suspicious" commodities to equal only one-eighth of the value of the coasting vessel's total cargo. Treasury also instituted a system of "floating bonds" that pegged the value of the cargo to its price in the West Indies, not to the price in the port of ostensible American destination. "The honest merchant," Jefferson believed, "has no objection to enlarge his bond in proportion as the temptation of foreign prices is enlarged."[29]

On April 25 Congress increased the required bond to three times the value of ship and cargo and allowed the customs collectors to detain suspicious vessels if the cargo, destination, port from which the vessel cleared, composition of the crew, or the previous record of the shipowner or captain elicited concern. Gallatin's actions, congressional law, customs' surveillance, and hard work decreased significantly the number of West Indian coasting violations. At summer's end, most of the illicit trade to the Caribbean involved ships that were licensed for the foreign trade and had sailed, generally at nightfall, without clearance papers.[30] This kind of evasion was on the increase because of the exceedingly high prices that American goods commanded in the British West Indies.

One way to measure the general effectiveness of the embargo in curtailing American exports to the Caribbean is to examine the West Indian price schedule on American produce. Since the American export trade was free of domestic restraint in 1807, the average prices that American commodities commanded in the West Indies through that year can be taken as a norm. The French islands are excluded because the contribution of the Royal Navy to the decline of America's exports there confuses an analysis of the embargo's effectiveness. But that contribution was great, and it increased the American desire to penetrate the British islands, thereby aggravating the task of enforcing the embargo where the administration wanted it most.[31]

For 1807, the average price of basic commodities in the British

[29] Treasury Department circulars of April 28 and May 6, 1808, outlined the grounds of detention. A Treasury circular of May 20, 1808, modified the certificate plan with the one-eighth ruling (Gallatin Papers, NYU, reel 16). TJ to Madison, June 3, 1808, Madison Papers, LC, reel 10.

[30] Gallatin to TJ, Aug. 6, 1808, Jefferson Papers, LC.

[31] In January 1808 the American consul in Saint Thomas warned that only the Royal Navy, not the embargo, could keep American vessels out of the West Indies

islands was: flour, $8.25 per barrel; cornmeal, $24.00 per barrel; tobacco, $8.00 per hundredweight; salt, $0.11 per pound. When the news of the embargo reached the West Indies in January, the fear of scarcity and the impact of speculation and hoarding drove up the price of flour to $40.00. But the scarcity did not result to the degree imagined, the speculation stopped, and the price began to drop steadily. America's consul in Surinam reported that the illegal shipments in January and February had "brought supplies to the West Indies sufficient for six months." The illegal traffic accelerated in the spring and summer. Philadelphia's collector informed Gallatin that "notwithstanding all that has been devised by government—the law of embargo is constantly . . . evaded," especially in flour (by "the thousands of barrels," he noted, and all of it destined for the West Indies). From the North the news was as grim. "In how great a degree is the Embargo evaded!" complained one New Englander. "How many thousands bls. of flour have been smuggled out—do the collectors do their duty?" He estimated that from Cape Cod alone the British West Indies "are glutted with provisions." Similar reports came from Baltimore and Petersburg. By July the price of flour had fallen to only $16.00 a barrel, still double the 1807 average, but much less than the $40.00 figure that accurately reflected West Indian fears at the embargo's onset. Nor was the $16.00 figure very firm. From the consuls in the West Indies came predictions of further price decreases.[32]

The reduction in the flow of produce to the West Indies was impressive in the last quarter of 1808. By the end of the year the price of flour had tripled from its 1807 average to $26.00 per barrel. Cornmeal had more than tripled to $80.00 per barrel. Salt had quintupled in price, and the market value of tobacco had increased

(James McGreggor to Madison, Jan. 28, 1808, Saint Thomas, Dispatches from Consular Officers, MS, NA). Similarly, the American consuls in the French islands of Martinique and Guadaloupe credited the Royal Navy, not the embargo, for the "noticeable decline in the importations of American provisions" into their islands (Archibald Cock to Madison, Feb. 25, May 31, June 3, 1808, Saint Pierre, Martinique, Dispatches from Consular Officers, RG 59, T431, reel 1; Lewis Formon to Madison, Mar. 30, 1808, to Robert Smith, July 23, 1809, Guadaloupe, RG 59, T208, reel 1; William A. Burwell to William Dickerson, Nov. 20, 1808, William Burwell Papers, LC).

[32] Average 1807 prices enclosed in James McGreggor to Madison, Jan. 2, 1809, Saint Thomas, Dispatches from Consular Officers, MS, NA. McGreggor to Madi-

sixfold to $50.00 per hundredweight. Yet the potential impact of these rises on English policy rested on the impact of these figures on the Caribbean economy. Latin American economic conversion lessened the impact. All through 1808 South American planters forsook the cultivation of sugar, coffee, and cotton in favor of tobacco, indigo, rice, corn, lumber, and timber staves. By 1809 Surinam alone was producing enough corn "to supply the whole West Indies."[33] Where there was suffering, it usually fell "on the lower class of people."[34] Although economic conversion and the embargo's uneven impact on the Caribbean people lessened the policy's effectiveness, continuing American evasions were still the major cause of the embargo's plight.

"Had it not been for the evasions of the law," the Saint Thomas consul believed, "the West Indies generally would long before this [have] been in a deplorable situation." From Antigua, the administration learned that the price of flour, often triple its 1807 level in most of the English Caribbean, was barely twice the 1807 figure "and in the other [neighboring] islands equally as cheap." "The numerous vessels that have been and are daily arriving" accounted for the dismal price figure. So large were existing stockpiles and so complete was England's anticipation of future American supply that America's consul in Surinam predicted in the fall of 1808 that the embargo would have no policy impact unless "continued another year *most strictly executed*."[35] This was Gallatin's greatest fear. Smuggling had thus far defeated the embargo. Yet the embargo's

---

son, Jan. 28, April 27, 1808, ibid.; T. Tufts to Madison, Feb. 25, 1808, Surinam, ibid.; John Shee to Gallatin, April 25, 1808, Philadelphia, RG 56, M178, NA, reel 22; Orchard Cook to John Quincy Adams, July 30, 1808, Adams Family Papers, MHS, reel 406; Gabriel Christie to Gallatin, Feb. 11, 1808, Baltimore, RG 56, M178, NA, reel 3; John Shore to Gallatin, June 5, Nov. 19, 1808, Petersburg, ibid., reel 19; McGreggor to Madison, July 1, 1808, Saint Thomas, Dispatches from Consular Offices, MS, NA.

[33] On Caribbean economic conversion, see Maurice Rogers to James Madison, Jan. 21, 1809, Cuba, RG 59, T55, NA, reel 1; William Savage to Madison, Jan. 20, 1809, Kingston, Jamaica, RG 59, T31, NA, reel t1; T. Tufts to Madison, April 4, 1809, Surinam, Dispatches from Consular Officers, MS, NA.

[34] James McGreggor to Madison, Jan. 2, 1809, Saint Thomas, Dispatches from Consular Officers, MS, NA.

[35] Ibid.; Joseph Warner Rose to Madison, Jan. 3, 1809, Antigua, Dispatches from Consular Officers, MS, NA; T. Tufts to Madison, Sept. 3, 1809, Surinam, ibid.

limited success in keeping American goods out of the Caribbean had triggered an upward spiral in West Indian prices that posed a compelling lure to the American entrepreneur and a major problem to the administration. Although the coercion of England had eluded the embargo in 1808, its flawed support among the American people rested on an implied agreement between them and the government that their obligation to suffer economic loss for high national ends would last only one year. As early as March 1808, Jefferson had recognized that the embargo courted serious domestic opposition if continued beyond the November 1808 session of Congress. William Eustis accurately captured New England's mood. "Knowing the active, restless temper of our own people," he wrote John Quincy Adams in April, "I am still inclined to the opinion that they will submit to the privations and distress of the Embargo until the Autumn."[36]

Northern commercial ports both submitted to the embargo and anticipated its repeal when the new Congress assembled. When prompt movement toward repeal did not occur, the embargo was doomed. Massive smuggling involving hundreds of vessels greeted this congressional failure in Massachusetts. Riotous mobs formed in Providence, Rhode Island, and sang Sons of Liberty songs in reply to the fifth embargo law. Especially in New England, but in Philadelphia, New York, Baltimore, and southern ports as well, the most severe opposition to the embargo came after the Jeffersonians' failure to satisfy the popular expectation to repeal the yearlong embargo.[37] Rising commodity prices in the Caribbean fueled the popular outrage. And by the fall, an additional problem confronted the administration. Through much of 1808 American goods commanded very small prices in European ports. This had aggravated the enforcement problem in the Caribbean by training the attention of potential lawbreakers on the West Indies. But by year's end, high prices existed everywhere, and the enforcement problem also had become universal.

[36] Eustis to Adams, April 21, 1808, Adams Family Papers, MHS, reel 406.

[37] Gallatin to TJ, Nov. 29, 1808, Jefferson Papers, LC; Jeremiah Olney to Gallatin, Jan. 25, 1809, Gallatin Papers, NYU, reel 18. In November, Congress asked Gallatin to send it a compilation of all evasions of the embargo, based on the reports of the customs collectors, and Gallatin complied on Jan. 24. The raw data of the compilation can be followed in Gallatin Papers, NYU, reels 17 and 18.

European Voyages

"We have never seen more gloomy times," Wilson Cary Nicholas's Norfolk banker and tobacco factor wrote him in October 1806. "Every market" for Virginia tobacco was "glutted." The previous month, Thomas Rutherfoord had made an equally dismal report for wheat. Its price in Norfolk was only a dollar a barrel. Because Norfolk was already glutted with 4,000 barrels of nonmarketable wheat, he advised Nicholas to keep his crop at home. Other Norfolk businessmen noted the same phenomenon. In February 1806 William Pennock reported that European prices no longer supported American expectations. "Our produce is too high and the export merchant has not a fair chance," he observed. In September he advised Nicholas that "was there not a single hogshead of tobacco made this year, there would be a sufficiency in Europe from last year's crop." In June, Moses Meyers wrote that American overproduction, English glut, and the Royal Navy's ability to focus American exports on British markets "compelled [American merchants] to land and sell in England at very depressed prices." The American consul in Liverpool noted much the same thing. More American ships, carrying more goods, had cleared into Liverpool in 1806 than in any prior year since Independence. In October 1806 he advised Jefferson that because southern planters "have so overdone the markets in Europe, they will have to find out others or curtail the culture." He offered an equally depressing picture for the future of southern tobacco. The bleak pattern held through 1807. Virginia cotton and tobacco factors continued to advise their clients to plant and sell less. So glutted was the cotton market in Liverpool—the first half of 1807 witnessed more than the entire 1806 American yield piling up in English warehouses—that not even the threat of Anglo-American rupture in December 1807 was able to drive up the prices. West Indian consuls reported that the gluts were so large in the Caribbean that only an embargo could save scores of mercantile fortunes.[38]

---

[38] Rutherfoord to Nicholas, July 18, Sept. [?], Oct. 22, 1806, Sept. 27, 1807, Pennock to Nicholas, Feb. 8, Sept. 22, 1806, Meyers to Nicholas, July 4, 1806, Wilson Cary Nicholas Papers, acc. no. 2343, UVa; James Maury to TJ, Oct. 22, 1806, July 21, 1807, Jefferson Papers, LC; Maury to Madison, Sept. 11, 1806, Jan. 28, July 23, Dec. 18, 1807, Liverpool, RG 59, M141, NA, reel L2. The embargo helped Virginia planters in other ways as well: "And although I have a right

Depressed prices and glutted markets supported the embargo on European voyages through much of 1808 because there was little incentive to sail to England. The embargo's success, however, drove up the prices in Liverpool and London markets to tempting levels. By December 1808 the policy confronted not only inflated prices in the West Indies but steeply rising prices in Great Britain as well. The economic bonanza that now awaited American traders in foreign ports fed the popular perception of oppressive government. This fusion of ideology and interest had created by year's end a nightmare for the Jeffersonians. The future demanded levels of enforcement that the past had not. But these would erode the embargo's lingering support, in Congress and the nation, and topple the policy. When Albert Gallatin outlined his proposals to the Senate committee, he knew their enactment would destroy the embargo before they registered any impact on the belligerent economies.

The Draconian Measures

Although triple bonding, the one-eighth rule, and detention had minimized coasting violations, pressures were again mounting on the trade by the end of 1808. Consequently, Gallatin asked Congress to raise to six times the value of ship and cargo the required bond on coasting voyages. He hoped the size of the potential loss would intimidate the potential lawbreaker. Since detention by customs had created inequities and annoying bureaucratic chores, Gallatin's new legislation did away with the clumsy process except in specified cases. In those areas, generally involving food, Gallatin's plan made executive guidelines obligatory on the collectors. In all the rest, coasters could sail if they found a surety to post the large bond. Because the size of the bond posed unacceptable risks to the nation's sureties, Gallatin's system promised to halt most legal maritime activity.[39]

---

to expect sundry payments, I must remark that I find those who can pay do not, but avail themselves of the common plea, THE EMBARGO" (William Smith to Wilson Cary Nicholas, Mar. 4, 1808, Wilson Cary Nicholas Papers, acc. no. 2343, UVa).

[39] Gallatin to William Branch Giles, Nov. 24, 1808, Gallatin Papers, NYU, reel 17.

By November, coasting violations did not challenge the embargo nearly as much as did smuggling without clearance papers. The embargo had always allowed vessels registered for the foreign trade to take on cargoes, but not to sail. Unless the law empowered the customs collectors to prevent the loading and to force the unloading of foreign-bound vessels, the immense coastline and the puny navy offered little challenge to would-be smugglers.[40] In April 1808 Congress had considered granting such powers. The Senate placed in its fourth embargo bill the power to prevent loading but limited it to those collectors in districts adjacent to foreign territory. On Gallatin's suggestion, the House extended the grant to all collectors. The Senate, however, struck out the House amendment. The April 25 embargo law which established the government's arsenal of weapons at summer's onset granted the power to those collectors specified in the original Senate bill.

The secretary of the treasury still hoped that the collectors would seize suspicious cargoes, from both ships and warehouses, if the president so instructed. But the customs officers thought executive approval insufficient legal protection. "Since the collectors will not place themselves in position to be sued," Gallatin informed Jefferson on July 29, "we must let the vessels go, and depend on [naval] force to enforce the embargo." Nor were the collectors to blame. Gallatin appreciated the extreme difficulties the lack of specific congressional authorization created for them. "We cannot expect [them] to risk all they are worth," he advised Jefferson. "Until the Congress meets [in November] we must depend entirely on force for checking this manner of violating the law."[41]

Smuggling broke the chain of embargo enforcement at its weakest link. If ships could be kept from sailing, the administration's war against embargo-breaking could succeed reasonably well. But once ships sailed, the administration was on the defensive. The problem—a lack of vessels and naval manpower to police the extensive coastline—worsened as the months of the embargo approached a year. The reports of the customs collectors graphed a steady rise in smuggling as the summer turned to autumn and the autumn to

[40] John Shee to Gallatin, April 25, 1808, Philadelphia, RG 56, M178, NA, reel 22; TJ to Gallatin, May 27, 1808, Gallatin to TJ, May 27, Nov. 29, 1808, Jefferson Papers, LC.

[41] Gallatin to TJ, July 29, 1808, Jefferson Papers, LC.

winter.[42] So did the consular reports from English port cities. In a frantic effort, the administration shuffled its ships and gunboats from port to port. In November, Gallatin requested ten more revenue cutters from Congress—a useless request because the navy did not have the men to operate them. Finally, the administration decided to focus on the West Indies by stationing its heavy ships—the *Chesapeake, Hornet, Wasp,* and *Argus*—at key points along the trade routes to the Caribbean. This decision cost the administration any chance of preventing transatlantic smuggling. The navy could not protect the embargo, and Gallatin largely ignored naval power in his final suggestions to the Senate. The bulk of his proposals aimed at preventing smugglers from ever sailing their ships from harbor.[43]

In Gallatin's scheme, only ships licensed and approved for the coasting trade could board cargo. He wanted Congress to legalize the notion that the act of loading except for coasting or fishing voyages was proof of fraudulent intent. His penalty for unapproved loading was forfeiture of ship and cargo. Prior to November, many merchants had argued that because the embargo made worthless their sailing vessels, they should be allowed to convert the ships to warehouses and accrue some profit. Jefferson thought the argument preposterous, a mere cover "to take advantage of the first northwester." If owners had a legitimate interest in conversion from ship to warehouse, they should not mind posting the same bond required of coasting vessels.[44]

Gallatin now wanted extended to officers in all customs districts the April legislation that had allowed customs collectors in districts adjacent to foreign territory to confiscate "unusual" deposits from ships, docks, and warehouses. He wanted this power conferred on the collectors secondarily through the president of the United States. Without such procedure, they would not place their financial futures

---

[42] In Gallatin's opinion, the smuggling was far worse than the customs records indicated: "Numerous evasions and violations have taken place, of which the official returns of the collectors herewith transmitted give but a partial account. For [it] cannot be concealed that illegal shipments and exportations of pot ash, flour, cotton, and other articles have been made to a much larger amount than might be inferred from a view of those returns" (Gallatin to Joseph B. Varnum, Jan. 24, 1809, Gallatin Papers, NYU, reel 18).

[43] TJ to Gallatin, Nov. 29, 1808, Robert Smith to TJ, Dec. 26, 1808, Jefferson Papers, LC.

[44] TJ to Gallatin, Nov. 16, 1808, ibid.

in jeopardy for the sake of the embargo. Private suits and state harassment had become so serious that in early November Gallatin advised Jefferson on methods to combat them.[45] These ideas he later forwarded to the Giles committee. He suggested that all civil suits against the collectors be tried in national courts. In these judicial proceedings, a Treasury Department ruling on the "reasonableness" of the seizure was sufficient protection against all damages.[46]

State interference threatened the collectors' work as much as private suits. This obstruction took several forms. Grand juries would not hand down indictments, district attorneys would not prosecute embargo violators, and when they did, judges and juries would not convict. The problem became especially severe in Massachusetts and Rhode Island after the passage, in January 1809, of the last enforcement act. John Quincy Adams told a friend that the grand jury, sitting for several weeks, had refused indictments against all forty persons charged with embargo violations. Embargo reform could not solve this particular problem; indeed, it often aggravated it. But it could prevent state interference in the collectors' pursuit of their duty. To that end, Gallatin asked the national legislature to prevent state courts from "wresting" away detained ships or confiscated property through attachments and writs of replevin. His proposals also branded state officials and local sheriffs who entered the customshouses under state law as "mere trespassers," subject to criminal penalty in national courts for their actions. Gallatin also requested reforms in the national judiciary laws "to protect our collectors against the encroachments of state officers."[47]

---

[45] Gallatin to TJ, Nov. 8, 1808, ibid.

[46] Gallatin to William Branch Giles, Nov. 24, 1808, Gallatin Papers, NYU, reel 17.

[47] Gallatin to TJ, Nov. 8, 1808, Jefferson Papers, LC; Gallatin to William Branch Giles, Nov. 24, 1808, Gallatin Papers, NYU, reel 17; Adams to Ezekiel Bacon, Dec. 21, 1808, to Giles, Jan. 16, 1809, Adams Family Papers, MHS, reel 135. The problems of judges, juries, and district attorneys was unremitting. Rhode Island: "We cannot enforce the embargo in R. Island with Howell for District Attorney and Barnes for Judge" (Gallatin to TJ, Jan. 6, 1809, Jefferson Papers, LC); Massachusetts: "Anticipate a non-execution of the embargo in Massachusetts by acquital on prosecution. This I think probable, and if so, do not perceive any remedy" (Gallatin to TJ, Oct. 5, 1808, ibid.); Pennsylvania: "You will reflect on the difficulty of persuading our courts and juries to adopt any construction that tends to enforce the embargo" (Alexander Dallas to Gallatin, July 30, 1808, Gallatin Papers, NYU, reel 17).

The protections that Gallatin demanded for his men were a direct assault on state judicial and police power. Their need arose from the recognition that in several quarters of the Union state courts and governments were threatening the embargo. This same danger triggered what Gallatin considered his most "arbitrary" request: that Congress place the state militias at the disposal of the federal revenue officers without the prior approval of the state governors. The request offended central beliefs in the Jeffersonian persuasion. Never before had the militias been removed from state control and placed under the authority of the federal establishment, and Gallatin made the request with "much regret." [48] Congress ignored the problem and simply authorized the state militias to aid the collectors. But the whole purpose of Gallatin's demand had been to ensure militia cooperation even in the face of state opposition. Consequently, he told Jefferson that Congress's hazy language still authorized "each collector to call . . . on such part of the militia as he himself may select" and that the matter required "immediate and deliberative consideration." The final decision was Jefferson's. Each interpretation risked something. If the governors were the medium, the administration risked noncompliance. If the collectors were the medium, the administration risked disobedience from both the governors and the militias. No presidential instructions to the nation's governors were forthcoming. As the administration contemplated the necessity of militia cooperation in the wake of the final enforcement law, Congress's vague authorization was its only lever. The power over the militia still lay on the state level. [49]

Nathaniel Macon called the last embargo law the harshest bill ever proposed by any administration, Federalist or Republican. [50] Gallatin had told the Senate in November that nothing justified his proposals except public opposition to the embargo and the expectation of a "daily increase" in evasions. The Jeffersonians had a beast in hand and could not, it seemed, let go. Simply because the embargo had become the nation's response to foreign danger, it had to be either enforced or abandoned. To mitigate its impact at home, to wink at

[48] Gallatin to William Branch Giles, Nov. 24, 1808, Gallatin Papers, NYU, reel 17.

[49] Gallatin to TJ, Jan. 10, 1809, Jefferson Papers, LC.

[50] Macon to Joseph Hopper Nicholson, n.d., Joseph Hopper Nicholson Papers, LC.

mounting evasions, equaled submission to the foreign edicts. It was ironic that Gallatin was the author of the draconian measures because, believing that war could no longer be avoided, he had offered his severe proposals to cure the congressional addiction to coercive embargo.[51] He produced ample evidence to show how each provision that he outlined—all essential to the embargo's future—would evaporate the remains of popular and political support and destroy the policy it was designed to promote. A foreign policy paper that he prepared for the House of Representatives better reveals Gallatin's views on embargo, war, and the nation's English crisis.

The Campbell Report

George Washington Campbell from Tennessee was the chairman of the House Foreign Affairs Committee. A House resolution charged his committee with preparing a summary of America's difficulties with Europe and suggesting policies in line with that summary. Campbell took Gallatin's advice. The final report submitted to the full House was substantially the same as the long letter Gallatin wrote the congressman. Because of the vagueness of Jefferson's last annual message, the Campbell Report comes closest to a full administration statement on the nature of America's foreign problems and their resulting policy needs; and it came down heavily for war. In the process it repudiated both coercive embargo and the expedients that Congress would legislate in the next three years.

Gallatin's analysis flowed from the failure of the previous summer's diplomacy. Given "that state of things," he began his letter to Campbell, "what course ought the United States to pursue?" Logic reduced the alternatives to war or embargo. But the nation wanted some "middle course" that "avoid[ed] the evils of both" and yet answered the requirements of "national honor and independence." "That illusion," Gallatin warned Congress, "must be dissipated. It is necessary that the people of the United States should fully understand the situation in which they are placed."[52] The halfway measure

[51] Samuel Smith to William Eustis, Dec. 4, 1808, William Eustis Papers, LC.

[52] Gallatin to Campbell, Nov. 1808, in Henry Adams, ed., *The Writings of Albert Gallatin* (Philadelphia, 1879), 1:443.

that most frightened Gallatin was the repeal of the embargo against all the nations of the world except England, France, and their allies. Such a policy was seductively honorable. The proponents of partial repeal argued that because belligerent mistreatment had called forth the embargo, it should deprive only them of American trade.[53]

The argument was both tempting and false. Gallatin used economic data and the likely aftermath of partial repeal to demolish it. What if the United States opened a trade with the nonoffending nations: Spain, Portugal, Sweden, Russia, and "the native powers of Africa and Asia." The export trade to these nations in 1807 totaled less than 15 percent of the gross American export trade. If the entire export sector crowded on that limited market, profits would vanish. Of greater weight was partial repeal's probable impact on each belligerent. Regardless of American intent, it would open an "indirect trade" with Great Britain. Here Gallatin was careful not to malign the patriotism of the American people. English commercial power alone was sufficient to produce it. Shortly after the trade began, American provisions would glut the legal markets. English ships would be waiting—at Saint Barthélemy, Havana, Lisbon, Cadiz, Göteborg—to buy American provisions at depressed prices and take them on to Great Britain and the Continent.[54]

What Gallatin did not mention, but what everyone knew, was that a British trade would result from American intentions as well. Merchants would calculate their interest. Rather than face depressed prices in the limited market, they would themselves sail to where the large profits awaited. If they sailed to both Great Britain and France, confiscations would increase at the cost of the defensive accomplishments of the embargo. If they sailed to Great Britain only, the merchants would affirm that England's claim to shape American trade with paper blockades and brute force was a valid one. At best partial repeal offered scant profit, succor to England, and tacit commercial alliance with Great Britain. At worst it promised war with France. It was better to calculate on profit only, Gallatin wrote Campbell, better to resume trade with Great Britain (it would get the trade anyway), and to announce publicly that France is the only aggressor and

---

[53] Joseph C. Cabell to Wilson Cary Nicholas, Dec. 26, 1808, Wilson Cary Nicholas Papers, acc. no. 5533, UVa.

[54] Gallatin to Campbell, Nov. 1808, in Adams, ed., *Writings*, 1:444.

that having no just reason to complain of Great Britain, "it is our duty to submit to her orders."[55]

Gallatin had utilized William Pinkney's London-based observations to prepare his report to Campbell's committee. Both men rejected partial repeal. Three of Gallatin's arguments against it— reward to Great Britain, unfairness to France, and the embarrassing admission that if profit be the soul of the nation, America should capitulate to the British orders, ply a safe and prosperous English trade, and explain somehow, in spite of the orders, impressments, and the *Chesapeake* attack, that France was the only enemy—have their exact counterparts in Pinkney's correspondence with the State Department. But when it came to Gallatin's discussion of war versus coercive embargo, Pinkney had been silent.

Gallatin omitted from his report all the indices that the American diplomat had cited to demonstrate the embargo's effectiveness as a coercive weapon.[56] His thoughts on the dangers and implications of permanent embargo were not original or his alone. They were quite commonsensical, and all Republican policy makers, including Jefferson, saw that permanent embargo was the surrender of the very economic interests that the administration had aimed to protect. The importance of Gallatin's admission rested on its public nature and on its relationship to other ideas in his statement to the Campbell committee. The French and British edicts, he told Congress, were "maritime war" against the United States, and the embargo was no match for them. For all its horrors, war was America's only recourse, "the ultimate and only effectual mode of resisting that warfare." Jefferson had seen this at the beginning of the 1808 diplomatic offensive. But approaching retirement made him incapable of acting on his earlier resolve and of discerning when persistence in the embargo became both a denial of America's commercial rights and a greater burden than the American people could bear.[57] By confronting Congress with the realities that Jefferson now ignored, Gallatin tried to

[55] Ibid.; see also Gallatin to Joseph Hopper Nicholson, Oct. 18, 1808, Joseph Hopper Nicholson Papers, LC.

[56] Pinkney to Madison, Sept. 7, 1808, Dispatches, Great Britain, Pinkney, vol. 16, NA.

[57] Gallatin to Madison, Sept. 9, 1808, Madison Papers, LC, ser. 2, reel 25; Gallatin to Campbell, Nov. 1808, in Adams, ed., *Writings*, 1:443–45; John Quincy Adams to William Branch Giles, Dec. 10, 1808, to Samuel Mitchill, Dec. 14, 1808,

jolt it into a consideration of war, just as his letter to Jefferson of November 15 had tried unsuccessfully to jolt the president in the same direction.

The Campbell committee reported out and the House of Representatives adopted three resolutions. It pledged the nation never to submit to the edicts of France and Great Britain. Since Congress adopted the body of Gallatin's letter as well as the committee resolutions, this pledge equated partial repeal with submission. Congress also resolved to harmonize America's treatment of equally offending nations by imposing nonimportation on France. This aimed to take advantage of the last remaining hope for settlement with England by removing a persistent British excuse for the lack of diplomatic accomplishment: American partiality toward France. In deference to that slim hope, the second resolution made France a coequal enemy with Great Britain and thereby imposed an obstacle to declaring war against England alone. The third resolution promised serious military preparations. They were all adopted in early December.[58] The major development during the next two months of the session was Congress's inability to avoid the partial repeal that the Campbell committee had branded submission. A minor episode was the attempt by the antiretreat forces, late in the session, to prevent the loss of the embargo's valid accomplishments through ill-timed repeal.

Repeal

President Jefferson was true to his last annual message. The final choice between war and embargo rested with the Congress of the United States. By November, Jefferson's hands-off policy was common knowledge among leading Republicans. To no avail, Gallatin and Madison, although disagreeing on the proper policy, urged him to anchor Congress to any policy that honored the spirited resolves of the Campbell Report. They feared that without presidential involvement and leadership, the national legislature would capitulate

to Joseph Anderson, Dec. 15, 1808, to Orchard Cook, Dec. 19, 1808, to Ezekiel Bacon, Dec. 21, 1808, Adams Family Papers, MHS, reel 135.

[58] On the "glorious spirit" of the "resolutions" see Isaac Coles to Joseph C. Cabell, Dec. 13, 31, 1808, Joseph C. Cabell Papers, UVa; Wilson Cary Nicholas to [?], Dec. 3, 1808, Samuel Smith Papers, UVa.

to its own fatigue and fears, ignore the harsh European realities that
crowded in, obey the naive popular demand for both trade and peace,
and abandon the embargo. Instead, Jefferson reposed his faith in the
Republican majority. He associated shouts against the embargo with
political villainy and party rage and imagined the congressional Republicans numerous and sound enough to defeat all Federalist attempts to subvert the embargo and bring on submission to Great
Britain. He preferred that his last congressional session do nothing
except strengthen the embargo and make provision for a special
summer session. By his own reckoning, the nation was "backed to
the wall," with no further retreat possible. But he refused to contemplate war and placed the whole burden of maintaining the embargo and the national interest on the shoulders of the Republican
congressmen.[59]

At the beginning of the November congressional session, New
England Republicans were as solid for the embargo as were the representatives from Jefferson's South. Ezekiel Bacon and Orchard
Cook, two influential Massachusetts congressmen, believed that
anything less than the embargo's continuation would betray the
Campbell Report and result in "the prostration of our commerce, our
independence, *our everything*." Either the complete or partial repeal
of the embargo they branded "a submission" and a mockery of the
Constitution that had aimed "to nationalize us and advance and defend our commercial rights."[60]

Although New England Republicans supported the embargo, few
of them thought it adequate to the nation's external needs or com-

---

[59] Nathaniel Macon to Joseph Hopper Nicholson, Dec. 4, 1808, Joseph Hopper
Nicholson Papers, LC; Samuel Smith to William Eustis, Dec. 4, 1808, William
Eustis Papers, LC; Orchard Cook to John Quincy Adams, Nov. 10, 1808, Adams
Family Papers, MHS, reel 406. On the dangerous implications of Jefferson's naive
faith in Congress's ability to meet this crisis without extreme executive prodding,
Thomas Rodney wrote: "he has left all to the wisdom and Patriotism of the legislature; . . . but there are times, and I have seen such, and so has the president, . . .
when the wisdom of the national councils was inadequate to the crisis, when the
nation was delivered by individual exertion and the favoring hand of decisive
[executive] action" (Thomas Rodney to Caesar Rodney, Dec. 13, 1808, Rodney
Family Papers, LC).

[60] Bacon to John Quincy Adams, Nov. 9, 14, 1808, Cook to John Quincy Adams,
Nov. 10, 1808, Adams Family Papers, MHS, reel 406; Bacon to Joseph Story, Nov.
4, 1808, Joseph Story Papers, LC.

patible with the economic aspirations of their region. Cook ridiculed
it as "warm water . . . utterly impotent as a coercive measure." He
"wish[ed] to God it were otherways" simply because the alternatives
were much worse: war or submission. Even among its supporters,
the embargo inspired little confidence and much hostility; for these
reasons its hold on the legislature was precarious and its survival
depended on energetic executive leadership. Cook was shocked that
the administration was not flooding Congress with reasons and
justifications for continuing the policy. By December 4 Pinkney's
"naked opinion" was the sum of the administration's proembargo argument. But Pinkney's celebration of the embargo was flatly contradicted by the official dispatches from John Armstrong in Paris
which maintained that "the E[mbargo] is a measure relished in
F[rance] and utterly disregarded in Eng[land]." If left to choose between the "opinion of minister against opinion of minister," Congress
would believe Armstrong because, Cook observed, "from various
sources we find abundance of evidence to believe Armstrong most
correct and that the embargo has not coerced in hardly any degree."
Yet in early December, Cook and most Massachusetts Republicans
wanted desperately to believe in the embargo. Receiving no support
from the administration, Cook asked John Quincy Adams, an important adviser to key Massachusetts Republicans such as Cook,
Bacon, and Joseph Story, "to give me the arguments."[61]

Adams's correspondence with the men from Massachusetts helped
cause, and also charted, Republican New England's retreat from the
embargo. When the congressional session opened, he located his
analysis primarily in the needs of foreign policy and national honor
and considered any trade with the belligerent nations an unspeakable
surrender to huckstering New England merchants. He had no faith
in the embargo as a coercive weapon because of the way he understood the stakes in the European war. Pride and national survival
were its issues, and weighed against these, the economic discomfort
that the embargo had inflicted counted for little. It "affects their
interests no doubt," he wrote Bacon in December, "but nations
which sacrifice men by the hundred thousands and treasure by the
hundreds of millions in war for nothing, or worse than nothing, pay
little attention to their real interests." Still, the embargo had re-

---

[61] Orchard Cook to Adams, Dec. 4, 1808, Adams Family Papers, MHS, reel 406.

deeming merit. It protected seamen and maritime property, prevented an insultingly foreign-taxed and foreign-licensed trade, and avoided war.[62] He found the "reasoning" behind the Campbell Report "so strong that I do not see how it can be successfully controverted." Militarily, the resumption of trade would fritter away the defensive accomplishments of the embargo and expose maritime ships, men, and wealth to English power. Economically, partial repeal promised only meager profit or profitable degradation. If Americans obeyed a nonintercourse act against the belligerents (partial repeal of the embargo), their goods would glut the legal markets and cause the profits to vanish. More likely, Americans would sail to the illegal and profitable markets, thereby offering humiliating witness to American greed.[63]

John Quincy Adams could not sustain his commitment to the Campbell Report because the context of his thinking began to change. An intense concern for internal harmony and the survival of the republican experiment challenged an earlier preoccupation with national honor that had shaped his understanding of America's predicament in the summer and early fall.[64] Beset by images of Federalist disloyalty—disunion "is the very point the tories are driving at," he now believed—he saw in the weakness, avarice, and discontent of his fellow New Englanders the ingredients of Federalist success. Adams feared that Jefferson, by clinging too long to the embargo, was playing Pompey to the Federalist Caesar.[65]

The congenital inability of a free people to withstand the assaults of partisanship and economic suffering made them susceptible to political infection, even to successionist schemes. Soon they would commit their trust and votes to the enemies of law, the Republic, and its independence. It mattered little that the majority of Americans were usually loyal and obedient to constituted authority. In almost medical fashion, Adams dwelt on the fragility of "their resolution"

[62] Adams to Ezekiel Bacon, Nov. 18, Dec. 21, 1808, ibid., reel 135.

[63] Adams to Nahum Parker, Dec. 5, 1808, to William Branch Giles, Dec. 10, 1808, ibid.

[64] In August, Adams prayed that Congress consider "no surrender of that inheritance which it is our sacred duty to transmit as we received it—unimpaired. In God's name let us have no sanctions of our admissions for British impressments or British taxation" (Adams to Orchard Cook, Aug. [?], 1808, ibid.).

[65] Adams to Ezekiel Bacon, Nov. 18, 1808, to Samuel Mitchill, Dec. 14, 1808, to Orchard Cook, Dec. 19, 1808, to William Branch Giles, Jan. 16, 1809, ibid.

and on the possibility that "the people" will "not prove true to themselves thro the long and severe trial they have to go through." The better part of policy was now to provide "a vent" for popular "passion" and discomfort. The internal turmoil that the English crisis had spawned triumphed over external matters in Adams's understanding of the embargo. It demanded partial repeal of the embargo.[66]

By mid-December, Adams's fear of social disorder had resolved the conflict between international stature and national tranquillity in favor of the domestic considerations. He was now ready to forgo the embargo's positive benefits. In November, he had thought it foolish and dangerous "to throw the whole burden of the controversy [with England] upon the calculations of mercantile speculation." By December, even as he hoped the nation's tradition of obedience to law would support a nonintercourse system, he was ready to place the responsibility for suffering at the door of the lawbreakers. If illicit trade resulted in foreign harassment, the national government was under no obligation to protect its prodigal sons. Nonintercourse with the belligerents and trade with the rest of the world placed the burden where the merchants "tell us it may be safely placed, exclusively at the risque of the individual speculation."[67]

Adams's opinions profoundly altered the perceptions of key Massachusetts congressmen. His arguments buttressed their fears, framed the retreat from the embargo in a socially valid context, and anchored their longings to escape the embargo to a respected New England authority figure.[68] So, too, did the opinions of Joseph Story, lately arrived from Boston to replace the deceased Jacob Crowninshield, and of Barnabas Bidwell, a long-standing favorite of Jefferson's whom the president had personally scouted for the Speakership of the House in 1806. Believing nonintercourse a useless foreign policy weapon, northern Republicans also came to believe that the postponement of the foreign crisis through partial repeal was small enough price to avert a crisis in self-governing institutions. By the end of December congressional support for the embargo had withered. Only a handful of Republicans from the North favored con-

[66] Adams to William Branch Giles, Nov. 15, 1808, to Orchard Cook, Dec. 8, 1808, ibid.

[67] Adams to Orchard Cook, Nov. 25, 1808, to William Branch Giles, Dec. 10, 1808, ibid.

[68] Ezekiel Bacon to Adams, Dec. 11, 1808, ibid.

tinuing it through the summer. Only among the congressmen of Georgia, South Carolina, and Virginia did the embargo still command sizable approval, mostly due to their loyalty to the president. Fears that the law now required levels of enforcement incompatible with republican society explained the erosion. "We begin to discover," Orchard Cook wrote John Quincy Adams on January 1, "that we have already more Embargo Law than can be enforc'd among a people totally adverse from such a measure."[69]

On December 28 northern Republicans told the administration that they could not support the embargo beyond March 4. The message was delivered in person by Cook to Gallatin. The men from the North wished simultaneously to repeal the embargo and pass a nonintercourse act against the belligerents, and they opposed defensive arming and letters of marque and reprisal until, as Cook put it, "by [our] losses our merchants shall call for it."[70] All knew the implications of partial repeal. American merchants would sail to illegal French and British markets. "Is it in your power," John Randolph asked Congress, "to direct their course after they cross the Gulf Stream?"[71] This trade would unleash another round of commercial abuse, for the international setting had not improved. And these acts of foreign hostility, John Quincy Adams's angry hopes notwithstanding, the national government could not ignore. The clandestine transactions would produce war and squander the military accomplishments that the embargo had performed at so high a domestic cost.

For these reasons, Gallatin pleaded for more time and asked Cook and his colleagues to support a June 1 repeal. The secretary of the treasury was stalling. He actually had a more comprehensive plan that he had not yet cleared with the president.[72] In it, Gallatin assumed war, recast the embargo in its original defensive mold, counted on executive-congressional cooperation to diffuse popular opposition to the embargo, and hoped that a bustle of activity might

[69] Cook to Adams, Jan. 1, 1809, ibid., reel 407.

[70] Orchard Cook to Adams, Dec. 29, 1808, ibid., reel 406; Cook to Adams, Jan. 1, 1809, ibid., reel 407; Cook, Jan. 31, 1809, *Annals*, 10th Cong., 2d sess., p. 1248.

[71] Randolph, Feb. 20, 1809, *Annals*, 10th Cong., 2d sess., p. 1464.

[72] Jefferson's views on policy can be followed in TJ to Thomas Mann Randolph, Nov. 22, Dec. 13, 1808, Jan. 2, 31, 1809, to Thomas Logan, Dec. 27, 1808, to William Eustis, Jan. 14, 1809, to Thomas Lomax, Jan. 19, 1809, to John Tyler, Jan. 19, 1809, to Thomas Leiper, Jan. 21, 1809, Jefferson Papers, LC.

yet produce a diplomatic miracle and preserve peace. His point of departure was the importance of simultaneously removing the embargo and declaring war against the nations that had not revoked their commercial edicts. A formal congressional report and a presidential address would communicate this new posture to the American people and the European belligerents. The report would "prefix" a resolution calling for a summer session during which, if necessary, war would be declared no later than July 1. In the meantime, the present Congress would enforce the embargo (the announcement of its summer repeal would make unnecessary oppressive enforcement measures), pass a nonintercourse act, adopt the 50,000-man voluntary army proposition, increase the regular army, make appropriations for fortifications, and increase the impost to counterbalance the decline in British import duties. Ideally, Gallatin hoped his plan would evaporate popular opposition to "permanent embargo," preserve the past accomplishments of the policy, and because it conveyed a presidential and congressional determination to fight, perhaps force a European reconsideration, thereby sparing the United States the need to go to war. That was why Gallatin wished to postpone the war declaration until July 1, "late enough," in his words, "to be better prepared and to have a last chance of a change in Europe."[73]

By his own reckoning, Gallatin's efforts to save the embargo through the spring failed, and the northern Republicans left the meeting still committed to early repeal, nonintercourse, and no military legislation. Their policies expressed their hopes—echoed throughout the land—that Great Britain might not resume its harassments and that the United States might yet peacefully limp its way through the European war. But they also recognized that the embargo had left an ambivalent legacy. While it had preserved the material resources of war, it had consumed the psychological ones. The nation "must again suffer" at foreign hands, they informed Gallatin, to recover its "war pulse."[74]

The embargo was doomed in Congress before the new year began. It was not "transient delusions" surfacing at the end of the session that killed it, as Jefferson believed, but doubts and fears that had

---

[73] Gallatin, personal memorandum, n.d. [late 1808 or early 1809], Albert Gallatin Papers, LC.

[74] Orchard Cook, *Annals*, 10th Cong., 2d sess., p. 1248.

been accumulating since November.[75] "What I had foreseen has taken place," Gallatin confided to his brother-in-law the day after his meeting with Cook. "A majority will not adhere to the embargo much longer. If war be not speedily determined on, submission will soon ensue. This entirely between us."[76]

Congress had reached an informal consensus to abandon the embargo before it put into law the draconian enforcement measures. These did not indicate a commitment to the embargo, nor did their passage mean that Congress changed its mind and suddenly and mysteriously decided to forsake the whole policy. All through December, northern and southern congressional dissatisfaction with the embargo had been mounting. Three days after Gallatin's fateful meeting with Orchard Cook, Republican Congressman John Rhea of Tennessee offered a resolution that would replace the embargo with nonintercourse, a resolution that Republican Joseph Anderson of Tennessee believed had the support of a majority of Republicans even though Jefferson opposed it. Nor did Anderson believe that Congress would pass the enforcement bills. Yet it did, but for political reasons. "Nothing," Anderson later apologized to John Quincy Adams, "but the necessity of preserving the union of the Republicans induced the passage of the Bill to which the Federal members greatly contributed by the many threats they threw out. We were therefore measurably compelled to take higher ground than perhaps strict prudence uninfluenced [by politics] would have justified. Yet this seems to me to be but a lame apology—but there is something of human nature in it."[77]

More than politics, however, silenced potential Republican embargo critics in November and December and drew from them the harsh enforcement bill in January. A debilitating fear of war made it difficult for them to contemplate any other policy. Jefferson's silence played to these fears and together they bound Congress hand and foot to economic isolation. By late December, Virginia's Wilson Cary Nicholas knew that the embargo had failed abroad and had created serious problems at home. He communicated these thoughts to the

[75] TJ to Thomas Mann Randolph, Feb. 7, 1809, to Alexander McCrae, Feb. 8, 1809, Jefferson Papers, LC.

[76] Gallatin to Joseph Hopper Nicholson, Dec. 29, 1808, Joseph Hopper Nicholson Papers, LC.

[77] Anderson to Adams, Jan. 1, 1809, Adams Family Papers, MHS, reel 407.

president and urged him to "give a tone to that part of the nation that is without taint [and] move them to some exertion." "Unless this can be done," he warned, "I see no remedy." This dismal letter communicated to the president the same ideas that the congressman had already given privately to his Virginia friends. But his personal attempt to move Jefferson off the rock of embargo ended with Nicholas clinging to the same stone. "I beg you Sir," he concluded, "to consider these as more the suggestions of a mind anxiously seeking the public good than as opinions conclusively formed. With such difficulties at every turn, I am disposed to cling to the embargo as long as there is anything to hope from it." Nicholas's letter went unanswered. By the time he brought his misgivings to the congressional floor, the sterner policies he desired could not command a majority. Both executive silence and congressional paralysis precluded a Republican move beyond embargo toward war and allowed men who knew better but hoped differently to elevate dreams over reason.[78]

On January 24, 1809, Nicholas offered the resolution that eventually resulted in the embargo's March 4 repeal. His goals were quite different, as to both timing and purpose. He favored a June repeal (three other repeal dates were also proposed from the floor, February 15, March 4, and John Randolph's "forthwith"), and he hoped its positioning in a strong package might yet change the European posture toward the United States. According to his resolution, the United States should "resume, maintain, and defend its navigation of the high seas" after June 1. His plan included both the defensive arming of American merchant vessels and the granting of letters of marque and reprisal against France and Great Britain. Although Nicholas hoped that the implementation of his resolution might preserve peace, it aimed at war, the only course, he told his colleagues, that "can extricate [the nation] from its difficulties." In keeping with this overall purpose, it also aimed to avoid the middle ground of partial repeal that would only weaken the United States militarily and strengthen England commercially. Between the congressional enactment of the resolution and June 1, the United States should ready itself for war, militarily and psychologically. If the belligerent nations resumed their harassment of American trade after June 1, Congress, meeting in special summer session, would declare war

[78] Nicholas to TJ, Dec. 22, 1808, Wilson Cary Nicholas Papers, LC.

immediately, thereby preserving most of the embargo's defensive accomplishments.[79]

Nicholas's ideas did not reflect an administration policy because, since November, the administration had no clearly defined and consistent program. The president had isolated himself from the doubts circulating in Congress and believed that its program to strengthen the embargo and to make provision for a special summer session "substantially decides the course they [the Republican majority] mean to pursue." Still thinking that the present session would take no final action on either the embargo or the foreign crisis, Jefferson was not even aware of Nicholas's plan, and the congressman's January 24 resolution came as a complete surprise.[80]

Madison continued to favor the embargo or some diluted form of economic coercion. Shortly after Cook's meeting with Gallatin, the New Englander took his misgivings directly to the secretary of state. He later reported that Madison was "inclined to hug the embargo, and die in its embrace." The heir apparent also opposed defensive arming and letters of marque and reprisal for "obvious and weighty reasons." He also opposed another plan circulating in Washington that had the present Congress repeal the embargo, resume trade, and declare war "contingent" on future European harassment because the idea was "not reducible to a fixed and practicable shape." For the secretary of state economic coercion, even in diluted form, still had validity long after the character of the European war and of the American people had defeated it.[81]

Only Gallatin favored policies consistent with those contained in the January 24 resolution. Both sets took the likelihood of war as their point of departure and attempted to salvage the embargo's de-

---

[79] Wilson Cary Nicholas, *Annals*, 10th Cong., 2d sess., pp. 1172, 1233.

[80] TJ to Thomas Leiper, Jan. 21, 1809, Jefferson Papers, LC.

[81] Cook to John Quincy Adams, Jan. 1, 1809, Adams Family Papers, MHS, reel 407; Madison to [?], n.d., Madison Papers, LC, reel 10. The editors of the microfilm edition of the LC Madison collection date this letter Jan. 31, 1809, and assume it was sent to Gallatin. Brant maintains that Madison was the invisible author of the Nicholas resolution because of the copy of the Nicholas resolution, dated Feb. 4, 1809, written in Madison's hand, in the Gallatin Papers (Brant, *James Madison, Secretary of State*, p. 477). The letter of Jan. 31, 1809, however, puts Madison against arming and contingent war and in favor of "repeal [of] the embargo no matter how soon as to all countries except Great Britain and France" and nonintercourse against the two belligerents.

fensive accomplishments from the wreckage of economic coercion. But Gallatin's support was insufficiently strong to ensure that the Nicholas proposals, rooted as they were in the harsh realities of European power, would command either the attention or the votes of a weary Republican majority anxiously longing to escape or ignore the difficulties that inevitably befell a peaceful, idealistic, yet avaricious neutral nation in a world at war.

The congressional Republicans were in as much disarray as the executive Jeffersonians. Only in the South did Nicholas's ideas command favor, and there the support contained pockets of opposition. John Randolph and his band favored immediate repeal and opposed nonintercourse against the belligerents. Several southerners supported Tennessean John Rhea's suggestion to replace the embargo with a nonintercourse act against the belligerents on March 4 and to forgo any military legislation whatever. David R. Williams was a loyal defender of the embargo from South Carolina who surprised everyone by proposing that complete repeal take effect on February 15. Because he blamed the embargo's plight on northern merchants, he wanted the embargo removed while northern ports were still icebound so that the instigators of American retreat would lose the race to the European markets to their more virtuous southern brethren. Although nonintercourse was preferred mostly in the North, and there for domestic reasons, some northerners, like Ezekiel Bacon, opposed it because it was unenforceable, while Madison's support for it weakened the southern opposition to a policy that, literally, had no friends.[82]

On February 1 the House of Representatives, sitting in Committee of the Whole, voted down a June 1 repeal date by a two-to-one margin and thereby ensured that the embargo would be repealed on March 4. Rather than accept this, a group of southern Republicans supported a resolution sponsored by George Troup of Georgia to table the Nicholas resolution for the life of the session and to postpone any decision on the embargo until the summer. The motion was soundly defeated, 26 ayes against 93 nays. All who voted for it were Republican: nineteen from the South, nine from Virginia alone. The Nicholas resolution had aimed both to resume trade and to defend it with military power. Its June repeal date made sense only in the

[82] Bacon, *Annals*, 10th Cong., 2d sess., pp. 1270–88.

larger contexts of military preparation and the preservation of what the embargo had accomplished at so high an economic cost. The June date was defeated in Congress because a majority of the nation's legislators opposed all policies that might lead to war. Stripped of its military and defensive purposes, the June date lost its rationale. "What ha[s] been already done," a Connecticut Federalist gleefully observed in describing the awful backfiring of the Nicholas resolution, "ha[s] excited the most pleasing hopes and joyful anticipations in the nation. Let us not disappoint them." Congress did not. On February 3 in Committee of the Whole it approved March 4 as the last day of the embargo.[83]

The Republicans caucused on Saturday evening, February 4, and the antiretreat forces tried to repair the damage. Congressmen Eppes, Jackson, Nicholas, and William Burwell of Virginia and Smilie of Pennsylvania along with Senators Smith from Maryland and Giles from Virginia begged, pleaded, and "pressed" the northern Republicans not to let the March 4 repeal stand as congressional policy. They began by demanding too much: "immediate or contingent war," Bacon of Massachusetts later reported. Finally, the Virginians offered to postpone consideration of war or any military legislation (defensive arming or letters of marque and reprisal) if the northern congressmen would help prolong the embargo until June 1. The northern Republicans rejected the very proposal that earlier they would have gladly accepted. As late as January 9 Bacon broke with the Massachusetts caucus and told John Quincy Adams that for the sake of Jefferson, he would support June repeal but that, unfortunately, "the Administration" opposed the policy. By February, Bacon thought "it would be triffling with the feelings and the interests of the people to disappoint the calculations which our vote on Friday must universally create." After the Republican caucus, Wilson Cary Nicholas confessed to Madison that "it has been our misfortune that the various expedients have been offered too late. At the beginning of the session, we could have carried any plan connected with the repeal of the embargo."[84]

[83] Vote on the Troup resolution, ibid., p. 1332; Jonathan O. Moseley, ibid., p. 1334.

[84] Brant, *James Madison, Secretary of State*, pp. 477–79; Gallatin to TJ, Feb. 4, 1809, Jefferson Papers, LC; Ezekiel Bacon to Adams, Jan. 9, 1809, Adams Family Papers, MHS, reel 407; Bacon to Joseph Story, Jan. 22, Feb. 5, 15, 1809, Joseph

Contradictory sets of truths supported the arguments of both those who favored speedy repeal divorced from some larger military purpose and those who favored blending the embargo's last months into a military and diplomatic framework that anticipated hostilities, depending on European actions, in the near future. On the one hand, coercion had failed, continued economic isolation risked massive popular disobedience, and the nation was ill-prepared, militarily and psychologically, for war. But on the other, simple repeal disguised in nonintercourse addressed none of the foreign issues, squandered what the embargo had already accomplished, and seemingly ensured future European harassment with America's commercial wealth spread dangerously across the oceans. That Congress chose simple repeal from these competing realities merely underscored its concern with constituent pressures, the weakness of the country, and its own antiwar sentiments. Although the retreat was engineered by New England Republicans, they were not proud of their handiwork. "Let [the merchants] defend themselves if they please," Bacon brooded. "And when they had rather fight with the nation . . . than be plundered, they will probably tell us so." The embargo died of democracy. "The genius and duty of Republican government," Orchard Cook concluded from what had passed, "is to make laws to suit the people, and not . . . make the people suit the laws." [85]

By February 4 Congress stood poised to repudiate completely the resolves of the November Campbell Report. So drastic had been the political change that Jefferson thought British power, through its monied influence, had corrupted "the legislative . . . authorities." He now hoped that the Republicans would have strength enough to add nonintercourse against the belligerents to repeal and "save our independence," but he thought even this "doubtful." His worst fears almost came true. Only by ten votes did the Republicans, mostly southern, manage to recommit the Nicholas resolution (the blank filled in with March 4) to the House Committee on Foreign Affairs. Also sent to the committee were resolutions for arming merchant ships and for making war contingent on future belligerent captures of

Story Papers, LC; Nicholas to Madison, Feb. 6, 1809, Madison Papers, LC, ser. 2, reel 25.

[85] Bacon to Joseph Story, Feb. 15, 1809, Joseph Story Papers, LC; Cook, *Annals*, 10th Cong., 2d sess., p. 1250.

American vessels. Already in committee, since December 31, was Rhea's nonintercourse resolution.[86]

The committee, chaired by Nicholas during Campbell's illness, took up all the resolutions on February 9, and the next day reported out a bill which simply added "the beggarly substitute of a non-intercourse" to the repeal of the embargo. Plans for contingent war and the defensive arming of merchant ships did not survive the committee meetings. Nicholas had discussed the proposed bill with Madison, and since the secretary of state opposed both defensive arming and contingent war, the likelihood is that they were not pushed at the February 9 meeting. On February 6 the full House had struck the letters of marque and reprisal clause from the Nicholas resolution, and Nicholas told Madison that although he might be able to get the clause put back in the Foreign Affairs Committee bill, he did not think it could pass the whole House. It did not appear in the final committee package. The bill that was reported out removed the embargo on all nations except France and Great Britain effective March 4; excluded French and British vessels from American ports, also effective March 4; and banned the importation of their goods in American bottoms effective May 20. This essentially decided the shape of congressional policy. But before this became law, the southern Republicans struggled a final time to deny what had been done.[87]

Although the Foreign Affairs Committee had added noninter-course to repeal at Madison's request, increasingly after February 9 southern Republicans viewed it with less and less favor. Nicholas castigated it as a betrayal of the embargo's original purposes. Campbell delivered the most sophisticated, involved, and far-reaching attack against it. He had been absent from Congress since it had approved the report bearing his name, and he was shocked, he told his colleagues, that they were "occupying a ground so different from that they occupied a few weeks ago." The particular change that angered him was the new relationship between nonintercourse and the embargo. Previously the goal had been to toughen the embargo by adding nonintercourse to it; now, he observed, Congress

---

[86] TJ to Thomas Mann Randolph, Feb. 7, 1809, to Alexander McCrae, Feb. 8, 1809, Jefferson Papers, LC.

[87] Wilson Cary Nicholas to Madison, Feb. 6, 1809, Madison Papers, LC, ser. 2, reel 25; Stephen White to Joseph Story, Feb. 18, 1809, Joseph Story Papers, LC.

was about to destroy the embargo's accomplishments with the expedient of partial repeal. "You have heretofore saved your property and seamen by the embargo. I conceive you are now about to throw at the mercy of Great Britain your whole commerce and seamen that have been so long preserved from her grasp." Campbell reminded his colleagues of their original conceptualization of the nation's dilemma, based on the November report drafted by Gallatin, reported by his committee, and approved overwhelmingly by the whole House. Consequently, the nation should keep the embargo until June, strengthen it with nonintercourse, hurry the work of military preparations, take the last chance of peace in Europe or change in the belligerents' policies toward the United States, and let the summer session vote war if the resumption of American trade saw a corresponding resumption of English harassment.[88]

These speeches began a flurry of congressional activity. John Clopton, a Republican from Virginia, moved to strike repeal from the omnibus bill. This set him apart from Republicans like Nicholas, Campbell, and Gallatin who wished to blend repeal into a sensible framework that comprehended both the failure of coercion and the probability of war. Clopton may have been speaking for Madison; at least he stated Madison's policy preferences and supported his stand with Pinkney's data on the embargo's impact on the English economy. But Clopton's quixotic attempt to turn the congressional tide failed.[89]

The Federalists then tried to strike nonintercourse from the committee package, thereby ending America's affair with commercial weapons. The amendment, sponsored by William Milnor of Pennsylvania, failed. But what began as a predictable Federalist attack soon developed more interesting possibilities. Four days after the vote on the Milnor amendment, the southern Republicans resurrected it as their own in a desperate attempt to force northern Republicans either to join them in more vigorous measures or to let the embargo's repeal, stripped of its soothing camouflage, stand as Congress's final answer to English abuse. These efforts failed because every congressman recognized them for what they were. The Federalists who had previously supported the Milnor amendment

[88] Wilson Cary Nicholas, *Annals*, 10th Cong., 2d sess., pp. 1443–47; George Washington Campbell, ibid., pp. 1475–85.

[89] Clopton, ibid., pp. 1451–60.

rejected an almost identical Republican proposal—only Daniel Verplanck broke ranks and voted in favor. Of the thirty-eight Republican aye votes, thirty came from the South, eleven from Virginia alone. In the meantime, the Senate had finally passed a bill of its own. In deference to the lateness of the session, the House decided on February 22 to table its own bill and to take up the work of the Senate instead.[90]

The Senate bill contained a letters of marque and reprisal clause that the House had already stricken from its own legislation. The clause, section eleven, was a tardy replica of the manageable war strategy that had underwritten Jefferson's unsuccessful summer diplomacy. Once the chief executive had determined that one of the belligerents had complied with American demands, and in this matter discretion was completely his, the clause bound him to resume trade with the complying nation and to issue letters against the other. The strategy attained some support because it might frighten both belligerents into repeal, or at least scale down the number of American adversaries.[91] Chances of success for either goal, however, were quite small. The strategy had completely failed the past summer. If France had not complied when it had everything to gain, it was unlikely that the outcome would be any different after the United States had passed a nonintercourse bill so heavily weighted in favor of the commercial interests of Great Britain. But the strategy resembled honorable policy, and this commended it to many congressmen who were sensitive on this point. But regardless of feasibility, the Senate desire to let the president play one belligerent against the other in pursuit of peace or manageable war outraged southern Republicans in the House. Federalists voted against section eleven because they had consistently opposed all administration attempts to combat the British imperial system. Northern Republicans voted against the clause because it was too bellicose. Southern Reublicans like David Williams from South Carolina and John Wayles Eppes from Virginia opposed the policy because its implications clashed with important assumptions they held about the character of Republican foreign policy. Section eleven's realpolitik offended them. They would not buy English trade with war against France, especially since impressments were nowhere mentioned in the proposed legislation.

[90] Ibid., pp. 1494–1500.
[91] James Holland, ibid., pp. 1503–6.

Seventy-four congressmen voted to strike the clause out of the Senate bill. Political affiliations have been determined for sixty-five of the aye voters. Twenty-three were Federalists, twenty were northern Republicans, and twenty-two were Republicans from the South. The defeat of the letters clause, Wilson Cary Nicholas told Ezekiel Bacon, "was done by the very same troops the administration had drilled for the service."[92]

After this defeat, the southern Republicans who opposed simple repeal tried to make the substance of section eleven compatible with the sensibilities of their regional brethren. Congressman Jackson from Virginia proposed that the nation deal with both belligerents independently. If the English failed to revoke their orders after a certain period of time, the president would instruct public vessels to wage maritime war, "grant permission to private vessels to arm as public privateers," and order the militia and regular army to invade contiguous British territory. Upon a French refusal to revoke its decrees, similar action would be taken. Although the Jackson amendment won immediate southern favor, it was too bold an action for so late in the session. It was the last gasp of a tired and frightened antiretreat southern Republican remnant, a frantic, unplanned attempt to avert, in the eleventh hour, without the support of either president or president-elect, the ruinous economic, emotional, and military implications of nonintercourse. Its very boldness deprived it of the votes needed for passage.[93]

On February 27 the House of Representatives approved the nonintercourse bill by a vote of 81 to 40. The bill pleased almost no one. Not the Federalists, who voted against it because of its paternity and its kinship with economic coercion; not the New England Republicans, who simply preferred it to war and embargo; and not the antiretreat block within the Republican party, located mostly in the South, who preferred it to outright submission.[94]

On the eve of his own inauguration, James Madison hoped that nonintercourse would pinch Great Britain and conform, at least distantly, to his ingrained notions on the power of economic coercion as a tool of diplomacy and a weapon of war. Nonintercourse would force

[92] Eppes and Williams, ibid., pp. 1510–18; Bacon to Joseph Story, Feb. 26, 1809, Joseph Story Papers, LC.

[93] *Annals*, 10th Cong., 2d sess., pp. 1523–30.

[94] Ezekiel Bacon to Joseph Story, Feb. 27, 1809, Joseph Story Papers, LC.

England to secure American commodities in roundabout ways. By "subjecting the supplies from the United States to the expense and delay of double voyages," Madison hoped that nonintercourse would make England suffer enough to reconsider its obnoxious orders. David Erskine, the British minister to the United States, knew better. England would soon have the American trade, he wrote his superiors, and from Americans themselves. Nonintercourse, he told them, was "a subterfuge to extricate [the administration] from the embarrassments of the embargo system." For three additional years the nation would pursue it and other "wretched expedients." The resulting humiliation would give the United States another reason apart from foreign oppression and the girth of its dream for "prosperous neutrality" to go, finally, to war.[95]

[95] John Dawson, *Annals*, 10th Cong., 2d sess., p. 1540; Madison to Pinkney, Feb. 10, 1809, Diplomatic Instructions, All Countries, vol. 7, NA; Ralph Ketcham, *James Madison, a Biography* (New York, 1971), p. 466; Perkins, *Prologue*, pp. 182–83, 223–60; Roger H. Brown, *The Republic in Peril: 1812* (New York, 1971), pp. 16–87.

JEFFERSON AND THE EMBARGO
Foreign Policy, Political Economy, Republican Law

A Discredited Weapon

After he left office, Jefferson steadfastly maintained that the embargo would have routed the British orders had the American people supported it a little longer.[1] It is unlikely, however, that an additional two, six, or twelve months of embargo would have changed British policy. For even if we concede to the Jeffersonians that John Quincy Adams was wrong and that the loss of American markets, raw materials, and food could have toppled the British system, the embargo's continuation through the spring and summer of 1809 would not have supplied the crucial difference because in its last few months evasions mounted and exports to Great Britain increased. Before the embargo was repealed in fact, it had already lost its ability to withhold American agricultural produce from foreign markets. By December 1808 embargo breakers were telling English policy makers that even if the Jeffersonians continued their experiment in self-denial, England could still count on a steadily rising supply of American raw materials.

Midway through the embargo's fifteen months, James Maury, the American consul in Liverpool, summed up for James Madison its economic impact on Great Britain. England's export sector had not suffered appreciably. In the first half of 1808, exports to the United States were "so much beyond expectation" that England used its own merchant ships in the traffic even though the embargo prohibited their leaving America with cargoes. More important to England was its burgeoning continental trade. So great was the European demand that England encouraged American vessels to make

[1] Peterson, *Thomas Jefferson and the New Nation*, p. 861.

the Anglo-European voyages. Those that did commanded "very high freights." But the American ships involved in this trade were not embargo breakers. They had been in European and English ports when the law had been passed and stayed in the Old World to reap the carrying profits that awaited them. America's economic weapons, according to Maury, had not prostrated the English export trade. The American market remained mostly available, and England's European market more than compensated for its partial loss.[2]

Although in theory it was not to be so, successful coercion, because of the weapons chosen, came to depend more on the stoppage of American exports than on the nonimportation of English goods. During the first two-thirds of 1808, a very small number of American ships—"a few straggling American vessels," Maury reported in late August—laden with cotton, grain, and tobacco cleared into English ports.[3] Ironically, the high volume of American exports in 1806 and 1807 accounted for this success by depressing the price and evaporating the profit on key agricultural commodities. Five-eighths of the 1807 cotton crop, for example, wound up in Great Britain.[4] The woefully low prices that resulted from this glut held through much of 1808 and offered little economic incentive to violate the embargo by transatlantic voyages. As a result, not one American vessel cleared into Liverpool during the first eight months of the year. Had there been no embargo, America's farmers would have sent their produce to England and absorbed the loss. Until recent times, agriculturalists have responded to depressed prices with increased production and panic selling. But the lack of financial reward encouraged popular support and contributed to the embargo's early strength against this type of violation.[5]

[2] Maury to Pinkney, Aug. 9, 1808, Maury to Madison, Aug. 23, 1808, Liverpool, Dispatches from Consular Officers, RG 59, M141, NA, reel L2.

[3] Maury to Madison, Aug. 23, 1808, ibid.

[4] Maury to Madison, Sept. 8, 1808, ibid.

[5] By July 1807 the importations of cotton into Liverpool exceeded the total value of the 1806 importations. Although American vessels were numerous in Liverpool, trade was dull and cotton prices were very low. In December the American consul reported that although "apprehension of a rupture with the USA appears rather increasing and has occasioned some advances in several articles of American produce," the fear had occasioned "none in cotton." Although prices did rise on all American produce, cotton included, in response to the embargo, by March 1808 the cotton schedules had again begun to fall (Maury to Madison, July 23, Nov. 19, Dec. 18, 1807, Feb. 6, April 20, 1808, ibid.).

The embargo's plight was that initial success promised ultimate failure because it depleted English reserves of American raw materials, drove their price to artificially high levels, and created inducements for the American entrepreneur that would eventually prove too attractive to let pass. After midyear, English cotton factors reported "a very rapid advance" on the price of raw cotton in Liverpool, mostly because of "none coming since the operation of the embargo." By the fall, prices had reached a dangerously high level. So did the price of wheat, because mildew had ravaged an "unusually promising" British crop. Autumn predictions from British agents in America that the embargo would continue through 1809 accelerated the upward spiral by triggering a mania of speculation within the English cotton houses. By mid-September, the price of American upland cotton had "already reached a price unprecedented." The import house of Cropper, Benson and Company noted in its September price list that "the increasing scarcity of cotton, together with very little expectation of the early removal of the embargo had caused a rapid advance on that article." Prices on old uplands, New Orleans, Sea Island, and "finer grades" had all risen. So had the price of tobacco, and qualities "fit for home consumption" were bringing 13½d. per pound. So devastating had been the mildew that Great Britain was importing American wheat from its Caribbean islands to feed its own people. The import house of James Hodgkinson and Company explained in its mid-September price circular that scarcity, rumors of the embargo's continuation, a horrible cotton crop in Brazil, and rampant speculation and hoarding had driven up the price of American cotton to unheard-of levels. Almost daily the price rose 5d. and 6d. a pound. In the week ending September 16, 6,500 bags of cotton had changed hands in the Liverpool market, with less than a quarter of the total actually leaving the market. The bulk of American cotton had become a floating speculative medium. It changed hands rapidly within the market, each buyer seeking another who would go a higher price and who, in his turn, would hold for awhile and sell to the next interested speculator.[6]

The high price for cotton held through October. On November 1 Maury predicted that Great Britain would have to "greatly curtail this branch of manufacture" unless fresh supplies of cotton arrived

[6] Maury to Madison, Sept. 8, 17, 1808, price circular of Cropper, Benson and Co., Sept. 17, 1808, price circular of James Hodgkinson and Co., Sept. 17, 1808, ibid.

from the United States. England's problem was scarcity, speculation, and hoarding. America's, on the other hand, was the embargo's very success, both confirmed and threatened by the tempting price level. On November 26 Maury reported the first instance of what soon formed an exasperating pattern. "The American schooner *Jane* is arrived here this evening (they say an embargo breaker) from Virginia with turpentine and cotton." The next day Maury learned that *Jane* was indeed an embargo breaker: it approached Liverpool with neither clearance papers nor bill of health. After a time in quarantine, it cleared into port and unloaded its cargo of 400 barrels of turpentine and 46 bales of cotton. High British prices, American popular frustration, and Congress's failure to move toward repeal all promised that the illegal voyage of the schooner *Jane* would not be an isolated event. By January, Jefferson and Gallatin had learned from their own customs collectors that cotton smuggling now posed the greatest threat to the embargo.[7]

More and more embargo breakers cleared into Liverpool in December and January. They came from northern, middle Atlantic, and southern ports; they came without register, sea letter, or Mediterranean pass. Sometimes they admitted openly to smuggling; sometimes they said they "were blown off course." They all brought with them cotton, tobacco, and wheat. On February 2 two American vessels that had left the United States in December cleared into Liverpool with several hundred bales of cotton. Four days later four more arrived with over 1,500 bales. By February 12 seven more had entered Liverpool laden with thousands of bales of cotton and bringing to twenty the number of ships that had sailed before the final enforcement measure was passed in January. All together, 5,796 bales of cotton entered Liverpool in American vessels that had violated the embargo in December and January. Fifty-four vessels departed America before the embargo's March 4 repeal. They carried with them about 21,000 bales of cotton, over 12 percent of the entire southern yield for 1810.[8]

[7] Maury to Madison, Nov. 1, 26, 27, 1808, ibid.; TJ to Gallatin, Jan. 20, 30, 1809, Gallatin to TJ, Jan. 9, 1809, Jefferson Papers, LC; Dearborn to Gallatin, Dec. 19, 1808, Gallatin Papers, NYU, reel 18.

[8] The figure of 21,000 bales of cotton is an approximation calculated from the Liverpool consular reports which detail the amount of illegal cotton that cleared into that port; see Maury to Madison, Dec. 13, 1808, Jan. 17, Mar. 6, 1809, to Pinkney,

Several things are important about the pattern of transatlantic embargo breaking. Both depressed prices in England and the American expectation of a November repeal contained this particular type of illegality through October 1808. The Liverpool and West Indian consular reports clearly show that although the embargo had not changed British policy by the fall, it had curtailed American exports. But the embargo's 1808 success drove up the English price levels and produced economic temptations that eager Americans legitimated with cries of oppressive or simply foolish government meddling. When partisanship, ideology, and aspiration fused, Americans openly and, they rationalized, courageously violated the embargo.

The amount of cotton and other agricultural commodities that cleared into Liverpool and other British ports in December, January, and February was crucial for three reasons. It provided the needed raw materials that spared the British manufacturing interest serious dislocation. It caused prices in the British market to turn downward, thereby ending speculation and hoarding and releasing countless bales that otherwise would have remained within the cotton trading centers as a hedge against further price increases. Finally, the physical presence of American ships, provisions, cotton, tobacco, and naval stores in British port cities destroyed the false hope that En-

---

Jan. 14, 26, Feb. 2, 6, 7, 11, 27, Mar. 9, 11, 14, 16, 18, 30, 1809, Liverpool, RG 59, M141, NA, reel L2. G. W. Daniels maintains that "considerable exports to Liverpool must have been made notwithstanding the embargo," and he estimates that about 25,000 bales of cotton entered Liverpool during 1808. But he makes no attempt to place the exports at various points in time ("American Cotton Trade with Liverpool under the Embargo and Non-Intercourse Acts," *American Historical Review* 21, no. 2 [1915–16]: 280). My own research confirms that the embargo was very effective until Nov. 1808, since over 21,000 bales entered after November, due in no small measure to disastrous prices in England. The overwhelming bulk of 1808 cotton entered Liverpool after the combination of exceedingly high prices and the refusal of Congress in November to move toward repeal drove the American merchant community to lawbreaking. Similarly, Louis B. Sears claims that the embargo was effective throughout 1808 because the price of American uplands cotton increased in 1808 by over 50% of its 1807 average (*Jefferson and the Embargo*, p. 287). But to appreciate the success and the failure of the embargo, it must be remembered that the 50% average increase that Sears cites combined both declining prices from Feb. 1808 until the early fall and a tremendously steep rise in the last quarter of the year. The total 1810 southern yield, 178,000 bales, is taken from Robert Fogel and Stanley L. Engerman, *Time on the Cross: The Economics of American Negro Slavery* (Boston, 1974), p. 44.

gland would bend beneath American economic pressure. Jefferson's faith that more time would have vindicated the embargo was based on frustration and bitterness, not on fact. It was the winter evasions and not the March repeal that spoiled the dream.

New England's President: Repudiation and Redemption

Several questions about Jefferson's involvement with the embargo remain unanswered and command attention. Why, at the end of his presidency, when his thoughts and hopes were increasingly on retirement, when, against the wishes and fears of cabinet members and congressional Republicans, he became almost a disinterested observer of the nation's English crisis, when this and much else pointed to Jefferson's final abdication of leadership, why, at this juncture, did he insist so passionately on complete public obedience to the embargo? There were, to be sure, the lingering pressures of office. The failure of the summer diplomacy and the president's refusal to face the meaning of that defeat and confront war left the embargo as the only alternative to submission and imposed on the American people either the obligation of obedience or the rigors of enforcement. But the answer is more complex and involves Jefferson's changing political economy and his constant ideas about Federalism, England, American character, and republican freedom.

Jefferson's frustrating struggle to protect foreign trade with diplomacy, military threats, and economic weapons finally soured him on a national economy bound to foreign markets. Ostensibly a weapon for the English crisis, the embargo became as well a means toward a different and happier American economy. All through 1808, the protection of interests within the existing economy gave way to the imperative of new beginnings. The battle ceased to be against an external foe and instead pitted the present against the future, a dependent against an independent economy, and the American producing classes, rural and urban, against merchant parasites. The embargo years witnessed Jefferson renouncing not only an economy tied to European war but, more audaciously, one tied to foreign markets generally. They showed him gladly renouncing the need to employ reason, persuasion, economic sanction, and military threat to protect markets the nation could not control, should not want, and was not entitled to. The embargo years showed him, finally, retreating to the safety and purity of an idealized and largely imaginary American economy grounded in native production, internal trade, domestic purchasing power, and republican labor.

The frustrations of protecting foreign trade rekindled in Jefferson an isolationist vision of American economic growth. The embargo was to set right the course of American economic development. Talking of future glory, it spoke of past betrayal as well. With it, Jefferson finally rejected the allures of both wartime neutrality and foreign trade that had cozened him and the nation into the pursuit of a dangerous and unrepublican commercial growth and personally applauded a republican path to economic greatness and national independence implicit in America's separation from the Old World, in the bounty of its domain, and in the freedom of its labor. Whether defending the embargo as defensive or coercive, Jefferson constantly celebrated it as a redemptive second chance. "There can be no question in a mind truly American," he wrote in February 1808, "whether it is best to send our citizens and property into certain captivity, or to keep them at home and to turn seriously to that policy which plants the manufacturer and the husbandman side by side and establishes at every door of every one that exchange of mutual labors and comforts which we have hitherto sought in distant regions and under perpetual risk of broils."[9] Damnation and praise of different kinds of economic activity became part of Jefferson's understanding of the embargo. The artisan and the farmer would benefit from the policy. So would the nation. So would shippers and merchants if they relocated their efforts primarily in the carriage of the goods of the American producing classes within the contours of a vibrant internal economy.

This transformation of the role of the merchant shipper marked a significant change in Jefferson's economic thinking. An economy resting on agriculture, foreign trade, and foreign industry, Jefferson's goal since the Revolution, had created equal standing in American society between the farmer and the merchant. The embargo years upset this balance and challenged the merchant class to renounce foreign trade or accept a marginal role in the nation's economic future. The frustrating maritime power of Europe, the seeming impos-

[9] TJ to Tammany Society, Columbian Order, New York, Feb. 29, 1808, Jefferson Papers, LC.

sibility of having both foreign trade and peace, a natural instinct to favor the producer over the trader, Jefferson's own involvement in the nation's quest for wartime profit, and the "rank fraud" of embargo violations all biased him against foreign trade and led Jefferson, finally, to choose and celebrate one side from each of several paired opposites that had maintained a harmonious balance in his view of the American scene until the national and personal traumas of the embargo years shattered it. Each of the cluster of paired opposites (producers and merchants, the interior and the seashore, "ephemeral wealth" and "solid wealth") fractured into antagonistic rivals, and Jefferson increasingly throughout 1808 became the champion of one side of a new dialectic that comprehended geographical, economic, vocational, and moral divisions within the Republic and, in its broadest sense, pitted the American producer against the American parasite.

"We behold in a temporary suspension of our commerce," a group of Philadelphia Republicans wrote Jefferson in March 1808, "an ephemeral and doubtful evil producing a great, a growing, and a lasting good. We see arising out of this cause the prolific sources of our internal wealth explored and with industry and ability directed through channels which, while they benefit the enterprising, [also] enrich our country with solid wealth and make our country more independent and happy." [10] Jefferson's new conception of the proper tack for American economic development loudly applauded the thoughts of the Philadelphia Republicans. Throughout 1808 he pointed to the positive good the embargo was effecting. "Homespun is become the spirit of the times," the president boasted in November.[11] The American people were turning their backs to the entrapments of trading wealth and rejecting "a dangerous doctrine" which Jefferson now saw went to sacrificing "agriculture and man-ufacturing to commerce, to calling all our people from the interior country to the seashore, and to convert[ing] this great agricultural country into a city of Amsterdam."[12] The embargo served the na-tional economic interests that were located in the soil and skills of the American producing classes. It aimed at the happiest of all economic

[10] Philadelphia Republicans to TJ, Mar. 1, 1808, ibid.

[11] TJ to Abraham Bishop, Nov. 13, 1808, to Marquis de Lafayette, Feb. 24, 1809, ibid.

[12] TJ to Thomas Leiper, Jan. 21, 1809, ibid.

convergences: individual prosperity and national growth and independence. And because the embargo favored real wealth, it marched to the rhythms of a Jefferson lyric on the idea of republican labor. The embargo years, then, transformed Jefferson's agrarianism. Once expressing almost exclusively the glories of agricultural work, it now encompassed productive labor generally. He now spoke of "planting" the manufacturer beside the husbandman. Their kinship was the quality of their labor. Artisans had become urban farmers, connected to their rural brothers of the same family by the nexus of productivity that defined the economic and moral dimensions of their occupational pursuits. In this new synthesis, the merchant was only cousin.

Wartime economic goals traduced the idea of productive labor and, by extension, jeopardized the nation's claim of living right by its traditions. Before the frustrations of defending the wartime trade, national leaders had reckoned the carrying business high in their accounting of American prosperity. Wilson Cary Nicholas had advised Jefferson in 1806 that its protection was worth a war.[13] The president's diplomacy with Great Britain had placed on its promotion as high a value as on the protection of the nation's seamen. But near retirement, Jefferson turned against this economic activity. In parts of the Union the desire for wartime profit was overwhelming respect for law and transforming illegality into proud, entrepreneurial ingenuity. Such behavior forced Jefferson to confront the greatest republican horror—massive civil disobedience to good and well-intentioned leaders—and jarred his faith in the strength of American character. The experience of the embargo had shaken the nation's commitment to law, majority rule, and the obligations of citizenship. In combating the lawbreakers, in his insistence on popular respect for the embargo, Jefferson was attacking the commercial spirit, the English spirit, that had visited such traumas on the nation.

Not only was this spirit eroding the legal and moral underpinnings of republican consensual government and undermining the meaning of 1800, it was also transforming America into "a mere headquarters for carrying on the commerce of all nations with one another." This trade did not enrich the nation, but "only a few individuals."[14] Native production, economic independence, the rural life, and national safety were all being sacrificed to a merchant class who, in John

[13] Nicholas to TJ, April 2, 1806, ibid.
[14] TJ to Benjamin Stoddert, Feb. 18, 1809, ibid.

Quincy Adams's phrase, "are as selfish and timid as riches can make them."[15] During the last six months of his presidency, Jefferson could not contain his hatred of this commercial class nor maintain his long-standing conviction that "the greatest prosperity" of the nation "depends on a due balance between agriculture, manufactures, and commerce." The balance constantly broke down when he dwelt on "the jealousy . . . among our commercial men" of their parasitical control of the nation's economy and when he brooded on the inequities of "honest men [farmers] religiously observing" the embargo and "the unprincipled along our seacoast and frontiers . . . fraudulently evading it."[16] His anger made more insistent his vision of a nation built on "solid wealth," internal growth, and economic independence from Europe. His passion for embargo enforcement spoke both to this anger and to the high national purpose now at stake. In his last official address to Congress, Jefferson intended to celebrate this vision as national accomplishment, to applaud the embargo for its contribution to the beneficent change, and to memorialize the artisan and the agriculturalist as the worthy classes within the American Republic. Dreams had become reality.

In the draft of his last annual message, the president noted the happy transformation in the purposes of American investment capital. More private money was going to internal improvement than to foreign trade. "The extent of this conversion," he wrote, "is far beyond expectation and little doubt remains that the establishments will now be permanent and that the mass of our future wants will be supplied among ourselves." Missing in the message was any praise or much succor for American shippers and traders in the export market. Jefferson came close to calling the embargo a blessed event. He outlined an American economic future pegged to the home market and isolation, underwritten by "the cheapness of raw materials" and the abundance and "freedom of labor," and protected from the calamity of foreign competition by congressional "protective duties and prohibitions." Ignoring the merchants dependent on foreign trade, the message, in Jefferson's draft, promised a bright future to the American

[15] Adams to William Branch Giles, Dec. 26, 1808, Adams Family Papers, MHS, reel 135.

[16] TJ to Thomas Leiper, Jan. 21, 1809, TJ to David Humphreys, Jan. 20, 1809, Gen. Henry Dearborn, "circular" to Governors of the States (in Jefferson's hand), Jan. 17, 1809, Jefferson Papers, LC.

farmer and skilled craftsmen. "The produce of the agriculturalist," Jefferson boasted, "will soon find at his own door that exchange for his wants for which it has heretofore traversed the ocean exposed to the dangers of that element, as well as of the rapine practiced on it."[17]

Albert Gallatin thought Jefferson's paragraphs on economic transformation "the most objectionable in the message" and "little less than a denunciation of commerce." The "avowal," he warned, "that a positive benefit is derived from the introduction of manufactures caused by the annihilation of commerce . . . will produce a pernicious effect and furnish a powerful weapon to the disaffected in the seaports and in all the eastern states." Beyond the fact that the growth in manufacturing establishments was not so great as Jefferson claimed, beyond the fact that the nation had not and could not create overnight an economic order independent of foreign commerce, Jefferson had dangerously revealed his hostility to commercial enterprise. Gallatin advised the president to "omit everything which looks like a contrast between commerce and manufactures and exaltation at the result." That foreign commerce was suffering and manufacturing was taking root, the secretary of the treasury insisted, "should be given as a consolation and not as a matter of congratulation."[18]

The new economy existed in Jefferson's imagination, and would take generations to implement in society. So it is understandable that Gallatin was confused when the president celebrated this romance as national accomplishment. But no matter. The celebration shows the rich stakes that Jefferson had invested in the embargo. It was redemptive enterprise that looked away from the present foreign crisis,

[17] TJ, rough draft of annual message, Nov. 8, 1808, ibid.

[18] Gallatin to TJ, received Nov. 3, 1808, ibid. Madison had suggested some reference to the positive good of the embargo, but his notes describe it in less celebrative and less total terms. "It is worthy of consideration that a portion of the industry and capital spared from those pursuits has been converted to internal manufactures and improvements. The extent of this conversion is far beyond expectation, and little doubt remains that the establishments formed and forming will under the auspices of cheap materials and subsistence, the freedom of labor from taxation with us, and the protection given by our commercial laws will become permanent, and that with the aid of household fabrics which needed a trial only to prove the durable advantages of extending them, the mass of our future wants will be materially diminished and the nation consequently liberated in an equal degree from that species of dependence" (Madison, notes for annual message, Nov. 1808, Madison Papers, LC, reel 10).

back to a noble agrarian past and forward to a new agrarianism that included all productive labor and that freed America, finally, from foreign economic bondage. With this the glittering prize, embargo enforcement was absolutely necessary and religiously sought. The long years of frustration in pursuit of a "prosperous neutrality" had finally soured Jefferson on the idea of a maritime future for the United States and relocated his vision of the nation's destiny in its internal economic capacities. By the close of his presidency, he cursed the same trade he had previously covered with the flag of national interest and honor. The carrying trade "brings us into collision with other powers in every sea," he lamented two weeks before leaving office. "This exuberant commerce is now bringing war on us." Jefferson's anger reflected more than the immediacy of war. It bristled with an anxious awareness that the trading spirit, and his administration's defense of it, had dulled the moral sharpness of the Republic and had diverted it from its unique New World economic mission.[19]

Toward the end of the embargo, angry New Englanders were convinced that the destruction of their foreign trade fulfilled the design of Jefferson's policy; that, in the words of the Boston Committee of Merchants, Traders, Mechanics, and Mariners, "the evident intention" of the embargo was "to unjustifiably depress an ill fated section of the union and on their ruin to erect the riches and glory of" the agricultural South.[20] So complete was their rage and so convinced were they that a crass sectional plot posed as national policy, these Bostonians ignored how much the southern economy also suffered and supported their opposition to tyrannous embargo with direct appeals to England's Magna Carta, omitting from their defense America's, and Jefferson's, famous Declaration. In one sense the Boston merchants were correct: Jefferson's policy had become anticommercial or, more precisely, a renunciation of commerce unconnected to American productivity and American markets. But in their haste to crucify, most New Englanders disregarded his previous commercial objectives that solidly welded his presidency to the New England interest. Between 1803 and 1808 Jefferson and Madison bound their diplomacy in the economic web of European war and defended all New England's commercial hopes, especially the lucra-

---

[19] TJ to Benjamin Stoddert, Feb. 18, 1809, Jefferson Papers, LC.

[20] Merchants, Traders, Mechanics, and Mariners (Boston), "Petition to Thomas Jefferson for Relief from the Embargo Policy," Dec. 28, 1808, ibid.

tive wartime carrying trade. In July 1808 the cabinet had decided that even if England revoked its orders "as to our own produce only," the United States would still reject such a settlement because it excluded the carrying trade. Virginian agrarians like John Taylor blamed the administration's fondness of northern commercial enterprise on Madison and his "predilection for the English navigation system." Another Virginian, Beverley Tucker, angrily compared the policy of embargo and stagnation "when the question is about our right to dispose of our own produce" with "all our [previous] clamour about the carrying trade, and our threats to go to war in defense of it." The Jeffersonians, a perceptive New Englander wrote in 1808, "are accused as being the enemies of commerce. I think this accusation cruel. They are indeed friendly to commerce *overmuch*. They waste themselves in defending it in all the immunities that its selfstyled *friends* claim for it." "All we contend for," Madison told Orchard Cook of Massachusetts in November, "is principally the interests of the north—the carrying trade in particular." When the New England Republicans deserted the embargo in December, Ezekiel Bacon noted that the administration "have been abandoned by that very interest for whose sake . . . they have been pushed to take the ground they have done." If Jefferson belonged to any region before 1808, he was New England's president. When he renounced both New England and foreign commerce at the end of his public run, his own involvement in the nation's quest for wartime profit shaped the severity of his act of rejection.[21]

The English in America

Had not Jefferson held certain assumptions on the moral qualities of a republican people and the moral deficiencies of the Federalist party,

[21] TJ, Notes on Cabinet Meeting, July 6, 1808, Jefferson Papers, LC; Taylor to Wilson Cary Nicholas, May 4, 1806, Wilson Cary Nicholas Papers, UVa; Tucker to John Randolph, Dec. 30, 1807, Tucker-Coleman Collection, Earl Gregg Swem Library, College of William and Mary (microfilm at UVa.); C. P. Sumner to Joseph Story, Dec. 1808, Bacon to Joseph Story, June 1, 1808, Jan. 22, 1809, Joseph Story Papers, LC; Cook to John Quincy Adams, Nov. 10, 1808, Adams Family Papers, MHS, reel 406.

his response to embargo breaking would not have been bitter disappointment, anger, an intense desire to scourge those who mocked the law and deserted their country, and a compulsion to prove, with force if necessary, that the idealized eighteenth-century republic of his imagination had withstood the assault of time and the temptation of self-interest. He would not have had to prove, in the words of a loyal Republican society, that during a crisis affecting community survival, "the rancorous spirit of party ceases its ravings, the clamours of discontent subside, the suggestions of mercantile inconvenience and disappointments are dissipated, and one united and magnanimous sentiment pervades every class of citizens: the government reposes with the confidence of the people, the people in the government."[22] Jefferson's attitude toward the Federalist party and a republican people dated to the 1790s and the American Revolution and affected in crucial ways his expectations for the embargo and his response to its evasions.

American politics in the 1790s was violent and embittered. During the decade economic and ideological antagonisms released hatreds and passions that threatened an early end to the nation's experiment in democratic self-government and union. That experiment outlived the political violence of the 1790s. Popular government moved toward stability and permanence in the United States when Jefferson and the Republican party contended successfully and peacefully for the leadership of the national government in 1800. Jefferson's first inaugural address, especially its idea that political difference need not slide into political war (an idea artfully expressed in the phrase "we are all republicans, we are all federalists"), elevated to party dogma a personal commitment to political harmony. His moderate stance toward the Federalist party during his first term brought him political victory in Federalist New England in 1804 and seemingly vindicated both his belief in political consensus and the sincerity of his own moderation.[23]

[22] Tammany Society, Columbian Order Number One, New York, to TJ, Feb. 16, 1808, Jefferson Papers, LC.

[23] On the nature and extent of political violence in the 1790s, see Marshall Smelser, "The Jacobin Phrenzy: The Menace of Monarchy, Plutocracy, and Anglophilia, 1789–1798," *Review of Politics* 31 (1959): 239–88; John R. Howe, Jr., "Republican Thought and the Political Violence of the 1790s," *American Quarterly* 19 (Summer, 1967): 147–65. The best recent treatments of Jefferson and the

Hanging an interpretation of Jefferson's political persuasion on consensus and conciliation, however, obscures very important aspects of his political thought and of his understanding of the dynamics of American politics. The peaceful words and kind policies of the first term camouflage Jefferson's hostile view of the Federalist party. Although this fact is relatively unimportant during Jefferson's first term, it is essential to an understanding of the domestic triggers of the president's enforcement policies.

Jefferson thought that in America political affiliation reflected the moral condition of men. "The division into whig and tory is founded in the nature of man," he wrote Joel Barlow in 1802. The whig-Republican was "healthy," "firm," "virtuous," "sound." The tory-Federalist was "weakly," "nerveless," "corrupt," "disaffected," sick. True Federalists were ill "beyond recall," mired in a state of "settled disaffection." They were also full of hate and "vengeful." Their status on the margin of American society rendered them "desperate and furious." But like the petty man who could not abide the happiness of others, the moral health of those about him made the Federalist a "disorganizer" and a sworn enemy of American freedom and contentment.[24]

Jefferson's first inaugural address was not an acceptance of the Federalist party, which he thought had no place and no legitimate role in American society and politics. The speech was only an invitation to good men of the Federalist persuasion, or, more accurately in Jefferson's mind, of the Federalist delusion, to join the Republican party; a statement that there was room for their talents in American politics if they would desert a "bitter" organization. The extent to which Jefferson was a political harmonizer amounted only to his commitment to the numerical and geographical expansion of the Republican party. His hatred of the Federalist party was constant. The difference between the last four years of the eighteenth century and

---

goal of political reconciliation are Morton Borden, "Thomas Jefferson," Morton Borden, ed., *America's Ten Greatest Presidents* (Chicago, 1961), and the works of Merrill D. Peterson, Dumas Malone, Richard E. Ellis, and Richard Hofstadter cited in the bibliographic essay. Carl Prince maintains that Jefferson's first-term patronage and removal policies mocked the reconciling phrases of his inaugural address ("The Passing of the Aristocracy: Jefferson's Removal of the Federalists, 1801–1805," *Journal of American History* 58 [Dec. 1970]: 563–65).

[24] TJ to Barlow, May 3, 1802, Lipscomb and Bergh, 10:320–21; TJ to Wilmington, Delaware, Citizens, Feb. 16, 1809, Jefferson Papers, LC.

the first four years of the nineteenth century was simply that in the first instance Jefferson organized a political following around his fears and hatreds and made them public, while in the second he maintained his opinions but did so quietly or in private correspondence. Politically astute enough to realize that the work of winning Republican converts from Federalist heresy would not be served by an open crusade against an organization which the votes of the people had discredited and rendered impotent, Jefferson reined in his political feelings for the sake of national harmony and political consolidation. Asked in 1801 why he was not crushing the Federalist sons as the Revolutionary whigs had crushed the tory fathers, Jefferson replied: "We are now justly more tolerant than we could have safely been then, circumstanced as we were." Openly in the late 1790s and privately in his first presidential term, however, Jefferson's attitudes toward the Federalist party were both negative and consistent.[25]

An appreciation of the political mentality of the Revolutionary generation is particularly useful for understanding Jefferson's encounter with his post-Revolutionary political enemies. Jefferson's view of American politics was remarkably similar to the way the Revolutionary whig viewed his political universe on the eve of the American Revolution. Formalism, fear, an abiding compulsion to see pattern where perhaps none existed, and a tendency to see conspiracies in the march of events were important characteristics of mid-eighteenth-century American political culture. The American whig, heir to an English radical tradition, perceived a divided society. Power always warred against liberty. This rather artificial political mathematics that equated government with power and the people with liberty ignored social tensions among classes at home. But it was quite real to the American colonial mind. Government, the apparatus of power, had always to be watched lest its naturally expansive tendency consume liberty and reduce the people to slavery.[26]

[25] TJ to John Page, Mar. 22, 1801, to William Branch Giles, Mar. 23, 1801, to Benjamin Rush, Mar. 24, 1801, to Henry Knox, Mar. 27, 1801, to Jacob Crowninshield, Mar. 29, 1801, Lipscomb and Bergh, 10:234, 240, 243, 245, 252.

[26] Bernard Bailyn, *The Ideological Origins of the American Revolution* (Cambridge, Mass., 1967), especially chap. 3, "Power and Liberty: A Theory of Politics," pp. 55–93.

Fear, then, characterized the American colonists' perception of their British governors. The Coercive Acts of 1774 propelled a submerged and inchoate fear to the surface of American political consciousness, sharpened it, and crucially altered England's image in the American political imagination, and in Jefferson's. No longer controlled by the integrity of the British constitution, English power was on the loose and on the march. Ministerial bribery had destroyed the independence of the House of Commons and poisoned it against the American people. Commons, king, and the English people became malevolent attackers of American freedom. Joining the attackers were those apostate to their countrymen: the American tories.

The recent history of imperial-colonial conflict achieved a different meaning in the American mind once trust in British virtue dissolved in the acid of the Coercive Acts. A pattern emerged from the welter of the past. British actions—stamp taxes, Townshend duties, the creation of juryless admiralty courts, the dissolution of colonial assemblies, standing armies, the Boston Massacre, the Coercive Acts themselves—were no longer comprehended as unconnected and unrelated events, but rather as integrated parts of a plot to deprive the American people of their liberty. The Declaration of Independence expressed the political mentality of a frightened Revolutionary generation. It charted British conspiracy and authorized violence and rebellion because of the threat it posed to the future of liberty in the American colonies. The importance of conspiracy, its pathological roots, its ability to attract a popular following, to win converts through deception, guile, and cunning; these were Jefferson's ideas on nineteenth-century Federalism that he brought with him from his Revolutionary past.

The president's attitude toward the Federalist party and its patron—toward "anglomen" and England—was a dramatic reenactment of the fears, suspicions, and antagonisms of the American Revolution. The Republican-Federalist conflict was to him a continuation of the ongoing encounter between liberty and power, virtue and villainy, between public health and social degeneracy. The Republican and the Federalist were reincarnations of the domestic antagonists of the American Revolution: the loyal patriot and the apostate tory. The Republican party was for Jefferson a simple regrouping of the popular movement of American citizens that had secured Independence. It was less a political organization than a social fraternity of patriot citizens, bound together more by affection than by the impersonal links of party machinery. When he spoke of Republican victories he did not describe political success, but rather social reformation and American triumph. "A new subject of congratulation has arisen," he wrote Gideon Granger in 1801. "I mean the regeneration of Rhode Island. I hope it is the beginning of that resurrection of the genuine spirit of New England."[27]

New England decency was vital to Jefferson's image of a united republican country. He solved the riddle of loyal New Englanders electing apostate leaders by locating Federalist victory in the enchanting power of political infection; in the triumph of cunning over simplicity, of guile over substance. He saw in the political process a constant dialectic of deception and perception. "Bad men will sometimes get in," he warned in 1801, "and with such an immense patronage, may make great progress in corrupting the public mind and principles." Evil leaders could confuse the people and turn a good society on itself in a morbid feast of republican autocannibalism. Jefferson's encounter with the American people—with their character and strength—was an ambiguous one. As strong, decent, and republican as the American people were, they could also become, he feared, "the instruments of their own bondage."[28]

These thoughts impelled Jefferson to place a high premium on the power of leadership and example and made him, finally, an eighteenth-century republican elitist. The relationship he perceived between social health and sound leadership was a behavioral one and approached the conviction that society would be sound or sick in proportion to the qualities of those in positions of political and social eminence. "Our people in a body are wise." This faith was always the source of Jefferson's optimistic vision of the nation's future. The popular wisdom so vital to national happiness was of the spirit and

[27] TJ to Granger, May 30, 1801, Lipscomb and Bergh, 10:259. For Jefferson, Republican victories, indeed republican society itself, rested on ethics, and ethics were grounded on the natural affections. Consequently, although the educated man should read "astronomy, natural philosophy, and mathematics," he need not read in ethics: "I do not place ethics on the list, because nature has not made a science of what the happiness of society makes it necessary every man should understand. Its dictates are written in the heart of every good man" (TJ to John Carr, April 28, 1807, Jefferson Papers, UVa).

[28] TJ to Moses Robinson, Mar. 23, 1801, to John Dickinson, Dec. 19, 1801, Lipscomb and Bergh, 10:237.

character, not of the intellect. And the people were wise, and therefore capable of self-government, because they were "under the unrestrained and unperverted operation of their own understanding." Good leaders and good people; the social circle was complete.[29]

But the popular understanding could be corrupted. The history of New England from 1765 to 1800 charted for Jefferson an immense political backsliding from Revolutionary patriotism to Federalist apostasy. The people were not to blame. What troubled him was that it seemingly did not matter that they did not share the principles of their spurious leaders. A clique of lawyers, judges, political and economic "adventurers," and clergy had played upon foreign crisis and economic interest in the 1790s, deceived the people, and captured power over them with their consent. Although Jefferson thought that New England was "as absolutely republican" as his native Virginia, the Federalist strategy had temporarily succeeded in the North. Still, he took as an article of faith that the Federalist method—to confuse, to frighten, to poison the public mind—must ultimately fail throughout the nation. Massachusetts "had drunk deeper of the delusion, and is therefore slower in recovering from it," he wrote Elbridge Gerry. But "your people will rise again," he assured him. "They will awake like Samson from his sleep and carry away the gates and posts of the city." By 1801 New England was just "recovering," just "escaping" from "the jaws" of a "ravenous crew." Because degenerate leaders could corrupt a republican social order, Jefferson vowed in 1802 to "take no other revenge, than . . . to sink federalism into an abyss from which there shall be no resurrection for it."[30]

Although Republican-Federalist conflict defined a crisis in American society, it did not describe a serious division among the American people. In Jefferson's imagination, the people were naturally Republican. Party differences represented the old antagonism between liberty and power and the moral qualities that each symbolized. The Republican party was not an engine of power, but a movement that the people led and supported to protect their own liberty and the nation's republican future. The Federalist party, an engine of power and fraud, never truly claimed the affections of the American popula-

[29] TJ to Joseph Priestley, June 19, 1802, ibid., 10:324–25.

[30] TJ to General Warren, Mar. 21, 1801, to Gerry, Mar. 29, 1801, to Levi Lincoln, Oct. 25, 1802, ibid., 10:231, 251–52, 339.

tion. Its illegitimate and temporary following owed to a passing dislocation in American society in the 1790s. Federalist outrages against American interest and ideology—the Jay Treaty, attempted war with France, the Alien and Sedition Acts, the army and taxation bills—called forth the Republican opposition, a movement that was neither narrow, seditious, nor politically partisan because it comprised the nation itself. It rose quickly to national triumph because its yeast was not political deception or personal gain, but the natural inclinations of the people themselves. And "among the people," Jefferson proclaimed in 1801, "the schism is healed." Stripped of the popular support it had never merited, all that remained of the Federalist house were its un-American pillars: "the clergy who have missed their union with the state, the anglomen who have missed their union with England, and the political adventurers, who have lost the chance of swindling and plunder in the waste of public money." Jefferson's political goals were gentle and revealed a personal urge to restore social love to the national community of Americans. Such a promising development was possible because its fulfillment hung on simple assumptions that neither economic, nor geographic, nor class difference threatened. In character and in central political beliefs the people, Jefferson trusted, were innately Republican. "The moment which should convince me that a healing of the nation into one is impracticable," he wrote immediately after his election, "would be the last moment of my wishing to remain where I am." [31]

All the American citizens who belonged to the Federalist party were not guilty by dint of their political association. Jefferson clearly distinguished among past "federal" administrations, American citizens who belonged to the Federalist party, and the organization itself. Federal administrations—especially Washington's—were past national administrations that carried the name "federal" because they accepted the tenets of constitutional federalism: separation of governing power on the national level, division of governing responsibilities between the states and the nation, and the elective principle. Though federal in name, they were republican in spirit. But the

---

[31] TJ to Gideon Granger, May 3, 1801, to Levi Lincoln, Aug. 26, 1801, ibid., 10:259–60, 275. For an elaboration on the relationship of ethics, human nature, and republicanism, see Yehoshua Arieli, *Individualism and Nationalism in American Ideology* (Baltimore, 1966), pp. 121–78.

Hamiltonian interest—"monocrats," "stockjobbers," "anglomen"—
transformed the federal administrations into a Federalist party that
had no commitment to republican values.

Perceiving a crucial difference between the legitimate federalism of
past administrations and the illegitimate faction that grew out of
them, Jefferson also believed that many worthy Americans had not
made the same distinction or, if they had, still wished to keep the
name "federal" while they followed a republican tack. "When speaking of [Federalism]," he wrote, "we never mean to include a worthy
portion of our citizens who consider themselves as in duty bound to
support the constituted authorities of every branch. These having
acquired the appelation of federalist while a federal administration
was in place, and have not cared about throwing off their name, . . .
are the supporters of the present order of things." Jefferson's worry
was "the other branch of federalists: those who are so in principle as
well as in name, disapprove of the republican principles and features
of our constitution and would, I believe, welcome any public calamity (war with England excepted) which might lessen the confidence
of our country in those principles and forms."[32] John Quincy Adams
made the same distinction. The "tories," he believed, "do not include
the whole Federal party, but they now *preside* over its policy. They
are the political descendants in direct line from the tories of our own
revolutionary war, and hold most of their speculative opinions." They
aimed at the destruction of "republican forms" and "submission to
Great Britain."[33]

The source of much of Jefferson's apprehension about the Federalist party was its suspect nationality. "Anglomen" who missed
their union with Great Britain, "tories" who craved submission to
Great Britain: their admiration for their patron made them unacceptable leaders in a republican culture. Their Jay Treaty not only had
sacrificed American agriculture to a monstrous paper interest; it also
tried to keep the United States chained to Great Britain with links of
credit and economic dependence. Their opposition to the Louisiana
Purchase further demonstrated a desire to confine America to the
eastern seaboard, under the influence of England. Jefferson's hatred
of Federalism, then, was part of a larger fear of Great Britain. Indeed,

[32] TJ to Michael Leib, June 22, 1808, Jefferson Papers, LC.
[33] Adams to Ezekiel Bacon, Nov. 18, 1808, Adams Family Papers, MHS, reel
135.

he saw in the Hamiltonian system—military power, aristocratic trappings of office, the splendor of state, and the creation of a paper fund through which the executive branch could corrupt, manipulate, and eventually dominate the peoples' representatives—a betrayal of the republican dreams of simplicity and separation of powers and a duplication of a dangerously sophisticated English model of government and society.

Not accidentally, Jefferson's moderate public stance toward the Federalist party during his first term coincided with a brief rapprochement in Anglo-American relations. With America temporarily free from foreign threat, the Federalist party lost its power and, in the absence of unsettling issues, its following as well. The Jeffersonians reduced taxes, expenditures, and the debt, purchased half a continent, secured the Mississippi for the West, and left the people free to prosper. Citizens repaid honest leaders with votes and confidence. Carefully Jefferson studied developments in the state elections and found ample justification for optimism. "Our well-meaning citizens" are fast "returning," he would note after Republican gain, "from the artifices practiced on them." All New England except Connecticut voted Republican in the canvass of 1804. By 1804 Federalism seemed to be a political oxymoron: deadly but not dangerous. "Monarchism," Jefferson commented late in his first term, "which has been so falsely miscalled federalism, is dead and buried, and no day of resurrection will ever dawn upon that. . . . It has retired to the two extreme and opposite angles of our land, from whence it will have ultimately and shortly to take its final flight."[34]

From more than a personal point of view, the Louisiana Purchase and the Republican victory in 1804 were the high-water marks of Jefferson's presidency. The first secured to the American people a landed empire for their experiment in liberty; the second confirmed Jefferson's dream of social harmony and his faith that the people, if their natural inclinations were not distorted, would choose their

[34] TJ to Joel Barlow, Mar. 14, 1801, to Thomas Paine, Mar. 18, 1801, to W. C. C. Claiborne, May 24, 1803, Lipscomb and Bergh, 10:222, 224, 392–93. Building on the themes of art, deception, and republican frailty and corruptibility, Jefferson explained his election to John Dickinson in this manner: "Our fellow citizens have been led hoodwinked from their principles, by a most extraordinary combination of circumstances. But the band is removed, and they now see for themselves" (Mar. 6, 1801, ibid., 10:217).

leaders wisely. To add the Floridas to the American domain, Gallatin noted in 1806, would complete the accomplishments of Jeffersonian philosophy and leaders.[35] But all went sour after the first-term triumphs. As Jefferson saw it, the problem was still England and the English in America.

The Embargo and the Revolution of 1800: Duty and Obligation in the Idea of Republican Freedom

During Jefferson's second term, as in the 1790s, Federalist merchants and politicians were aggravating popular suffering and foreign crisis. Their trickery and the ease by which their legal manipulations and illegal evasions of the embargo laws lined their pockets confused, corrupted, and tempted the republican citizenry. If the people had been left alone, Jefferson believed, then the embargo would not have required an extensive enforcement apparatus. But such was not the case. Enforcement became a governmental duty both to rout and punish Federalist evasions and to keep these activities from poisoning the larger social order. So it was that Jefferson protected his image of a virtuous America and found solid reasons, rooted in Federalist cunning and republican frailty and corruptibility, to justify the harshest enforcement measures. Embargo violations risked far more than the embarrassment of a foreign policy weapon. Obedience to it had become implicated in the meaning and survival of the Revolution of 1800.

The Revolutionary leaders, Jefferson among them, recognized the problem of the morality of authority in a free society. The 1776 Declaration that rejected imperial rule also tried to preserve the bases of governmental authority in the future American state. The deadly conspiracy against American freedom that the Declaration unfolded justified the approaching Revolution. Yet, Jefferson was just as anxious to distinguish between illegitimate authority and governments that merely vexed their people with "transient grievances." The distinction was important not only to the moral foundations of the Re-

---

[35] Gallatin to TJ, Oct. 13, 1806, Jefferson Papers, LC.

bellion but also to the legitimacy of authority in the post-Revolutionary American world. Not until 1800 did Jefferson think the matter settled.

Although the Constitutional Convention of 1787 established the legal foundation of a national government, the blueprint could not measure performance and consequently could neither judge the morality of national political power nor establish an ensuing popular obligation to obey the decisions of a just state. The goals and methods of Federalism had by 1799 destroyed the moral credentials of the incumbent national authority and freed the citizens to dismiss it, peacefully, from power. In Jefferson's view, the election contest of 1800 became an important referendum on governing authority in America. The returns bound the future of national power to the ideology and personnel of the Republican movement. Because they rested on wide suffrage and ample information, their outcome democratically established Republican authority and therefore created obligation in the larger social community. Law, authority, and freedom became inseparable as a consequence. This was the legacy of 1800 as Jefferson understood it; not the legitimacy of dissent and political parties, but the moral authority of republican law and Republican leaders.[36]

Thomas Jefferson and John Randolph had little in common. Their personalities clashed, their politics diverged, and their public purpose differed. Jefferson was concerned with applying liberal principles to nation building through time, Randolph with protecting agrarian principles against time. Randolph's self-imposed role as conscience of the Republican party led him to oppose the administration on judicial reform, the Yazoo lands settlement, political consolidation with moderate Federalism, foreign policy, and the embargo. Yet both Randolph and Jefferson held specific definitions of political freedom and republican citizenship that explain Jefferson's anger and actions regarding the embargo evasions. In the midst of a characteristic exploration of Jeffersonian policy, Randolph hit the mother lode of Jeffersonian political belief. "Obedience to law," he reminded his fellow congressmen, "is the vital principle of every government pretending

---

[36] For a differ.nt interpretation of the Revolution of 1800, stressing individualism and political dissent, see Daniel Sisson, *The American Revolution of 1800* (New York, 1974).

to be free."[37] Eight years before, Jefferson had tied the permanence of republican institutions and the promise of American tranquillity to "that love of order and obedience to the laws which so remarkably characterize the citizens of the United States."[38] Jefferson never imagined an oppressive state. He was sure that American citizens would support just, necessary, and majoritarian law by "the investigation of reason." But if reason led them to oppose the laws, they must ignore their own dictates and "acquiesce in what their country shall authoritatively decide and arrange themselves faithfully under the banners of the law."[39] The events of 1800 had created a community of consent that became the nation's sword and shield. "The government," Jefferson believed, "which can wield the arm of the people must be the strongest possible." Activities that ignored the law or abused it for selfish purpose exposed the law to laughter and weakened the bond between freedom and authority in a republican government.[40]

The popular and judicial reactions to the Burr conspiracy of 1807 and the ensuing treason trial in John Marshall's court reminded Jefferson of the embargo's strengths and weaknesses. The people's response was exhilarating and proved that neither Burr nor his fellows "knew anything of the people of this country." "A simple proclamation," Jefferson happily observed, "informing the people of these combinations and calling on them to suppress them provided an instantaneous levee en mass of our citizens wherever there appeared anything to lay hold of and the whole was crushed in one instant." To a friend in Pennsylvania, Jefferson wrote that the popular response to the Burr conspiracy was the "proof . . . of the innate strength of our government," and "one of the most remarkable which history has recorded. . . . The moment a proclamation apprised our fellow citizens that there were traitors among them, . . . they rose upon them wherever they lurked and crushed by their own strength what would have produced the march of armies in any other country."[41]

The embargo, too, was a simple proclamation. It warned the

[37] Randolph, *Annals*, 10th Cong., 2d sess., p. 1466.
[38] TJ to Benjamin Waring, Mar. 23, 1801, Lipscomb and Bergh, 10:235.
[39] TJ to Tammany Society of Washington, Dec. 14, 1807, Jefferson Papers, LC.
[40] TJ to Isaac Weaver, June 7, 1807, ibid.
[41] TJ to the Marquis de Lafayette, May 26, July 14, 1807, to Pierre Dupont de Nemours, July 14, 1807, to Isaac Weaver, June 7, 1807, ibid.

people of danger, and its expected support flowed from their attachment to republican law and the inclination of the American people to "faithfully arrange themselves under the banner" of government.[42] The initial embargo legislation was completely lacking in refinement and enforcement apparatus. As Gallatin wrote Jefferson within days of its passage, what of "the coasting trade . . . what of penalties"? In fact, the whole career of the embargo saw the government racing to throw legislative barriers in the path of the onrushing American entrepreneur. "Each hour teems with fresh and unusual applications and various reasons" to escape the law, the customs collector in Philadelphia informed Gallatin a few days after he had posted notice of the embargo in the port. "Nothing that ingenuity could devise to counteract . . . the law imposing an embargo has been omitted," the Philadelphia officer observed two days later.[43]

No doubt the embargo's sudden adoption contributed to the omissions of the coasting trade and financial penalties. But there was more to these omissions than haste and legislative sloppiness. Jefferson's understanding of the American people—their attitudes toward law and duty—and the meaning of his own election, a set of beliefs affirmed by the popular response to the traitor Burr, convinced him that in a republic, only a simple proclamation was necessary.[44] All through the embargo, Jefferson believed that this simple proclamation attracted the support of the overwhelming majority of American people. "If clamours ensue," he wrote in August, "it will be from the few only who will clamour whatever we do."[45] But did the treachery of the Federalist rump require so massive an enforcement effort? It did, and again the Burr conspiracy illustrated why. Whom the people had crushed, the courts had set free. About Burr's acquittal Jefferson wrote: "Never will chicanery have a more difficult task than has been

[42] TJ to James Sullivan, Aug. 12, 1808, to Gallatin, Sept. 5, 1808, to William Eustis, Jan. 14, 1809, to Jonathan Law, April 13, 1809, Jefferson Papers, UVa.

[43] Gallatin to TJ, Dec. 22, 1807, John Shee to Gallatin, Dec. 29, 31, 1807, Gallatin Papers, NYU, reel 15.

[44] TJ to Loudoun County, Virginia, Republicans, care of Armistead T. Mason, n.d., to Abner Watkins, Dec. 21, 1807, to Adams County, Pennsylvania, Democratic Citizens, Mar. 20, 1808, to Benjamin Smith, May 20, 1808, to Philadelphia, Pennsylvania, Citizens, Feb. 3, 1809, to Wilmington, Delaware, Citizens, Feb. 16, 1809, to Republicans of Annapolis, Maryland, Feb. 17, 1809, to Daniel Tompkins, Feb. 24, 1809, Jefferson Papers, LC.

[45] TJ to James Sullivan, Aug. 12, 1808, ibid.

now accomplished to warp the best of the law." The consequences of the Marshall decision mortified Jefferson. How strong was the Union if disunionists escaped punishment through, of all things, the legal and judicial process? How sound were our "fixed laws to guard us equally against treason and oppression" if sophistry could defeat the law? How permanent a popular attachment to law—the main prop of a republican society—could the nation anticipate if the lawbreaker used the law to enrich himself, mock the loyal, and escape punishment? For Jefferson, the parallel with the embargo was compelling.[46]

The nation's "anglomen" had involved the embargo in a genuine crisis of law, obedience, and authority in Jefferson's Republic. This domestic crisis assaulted crucial notions that Jefferson held about the meaning of citizenship and freedom in a political society formed and dependent on the representative principle, and it came to overshadow in significance the problem in foreign affairs, particularly with England, that had brought the embargo into being. He strove to enforce the embargo because democratic fairness demanded an equal measure of suffering for all and because, on the verge of retirement, he could neither confront war nor abide submission. He strove to enforce the embargo because it announced his rejection of English forms of economic activity and offered a means toward establishing a future economy freed from a dangerous dependence on foreign trade. But equally important, he strove to enforce the embargo because on voluntary obedience to republican law hung his understanding of American character and his belief that Americans were chosen, fitted out, to exist as a free people. John Quincy Adams and Albert Gallatin thought that Americans had "grown fat on prosperity" or were never really different from the mass of enterprising and selfish humanity. Jefferson could not accept their beliefs without shattering his American hopes. Unable to accept that embargo breaking was consistent with the nation's economic and entrepreneurial character, he chose instead to believe that the mass of "good citizens" either supported the law or were seduced into treason by Federalist intrigue and merchant avarice. These activities risked dangers far greater than clandestine trade and economic submission to England. They ridiculed the law and endangered the accomplishment of 1800, the

[46] TJ to William Thompson, Sept. 26, 1807, ibid.

links of affection that bound good citizens and good leaders in a just republican state. Once Jefferson had made these associations, complete enforcement of the embargo became both necessary and within the constitutional powers of republican rulers. Jefferson's enforcement policies did not reveal a dark side to his encounter with civil liberties; they merely combated the enemies of the Republic in proper eighteenth-century fashion.[47] And if good people lost sight of the law, they too must be reminded, harshly if need be, of the duties and obligations in the idea of American freedom.

[47] The "darker side" aspect to Jefferson's handling of the embargo has been explored by Leonard Levy, *Jefferson and Civil Liberties: The Darker Side* (Cambridge, Mass., 1963), pp. 93–141.

ESSAY ON THE SOURCES

The following essay does not include every book or article that I have looked at or read in the course of studying Thomas Jefferson and writing this book; nor does it include all the books and articles written about the Jeffersonian period. The reader is referred to the comprehensive bibliographies in the two major works of recent Jeffersonian scholarship: Dumas Malone, *Jefferson and His Time* (Boston, 1948—), and Merrill D. Peterson, *Thomas Jefferson and the New Nation* (New York, 1970). It does include all the material that forms the documentary basis of this study and that has helped me to clarify in my own mind my stance toward the American Revolution, the political history of post-Revolutionary America, republicanism, Thomas Jefferson, and his presidency.

Manuscript Collections

The microfilm edition of the Jefferson Papers in the Library of Congress was an essential part of my research and the documentary basis of this study. I used reels 45–70 of this edition. Less complete were the Jefferson papers at the University of Virginia, Charlottesville, and the Archives Division, Virginia State Library, Richmond. The microfilm edition of the Albert Gallatin Papers, New York University, New York City, was invaluable, not only for Gallatin's contributions to and criticisms of policy and his relations with Congress but also for his almost daily correspondence with Jefferson and the customs collectors about the embargo, its evasions and enforcement. I used reels 10–20 of this collection. There is also a small collection of Gallatin materials at the Library of Congress that yielded some of his personal memorandums about policy options in 1808. The James

Madison and James Monroe Papers at the Library of Congress were also invaluable. I used reels 6–10 of the microfilm edition of the Madison Papers, as well as reels 25–26 of series 2 of this collection, formerly segregated as the William Rives collection. I used reels 3–4 of the Monroe Papers. There is a smaller collection of Madison Papers at the University of Virginia that was invaluable because it contains several important letters about the relationship between Jeffersonian commercial goals and the Republican tradition of economic development. There is also a microfilm edition of all the Monroe papers housed in Virginia repositories. I used reel 12 of this edition at the Archives Division, Virginia State Library.

The other members of Jefferson's cabinet did not leave extensive paper collections, but many of the letters of Dearborn, Smith, Rodney, and Granger are in the Gallatin, Madison, and Jefferson Papers. The Robert Smith Papers at the Library of Congress were disappointing. But the Samuel Smith Collection, MS 1790, and the Robert and William Smith Papers, MS 1423, at the Maryland Historical Society, Baltimore, contain useful material about the secretary of navy. Also helpful in this regard were the Samuel Smith Papers at the Library of Congress and the University of Virginia. The Rodney Family Papers, 1771–1824, Library of Congress, revealed more about the family than the attorney general.

There are many collections of the political and ideological leaders of the Republican movement, some very valuable, some less so. I have used:

Library of Congress: The Nicholas Biddle Papers contained several important observations about the Monroe-Pinkney negotiations and Jefferson's policy during the *Chesapeake* discussions. The Barnabas Bidwell Papers, the William Burwell Papers, and the George Washington Campbell Papers, 1793–1844, 1804–1886, Letterbooks, 1803–1811, were less useful. The William Eustis Papers contained many important letters about public policy and New England Republicanism. The Phillip Barton Key Papers, Nathaniel Macon Papers, William Pinkney Papers, and the Levi Lincoln Papers and Lincoln Family Papers were less useful. The Wilson Cary Nicholas Papers were invaluable on public policy, congressional activity, and the Virginia political scene. The Joseph Hopper Nicholson Papers yielded many important letters about politics and diplomacy; especially valuable was his correspondence with Albert Gallatin. The John Randolph–James Garnett Correspondence, the John Randolph Papers, the John Randolph Letterbooks, 1801–1834 and undated series, and the Randolph Family Papers, 1773–1833, 1806–1832, all contained useful material. The Samuel Smith Papers, Letterbooks, and Scrapbooks were less useful, as were the Richard Stanford Papers. The Joseph Story Papers contained a wealth of information about New England Republicans and the embargo.

The Maryland Historical Society: The William Pinkney Letterbooks, MS 661, contained a wealth of information about Jefferson's English diplomacy. The William Pinkney Papers, MS 1338, were less useful for my purposes. The Samuel Smith Collections, MSS 1424 and 1790, yielded some important information, as did the Robert and William Smith Papers, MS 1423, and the Smith Papers, MS 766.

The University of Virginia: The Burwell Family Papers were not useful for my work. The Joseph C. Cabell Papers, the John Hartwell Cocke Papers, and the Edgehill-Randolph Collection range across a wide variety of subjects, political and economic, and all were useful in my research. The William Branch Giles Papers were less useful. The Wilson Cary Nicholas Papers were invaluable, as were the John Randolph Papers and the Randolph Family Papers. The Samuel Smith Papers contained much useful information about commercial diplomacy and the Monroe-Pinkney Treaty not found in the Library of Congress collection. The Creed Taylor Papers were also helpful.

Virginia State Library: The John Randolph papers contained in the Archives Division were extremely helpful. They are identifiable according to many accession numbers, but all the available Randolph material is indexed in a general calendar of Randolph papers by date of acquisition.

The College of William and Mary: The Tucker-Coleman Collection (available on microfilm at the University of Virginia) contains useful material about a variety of public figures and issues.

Massachusetts Historical Society: The microfilm edition of the Adams Family Papers in the Massachusetts Historical Society was immensely rewarding. Not only does it contain the letters, diaries, and jottings of John, John Quincy, and Abigail, but the father's and especially the son's correspondence with New England Republicans like Orchard Cook, Ezekiel Bacon, Joseph Story, Nahum Parker, and many others revealed the timing and motivations of New England's actions during Jefferson's English crisis.

Unpublished Government Documents

The National Archives is a storehouse of manuscript and microfilm material on the operations of the State and Treasury departments. For foreign policy, I used Diplomatic Instructions, All Countries, vols. 6–7. These bound manuscript volumes contain much material that is not reproduced in the *American State Papers*. All the dispatches and private letters from James Monroe and William Pinkney, as well as copies of communications to the American ministers from British officials, are found in Dispatches, Great Britain, Monroe, Monroe and Pinkney, Pinkney, vols. 10–17. Their use was essential.

The amount of material in the National Archives relating to embargo enforcement and effectiveness is staggering. It is readily available on microfilm. I used: Letters Sent to Collectors of Customs, RG 56, M175 (mostly Treasury Department Circulars); Correspondence of the Secretary of the Treasury with the Collectors of Customs, 1789–1833, RG 56, M178, Alexandria, Norfolk, Petersburg, and Richmond, Virginia; Baltimore, Maryland; Boston, Massachusetts; Beaufort and New Bern, North Carolina; Charleston, South Carolina; New Orleans; Philadelphia, Pennsylvania; and Providence, Rhode Island.

As important as the correspondence of the customs collectors are the microfilm and manuscript collections of Dispatches from Consular Officers, RG 59. Some of them were essential in measuring the impact of the embargo on foreign economies, European and Caribbean, because they contain reports on American ships entering the ports, number of impressments, and the price levels on American commodities. I used the consular reports for: Alicante, Spain, microcopy, T357; Amsterdam, Holland, M446; Antwerp, Belgium, T181; Barcelona, Spain, T121; Bilbao, Spain, T183; Bordeaux, France, T164; Bremen, Germany, T184; Bristol, England, T185; Falmouth, England, T202; Genoa, Italy, T164; Guadaloupe, French West Indies, T208; Hamburg, Germany, T211; Kingston, Jamaica, T31; La Rochelle, France, T394; Leeds, England, T474;

Le Havre, France, T212; Leghorn, Italy, T214; Liverpool, England, M141; London, England, T168; Malaga, Spain, T217; Malta, T218; Marsailles, France, T220; Martinique, T431; Naples, Italy, T224; Paris, France, T1; Rome, Italy, T231; Saint Croix, T233; Saint Kitts, T234; Saint Thomas, Virgin Islands, T350; Antigua, MS; Havana, MS; Saint Thomas, MS; Surinam, MS.

Published Government Documents

Walter Lowrie and Matthew S. Clarke, eds., *American State Papers, Foreign Relations*, vols. 2 and 3 (Washington, D.C., 1832), is a convenient collection of much pertinent diplomatic source material, but it is incomplete. I complemented them with manuscript and microfilm material deposited in the National Archives. *Debates and Proceedings in the Congress of the United States* (Washington, D.C., 1834–53): I made extensive use of these *Annals* for the Ninth and Tenth Congresses.

Published Correspondence

There are three major publications of Jefferson's correspondence. Julian P. Boyd and others, eds., *The Papers of Thomas Jefferson* (Princeton, N.J., 1950—), will one day be the definitive edition of all of Jefferson's writings and correspondence. To date, its completion falls almost a decade short of the beginning of Jefferson's presidency, but it is invaluable for the years it does cover. I have also used, but not as extensively, Paul Leicester Ford, ed., *The Works of Thomas Jefferson* (New York, 1905), and Andrew A. Lipscomb and Albert Ellery Bergh, eds., *The Writings of Thomas Jefferson* (Washington, D.C., 1907). James D. Richardson, ed., *A Compilation of the Messages and Papers of the Presidents, 1789–1908* (New York, 1908), contains Jefferson's addresses and messages to the Congress. Henry Adams, ed., *The Writings of Albert Gallatin*, vol. 1 (Philadelphia, 1879), contains some of Gallatin's important correspondence with Jefferson and the Congress.

Secondary Literature

Scores of books and articles have given me information, leads, frames of reference, and pleasant challenges to my own understanding. Biographies of Jeffersonian leaders are especially good. Nathan Schachner, *Thomas Jefferson, a Biography* (New York, 1951), is careful, lengthy, and detailed. It incorporates some of Jefferson's letters located in the New York Public Library. A more recent one-volume study that analyzes Jefferson's public life and political thought in the context of American democrary and nationality is Merrill D. Peterson, *Thomas Jefferson and the New Nation* (New York, 1970). Dumas Malone, *Jefferson and His Time* (Boston, 1948—), aims toward definitiveness in six volumes. Five are done to date. His volumes on the presidential years, *Jefferson the President, the First Term* (Boston, 1970) and *Jefferson the President, the Second Term* (Boston, 1974), are both judicious and helpful. Fawn M. Brodie, *Thomas Jefferson, an Intimate History* (Boston, 1974), offers sensitive and sensible insights into Jefferson's temperament, familial relations, and fascination with growth and decay. Forrest McDonald's recent *Presidency of Thomas Jefferson* (Lawrence, Kans., 1976) brilliantly refines our understanding of Jefferson's republicanism, then faults him for trying to implement his ideas in action.

Irving Brant's five volumes on James Madison (1941–61) form the definitive Madison biography. His *James Madison, Secretary of State, 1800–1809* (Indianapolis, 1953) is a valuable study of Madison's involvement in diplomacy and policy (although I occasionally view Madison's role and preferences differently), especially on the months between election and inauguration. Brant's *James Madison, Father of the Constitution* (Indianapolis, 1950) is a solid study of Madison's constitutional nationalism in the 1780s. Ralph Ketcham's *James Madison, a Biography* (New York, 1971) ably complements Brant's focus on nationalism with its own attention to Madison's republicanism.

Albert Gallatin awaits a comprehensive modern biography. Alexander Balinky's *Albert Gallatin: Fiscal Theories and Policies* (New Brunswick, N.J., 1958) is critical of Gallatin's treasuryship, while Raymond Walter's *Albert Gallatin: Jeffersonian Financier and Diplomat* (New York, 1957) is generally praiseworthy.

One other biography, more accurately an essay or an appreciation, bears mention. Albert Jay Nock, *Jefferson* (Clinton, Mass., 1960), has little to say about the embargo other than it was "the most arbitrary, inquisitorial, and confiscatory measure formulated in American legislation up the period of the Civil War." Nock's observation says more about his principled dissatisfaction with Jefferson's assault on property and liberty than it does about the policy in the twin contexts of foreign relations and republican belief. Yet Nock has a fine sense of Jefferson, especially evident in his awareness that Jefferson's understanding of political issues, particularly the differences between Republicanism and Federalism, turned on moral differences among men. Leonard W. Levy, *Jefferson and Civil Liberties: The Darker Side* (Cambridge, Mass., 1963), measures Jefferson's embargo against the requirements of individual liberty. My own thought is that the embargo brought to the surface an agonizing tension, if not a contradiction, buried deep in the ideology of republicanism itself, a tension between freedom and obligation, and that Jefferson's enforcement policies must be measured against the eighteenth-century meaning of republicanism. Very important in this regard are Gordon S. Wood, *The Creation of the American Republic* (Chapel Hill, N.C., 1969), Yehoshua Arieli, *Individualism and Nationalism in American Ideology* (Baltimore, 1966), and Fred Somkin, *Unquiet Eagle: Memory and Desire in the Idea of American Freedom* (Ithaca, N.Y., 1967).

A basic theme of this study is that Jefferson's ideas on American character, republicanism, Great Britain, and toryism-Federalism were formed during the Revolutionary struggle against England and "anglomen." My understanding of Jefferson's eighteenth-century inheritance owes much to Bernard Bailyn, *The Ideological Origins of the American Revolution* (Cambridge, Mass., 1967), and *Pamphlets of the American Revolution* (Cambridge, Mass., 1965); Caroline Robbins, *The Eighteenth-Century Commonwealthman* (New York, 1968); H. Trevor Colbourn, *The Lamp of Experience: Whig History and the Intellectual Origins of the American Revolution* (Chapel Hill, N.C., 1965); and Pauline Maier, *From Resistance to Revolution: Colonial Radicals and the Development of American Opposition to Britain, 1766–1776* (New York, 1972).

For Jefferson, the party battles of the 1790s embraced a continuation of the struggle between England and America, nationality and foreign domination, and health and sickness in the American political and social order. Excellent treatments of 1790s are Paul Goodman, "The First American Party System," in William Nisbet Chambers and William Dean Durnam, eds., *The American Party Systems: Stages of Development* (New York, 1967); John R. Howe, Jr., "Republican Thought and Political Violence in the 1790s," *American Quarterly* 19 (Summer, 1967); Marshall Smelser, "The Jacobin Phrenzy: The Menace of Monarchy, Plutocracy, and Anglophilia, 1789–1798," *Review of Politics* 21 (1959); Richard Hofstadter, *The Idea of a Party System: The Rise of Legitimate Opposition in the United States, 1780–1840* (Berkeley, Calif., 1969).

The movement for a constitutional and governmental reform in the 1780s and the falling out between northern and southern nationalists in the 1790s have been ably treated. On the ideological and class dimension of the 1780s debate see Wood, *The Creation of the American Republic*. On the fiscal thought of 1780s nationalists, see E. James Ferguson, *The Power of the Purse* (Chapel Hill, N.C., 1961). On the importance of foreign trade and foreign markets to the nationalism of the 1780s and the falling out of the nationalists in the 1790s, see Frederick Marks III, *Independence on Trial: Foreign Affairs and the Making of the Constitution* (Baton Rouge, La., 1973); Charles Beard, *Economic Origins of Jeffersonian Democracy* (New York, 1915); Paul Varg, *Foreign Policies of the Founding Fathers* (East Lansing, Mich., 1963); Jerald A. Combs, *The Jay Treaty: Political Battleground of the Founding Fathers* (Berkeley, Calif., 1970); and Joseph Charles, *The Origins of the American Party System* (Williamsburg, Va., 1956). Jackson Turner Main, *The Anti-Federalists, Critics of the Constitution, 1781–1788* (Chicago, 1964), locates 1780s political Antifederalism in economic considerations and marketplace realities. His Antifederalist is generally economically provincial, concerned with subsistence, and dwelling beyond the arc of commercial enterprise. Cecelia M. Kenyon, "Men of Little Faith: The Antifederalists on the Nature of Representative Government," *William and Mary Quarterly*, 3d ser., 12 (1955), finds that frightened and uncompromising views on the dangers of political power and national consolidation characterized most Antifederalists. Forrest McDonald, *The Formation of the American Republic, 1776–1790* (Baltimore, 1965), likewise attaches Antifederalist opposition to the Constitution to fears of political consolidation, albeit in his idiosyncratic fashion.

Antifederalists, however, did not lead the opposition to Federalist executive policy in the 1790s; Republican leaders had largely supported and actively created the constitutional settlement of 1788. Although Jefferson did not have a loud voice in the American debate on the Constitution, he favored reform because he understood the relationship between domestic political consolidation and the improvement of America's trading relationship worldwide. Merrill D. Peterson, "Thomas Jefferson and Commercial Policy, 1783–1793," *William and Mary Quarterly*, 3d ser., 22 (1965), addresses Thomas Jefferson's involvement in and attitude toward America's commercial failure abroad in the 1780s. Richard E. Ellis, "The Political Economy of Thomas Jefferson," in Lally Weymouth, ed., *Thomas Jefferson: The Man, His World, His Influence* (New York, 1973), stresses the importance of agricultural productivity, foreign purchasing power, and tranquil oceans in Jefferson's economic vision. He also inverts the traditional wisdom by crediting Jefferson with foreign policy realism and Hamilton with visionary idealism. Also helpful are William D. Grampp, "A Re-examination of Jefferson's Economics," *Southern Economic Journal* 12 (1946), and Joseph Spengler, "The Political Economy of Jefferson, Madison, and Adams," in Donald Kelly Jackson, ed., *American Studies in Honor of William Kenneth Boyd* (Durham, N.C., 1940). Although he does not comment on the conflict between land and water in Jefferson's political economy, Julian P. Boyd, "Thomas Jefferson's 'Empire of Liberty,'" *Virginia Quarterly Review* 24 (1958), catches the crucial importance of orderly expansion across the continent to Jefferson's political and economic definition of the Union. See also Drew R. McCoy, "The Republican Revolution: Political Economy in Jeffersonian America, 1776–1817" (Ph.D. diss., University of Virginia, 1976), which focuses "on the ideological origins and influence of a Jeffersonian conception of republican political economy, which emphasized expansion across space—the American continent—as an alternative to development through time, with its attendant corruption and decay." In a less complimentary way, Robert McColley, *Slavery in Jeffersonian Virginia* (Urbana, Ill., 1964), locates Jefferson's interest in territorial expansion in the needs of the South's slave economy.

Studies of Jefferson's presidency are as thoughtful and informative as studies of Jefferson's life and thought. The standard and the model is Henry Adams, *History of the United States during the Administrations of Jefferson and Madison* (New York, 1891–93). Although he said much more, one of Adams's crucial observations was that Jefferson in power was far different from Jefferson in opposition. Recent historians have refined this to mean that Jefferson effected political and regional conciliation with Federalism and New England, thereby sparing the nation a continuation of the party rage of the 1790s, and secured to the nation both the tradition of peaceful transfer of governing power from one political party to another and the blessings of what Henry May calls "the Didactic Enlightenment." The previously mentioned works of Hofstadter, Malone, and Peterson are important in this regard. See also Morton Borden, "Thomas Jefferson," in Morton Borden, ed., *America's Ten Greatest Presidents* (Chicago, 1961), and Richard E. Ellis, *The Jeffersonian Crisis, Courts and Politics in the Young Republic* (New York, 1971). Basic to all these studies is the sincerity of Jefferson's inaugural words, "we are all republicans, we are all federalists." Although the Republican movement captured New England in the first decade of the nineteenth century—in this regard see William Robinson, *Jeffersonian Democracy in New England* (New Haven, 1916), and Paul Goodman, *The Democratic-Republicans of Massachusetts: Politics in a Young Republic* (Cambridge, Mass., 1964)—my own feeling is that Jefferson's rapprochement with Federalism in the first term was made possible by foreign factors and obscured his consistently fearful attitude toward the organized Federalist party. Carl Prince, "The Passing of the Aristocracy: Jefferson's Removal of the Federalists, 1801–1805," *Journal of American History* 57 (Dec. 1970), asks for a modification of Jefferson's policy toward political opposition in light of his first-term patronage and removal policies. Other works on Jefferson's presidency have proved valuable. Noble Cunningham, *The Jeffersonian Republicans in Power, 1801–1809* (Chapel Hill, N.C., 1963), clarifies the organization of the party and the relationship between the various state parties and the national administrations. It has also been helpful in determining the political affiliations of several congressmen. Sanford Higgenbotham, *Keystone in the Democratic Arch: Pennsylvania Politics, 1800–1816* (Harrisburg, Pa., 1952), and Carl E. Prince, *New Jersey's Jeffersonian Republicans* (Chapel Hill, N.C., 1967), are two fine state studies of the Republican movement. Leonard White, *The Jeffersonians: A Study in Adminis-*

trative History (New York, 1951), charts the day-to-day administration of government. C. Peter Magrath, *Yazoo: Law and Politics in the New Republic* (Providence, 1966), deals with the legal and political implications of the Yazoo lands issue. Frank A. Cassell, *Merchant Congressman in the Young Republic: Samuel Smith of Maryland, 1752–1839* (Madison, Wis., 1972), deals very critically with Jefferson's handling of the English threat to American commerce in 1806–9.

Several recent studies extend our knowledge of Federalism and, interestingly, relate its animus to the Jeffersonian movement to its own understanding of the American Revolution and the principles of republican government and society. Linda K. Kerber, *Federalists in Dissent: Imagery and Ideology in Jeffersonian America* (Ithaca, N.Y., 1970), brilliantly uses politics, literature, theories of education, and science to chart the Jeffersonian threat to the Federalist world view. James T. Banner, *To the Hartford Convention: The Federalists and the Origins of Party Politics in Massachusetts, 1789–1815* (New York, 1970), deals with the social, intellectual, and economic foundations of Federalism in one state and its organizational response to the Republican ascendancy. David Hackett Fischer, *The Revolution of American Conservatism: The Federalist Party in the Era of Jeffersonian Democracy* (New York, 1967), relates Federalist inability to organize effectively in response to the Jeffersonian threat to old-school attitudes, dating to the pre-Revolutionary colonial past, about the relationship between rulers and citizens in a stable republic. John Howe, *The Changing Political Thought of John Adams* (Princeton, N.J., 1966), details in admirable fashion Adams's rather pessimistic republicanism. In this regard, see also Peter Shaw, *The Character of John Adams* (Chapel Hill, N.C., 1975). Manning Dauer, *The Adams Federalists* (Baltimore, 1953), is an older study that clarifies the split between the Adams and Hamiltonian Federalists. Gerald Stourzh has put Hamilton back into the republican movement and in the process expands our understanding of eighteenth-century republicanism in his brilliant book, *Alexander Hamilton and the Idea of Republican Government* (Stanford, Calif., 1970). Richard H. Kohn, *Eagle and Sword: The Beginnings of the Military Establishment in America* (New York, 1975), captures the Federalist mood on the issues of liberty and authority in a self-governing society through a careful and gracefully written analysis of Federalist military policy and civil-military relations. Richard Buel, *Securing the Revolution: Ideology and American Politics, 1789–1815* (Ithaca, N.Y., 1972), differentiates Jeffersonian and Federalist republicanism on the central issue of the binding power of public opinion on political leadership. Henry May, *The Enlightenment in America* (New York, 1976), makes much the same point (although his important book does much more) through his association of Adams with the Moderate Enlightenment, Jefferson with the Revolutionary Enlightenment, and the post-1800 compromise with the Didactic Enlightenment. Merrill D. Peterson, *Adams and Jefferson: A Revolutionary Dialogue* (Athens, Ga., 1976), sees the disagreement between Adams and Jefferson on the meaning of the American Revolution, of republicanism, as one between traditionalism and modernity.

The major problems of Jefferson's second term were English impressments and maritime power, European war, and American economic aspirations and the harsh antagonisms that resulted. Vernon G. Setser, *The Commercial Reciprocity Policy of the United States, 1774–1839* (Philadelphia, 1937), studies America's attempt to achieve equitable reciprocity with the trading nations of Europe. James F. Zimmerman, *Impressment of American Seamen* (New York, 1925), is a basic study of the impressment dilemma. The carrying trade both embarrassed Republican ideology and confounded Republican foreign policy. Douglass C. North, *The Economic Growth of the United States, 1790–1860* (New York, 1968), and John H. Coatsworth, "American Trade with European Colonies in the Caribbean and South America, 1790–1812," *William and Mary Quarterly*, 3d ser., 24 (1967), document its profitability. Bradford Perkins, *Prologue to War: England and the United States, 1805–1812* (Berkeley, Calif., 1968), is exhaustively researched and provides the definitive treatment of English policy and belief during the years before the War of 1812. His *The First Rapprochement: England and the United States, 1795–1805* (Philadelphia, 1955) is a valuable treatment of a quieter time in Anglo-American affairs. An unduly critical treatment of Jefferson's conduct in the Monroe-Pinkney negotiations is Anthony Steel, "Impressment in the Monroe-Pinkney Treaty, 1806–1807," *American Historical Review*, 57 (1952). Harry Ammon, *James Monroe and the Quest for National Identity* (New York, 1971), deals with the negotiations from Monroe's vantage point.

Several studies deal with Jefferson's embargo. Walter Wilson Jennings, *The American Embargo, 1807–1809* (Iowa City, 1921), deals with its domestic impact. Louis Sears, *Jefferson and the Embargo* (Durham, N.C., 1927), locates the policy in Jefferson's pacifism. Wolford L. Thorp, "Democratic-Republican Reaction in Massachusetts to the Embargo of 1807," *New England Quarterly* 15 (1942), follows its political career in one state. G. W. Daniels, "American Cotton Trade with Liverpool under the Embargo and Non-Intercourse Acts," *American Historical Review* 21, no. 2 (1915-16), assesses the impact of the embargo on the English cotton economy. Lawrence S. Kaplan, *Jefferson and France* (New Haven, 1967), calls the embargo a concession to France and an acquiesence in Napoleon's Continental System motivated, in part, by Jefferson's desire to secure French cooperation in the American desire for the Floridas. Richard James Mannix, "The Embargo: Its Administration, Impact, and Enforcement" (Ph.D. diss., New York University, 1975), discounts the embargo's importance to either Jefferson or American foreign policy and studies it purely as an administrative chore falling in Gallatin's orbit in Treasury. More than most historians, Bradford Perkins and Dumas Malone recognize the shifting purpose of the embargo and stress the importance of defensive precaution in Jefferson's early formulation of the policy.

INDEX